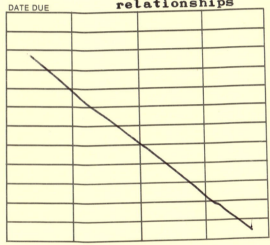

# The Heart's Events

# The Heart's Events

## The Victorian Poetry of Relationships

PATRICIA M. BALL

UNIVERSITY OF LONDON
THE ATHLONE PRESS
1976

*Published by*
THE ATHLONE PRESS
UNIVERSITY OF LONDON
4 *Gower Street, London* W C I

*Distributed by*
*Tiptree Book Services Ltd*
*Tiptree, Essex*

*U.S.A. & Canada*
*Humanites Press Inc*
*New Jersey*

© *Patricia M. Ball* 1976

ISBN 0 485 11163 2

*Printed in Great Britain by*
WESTERN PRINTING SERVICES LTD
BRISTOL

FOR MARGARET

The Song should have no incidents,
They are so dull, and pall, twice read:
Its scope should be the heart's events . . .

PATMORE

# Contents

CREDICRED CREDICRED CREDICRED CREDICRED CREDICRED CREDICRED

# INTRODUCTION

# 'Let us be true to one another'

*∽ I ∽*

Arnold's cry in *Dover Beach* rings through many other Victorian poems, though the tone is not always one of desperation, and the sentiment may be expressed in joy or with irony as well as in varying shades of grief, hope and bitterness. The poets of the time are so much drawn to the theme that it—the poetry of relationships—emerges as one of the central areas of Victorian poetic exploration, and I want to suggest that we have not yet appreciated the full vigour and variety of their enterprise in this field.

The first point to stress is that the mid-century poets largely discover and develop the theme for themselves. They are, perhaps surprisingly, repairing a Romantic neglect rather than following their predecessors' lead, for though the Romantics frequently make use of personal situations in their poetry, those situations are rarely concerned with shared emotional experience. They are not poets commonly moved to take as their creative centre either the history, the crises or the key moments of a relationship. This is not to contradict the obvious, that they are acutely aware of psychological happenings, but it is to limit their field of poetic interest to a more exclusively individual alertness. Love is a concept potent enough in Romantic poetry, certainly, but it appears as a vision not as it may be known in the dramatic actuality of a relationship. Realism is dissipated, as in the extreme example of *Epipsychidion*; and even in such a sensitive study as Margaret's widowed decline in *The Ruined Cottage*, the poetry is essentially interested in something else—the solitary woman. It is a poetry inspired by the idea of the autonomous self, an independent adventure not a shared expedition.

But if the Romantic poet refuses emotional journeying with another person as his theme, the Victorians not only welcome,

I

they specialise in it. They are fascinated by the challenge of recording the psychological repercussions when two lives are brought into intimate conjunction. The working out of such a history is compelling to these poets, as it weaves or unweaves the personalities involved and brings about a calamitous or ecstatic realisation of their own being and potential. The poetic centre remains the individual, but his or her world now expands to contain two people, caught willingly or unwillingly in each other's emotional web.

Arnold helps us to see what underlies this development. Although the mood of *Dover Beach* should not be taken as a general index to Victorian feeling, it is revealing in its insistence that, amid uncertainty and confusion, a possible rock of salvation is to be found in the loyalty of individuals to each other. In *The Buried Life* he offers more explicit reasons why the intimacy of lovers is to be aspired to and clung to when found. 'Let me read there, love! thy inmost soul', he asks of her 'limpid eyes' as they gaze at him, and the whole poem is a plea for love as a means of access to the deeper layers of being. The subterranean depths of the soul are all but lost to the world-distracted mind:

Only—but this is rare—
When a beloved hand is laid in ours,
When, jaded with the rush and glare
Of the interminable hours,
Our eyes can in another's eyes read clear,
When our world-deafened ear
Is by the tones of a loved voice caressed—
A bolt is shot back somewhere in our breast,
And a lost pulse of feeling stirs again.
The eye sinks inward, and the heart lies plain,
And what we mean, we say, and what we would, we know.

The rarity of such a moment is as important to the poem as its occurrence. The lovers do not automatically bring its peace and enlightenment to each other, as the poem's opening lines indicate, where 'gay smiles' and the flippant 'war of mocking words' leave no room for other kinds of communication. Thus Arnold acknowledges that relationships, however close, are not to be summarised by any ideal vision of what they can achieve.

2

Ardently though he may wish it otherwise, he is as aware as Meredith that answers can be dusty, that loving is not a simple matter of exalted happiness ever after, and also that moods of varying kinds make up the emotional exchange. *The Buried Life* is a miniature of much which preoccupies the poetry of his time.

Love—understood as commitment to another—is tested, questioned and found wanting in this poetry as well as explored as an experience of great potency. It is seen both as a force and as a guiding compass in development, an agent promoting personal awareness. Its breakdown is seized on as a theme of paramount importance, sometimes affirming these attributes from the reverse point of view. And some of the poems register a sense of strain that so much weight is felt to fall on the curious chance that one human creature becomes implicated in the nature of another, to affect and be affected in an experience that conditions and even determines the life of each. But all acknowledge that it is so.

Some idea of the energy expended on the theme is already apparent from this survey of its implications. But the range of poems which can be gathered to illustrate it provides further evidence. They are diverse as well as numerous. There is no uniformity of feeling, or of language and structure, even among poems I have been able to group within a chapter. Each poem finds its own way of rising to and embodying the common theme, and in the interpretation of the latter there is considerable licence.

In the first place, there is no ruling convention on what may be assumed to constitute, for poetic purposes, a crucial relationship. No equivalent of courtly love, no insistence on physical connotations, nor yet on the denial of them. The requirements for a profound emotional experience, as the Victorian poets see them, are simply two people moved by each other. They may be sexually stirred, but this aspect is in itself neither obligatory nor the dominant area of interest, and when it is important, it too is shown in its variety, with other elements of temperament and situation influencing it and making the poem.

The poets are, however, very ready to take the marriage relationship as their territory. This is a further sign of their rejection of a chivalric or romantic ideal, and their preference for love on the earth not in the clouds—love envisaged, that is, as a daily sharing of lives, a matter of history rather than dream. But here too the range is considerable, and only realism of perception unites Meredith's suffering partners with Mrs James Lee's despair, or Patmore's ideas on wives and husbands with Clough's.

Other contrasts and freedoms will be better demonstrated in the course of comparative discussion on the poems themselves. And the whole nature of this versatile, responsible and sensitive poetry can only be appreciated by the same direct means. All I want to provide here is a rough sketch map to suggest what the consequences are when Victorian poets examine and ponder the exhortation, 'Let us be true to one another'.

ᥤ 2 ᥤ

To add a little more to the map, I can introduce generally some of the structural implications of this material, especially in the field of the long poem. Technical resource and themes of emotional involvement are aspects of a single poetic ambition, for Victorian poets set up new concepts of the long poem, or the lyric group, principally in order to accommodate two of their central notions: first, that change—whether of growth or decay —is integral to love and, secondly, that the inner life as it is affected by close relationships evolves with a logic of its own which is not merely that of temporal sequence. The technical energy is generated by the pursuit of psychological realities and out of the consequent need for poems longer than the single lyric unit. It is an energy which is hostile to narrative in the simple sense, even while it appropriates some story-telling characteristics by admitting the question, 'and then?'.

In his Prologue to *The Angel in the House*, Patmore originally included the lines I have adopted as epigraph:

> The Song should have no incidents,
> They are so dull, and pall, twice read:
> Its scope should be the heart's events . . .

Patmore's devaluation of incident in favour of inward action is

4

not an attitude he cancelled with the lines. It offers the key to his and his fellow poets' approach to their material. Their effort is to break down or punch holes in narrative sequence, or otherwise to subordinate it to, and make it serve, the investigation of the individual, not as he acts, but as he is and as he becomes.

It is misleading therefore to describe Patmore's poem or any of the others as a verse-novel. Both novelists and poets are better understood if the nature of their activity and its goals are kept distinct. The poets are not vainly trying to poach on the provinces of fiction, for they are pursuing a different quest, one leading them away from rivalry. To their imagination, the process by which event becomes the heart's event is the magnet, whereas to the novelists, event can be honoured for itself and its drama; the transfer to the deeps of personality and the inner crises need not, often does not, occur. Where relationships are acutely read—as in what F. R. Leavis calls George Eliot's 'psychological notation'—there is an intensification of narrative rather than a violation or disruption of its importance. The pressures are not the same as those which induce the poets into their lyrical researches: theirs is the more naked art and the more concentrated in its study of the mysteries of emotional bonds. I do not intend to exalt *James Lee's Wife* at the expense of *Middlemarch*, which would be stupid. But in stressing the fruitful divergence of poet from novelist, I do wish to redress a balance which has gone against the poets, for their explorations are no less vital, no less serious, no less sophisticated and certainly no less aware of the potential of their chosen forms and structures than those of their prose contemporaries.

This independence is the more noteworthy because in some ways the poets seem nearer to the novelists than they are to their poetic predecessors. They mostly set their poems in society, for instance: the conventions, opportunities, and constraints of contemporary life form an active part of their theme. To put this simply, more people have names in Victorian than in Romantic poems; they are known in terms of time, place and parentage. The poetry of relationships is a matter of Felix Vaughan and Honoria, daughter of the Dean; Philip Hewson and Elspie Mackaye of the bothie of Tober-na-Vuolich; Maud

5

and her family at the Hall; Claude and the Trevellyns in Rome; or Marguerite in a Swiss village. Such specification is to Wordsworth's Lucy as the body to the ghost. But if it anchors the poems firmly in the world the novelists also inhabit, the poets' object is not verisimilitude for the benefit of narrative conviction, but a recognition that the commitment of individuals and its consequences involves the whole history of those individuals.

In short, this is another route by which the poets arrive at their grasp of psychological process. What lovers become together cannot be separated from where they live, how they live, who their families are, and all that has been. If *Maud* is an expression of this insight at one painful extreme, *The Angel in the House* builds upon it too at another. And structurally, as I have said, these and my other examples thrive on resisting the novel, or the narrative pull of such detail, exploiting it in their own way for ends as technically distinctive as they are psychologically rewarding.

### ↜ 3 ↝

Despite the fact that the poetry of relationships is a mid-century phenomenon, a distinctively Victorian development, it is still possible and I think helpful to approach it from a Romantic direction. First, because this poetry belongs to the same general area of imaginative vision. While the appreciation of time as a factor in the psychological life is an important Victorian perception in this particular field of relationships, it is not of course these poets who first respond to the notion of experience as process in a wider sense. For Wordsworth, the child is father of the man, and *Tintern Abbey* in little and *The Prelude* on the major scale see the influence of past on present as a crucial element in the formation of the moral nature, and the idea of formation itself as the key to the interpretation of the individual life.

Change and growth could be termed Romantic values. Keats discovers that leaving the Chamber of Maiden-Thought for 'dark passages' is the way of maturity not of deprivation; the concept of living as an exercise in learning and becoming a 'Soul' is his dominant obsession. To chart the inner history of the individual is therefore a Romantic task accepted with enthusiasm and regarded as imperative if a full consciousness of identity is to be reached, despite an equally strong celebration of timeless moments of experience.

Historical ambition is not discarded by the Victorian poets, and the proposition that living is a dynamic, evolving, and essentially educative process is likewise—and perhaps more literally—accepted. But to them, identity is a more contingent concept, and the feeling of its growth and development is best recognised in one specific area of life. 'A world of pains and troubles', or alternatively, nature and solitude, make the Romantic soul: the Victorian's sense of identity is born of his most intimate relationship. The later poetry explores the implications of loving and being loved with a thoroughness, a social and personal realism and a sensitivity which is not found earlier, although that earlier vision in its fundamentals can be said to make this concentration possible.

Secondly, and more directly helpful in providing bearings for the poems I want to discuss, there are occasions in Romantic poetry where love is represented not as a predominantly subjective or ideal condition, nor as a private epiphanal moment, but as an invasion of the personality by another, giving rise to a new situation and demanding a recognition of another sensibility, if only because the force of impact makes it impossible to ignore. And there are poems where this experience has to be dealt with as a developing, or at any rate changing, situation, so that the single lyric unit comes under narrative pressure. The result is an incipient poetry of relationships.

I want therefore to start with two Romantic examples to indicate these beginnings, both to acknowledge the links and to emphasise the degree to which the Victorians went beyond their predecessors, technically and substantially, in making this theme their own.

# 'The Difference to Me'

## Wordsworth: the Lucy Poems;
## Byron: Poems of the Separation

∽ I ∽

These poems suggest the two poles of Romanticism when it deals with relationships in their actuality: at one, the quiet but intense grief of bereavement, at the other, the more violent explosion of marital breakdown. Both have their Victorian counterparts. The contrasts between the two are important, but what they have in common is fundamentally relevant to Victorian developments. For Wordsworth and Byron, the experience of loss, of something overwhelming happening to them, was an incentive to repeated composition, not an event which could be adequately assimilated in a single poem. 'The difference to me' is a theme with narrative content, prompting them to an imaginative effort which is not just an expression of pain, but which strives to articulate an extended process of inner shock with its varying aspects and changing lights. Seeing how they do this and what is involved in it, will prepare the way for an understanding of the far more intensive Victorian scrutiny of the heart's events.

∽ 2 ∽

When he sent 'I travelled among unknown men' to Mary Hutchinson in a letter of 29 April 1801,[1] Wordsworth directed her to read it after 'She dwelt among the untrodden ways'. Three of the four poems which were written earlier in Goslar had been grouped together at their first publication in the second volume of the *Lyrical Ballads* of 1800: 'Strange fits of

[1] *The Letters of William and Dorothy Wordsworth*, ed. E. de Selincourt, revised C. L. Shaver (1967), i, p. 333.

passion', 'She dwelt among the untrodden ways', 'A slumber did my spirit seal'. 'Three years she grew in sun and shower' appeared later in the same volume, but in Wordsworth's final arrangement of his poems, it precedes 'A slumber did my spirit seal' in the section called 'Poems of the Imagination', and the other three stand together under the heading 'Poems founded on the Affections', their order unchanged from his first thoughts.

This outline helps in an attempt to assess how far Wordsworth saw the five lyrics, now commonly classified as the Lucy poems, as related pieces. It shows that on the one hand he regarded their being placed in a certain sequence as important, but on the other that he did not view all five as poems uniform in kind or appeal. His mixed attitude encourages a reading of them which is equally undogmatic: they are neither one poem broken into five parts, nor are they five independent poems. But they stand as an interesting experiment in handling event as feeling, one of the few Romantic ventures into bringing together what happened in and to a relationship and its psychological import.

Do the Lucy poems, then, tell a story? It is possible to summarise them so that they do. The speaker of the poems loved a girl of grace and beauty called Lucy, who lived in a secluded country spot and occupied herself with the usual domestic employments. He used to visit her frequently at her cottage, his horse knowing the path there without any guidance. The love affair was happy, the lovers trusted each other, Lucy being ready to tease him for his moods. Despite being momentarily visited by inexplicable fears that she might die, the lover is shocked when that event occurs, and his view of his native place, and the earth in general, remains deeply affected by it.

There is no need to labour the point that such a bald account conveys nothing of the poems' character: it is an obvious way of demonstrating that theirs is a lyric vitality. None the less, that lyricism does depend upon the narrative or historical framework, slight though it is. The first point to consider is how Wordsworth uses and also subdues the element of narration.

A clue to his attitude towards the presence or absence of a determining story shape can be found if I admit that in my sketch I cheated to the extent of using a stanza found only in the manuscript version of 'Strange fits of passion'. There the poem does not end at, '"Oh mercy!" to myself I cried, "If Lucy should be dead!"'', but continues:

> I told her this: her laughter light
> Is ringing in my ears:
> And when I think upon that night
> My eyes are dim with tears.

De Selincourt calls this an 'eminently Wordsworthian' conclusion, even if the poem 'may be the better' for its omission.[2] But there is more to consider both in the stanza itself and in the poem, with and without it. It is, first of all, the only moment in the five poems where Lucy is actively present: even here of course her laughter has the poignancy of being remembered— this with its simple irony is the emotional point. But still she is allowed a reaction which not only hints at her independent personality but gives substance to the lovers' relationship. The speaker's spasm of foreboding, his sense of hypnotic unreality and fear, are challenged and gently criticised by the 'light laughter': two people are impinging upon each other, and the alchemy of giving and receiving is momentarily seen at work.

For this reason alone, 'Strange fits of passion' with the additional stanza is a very different poem from the final version without it. The range of implication is greater once Lucy's voice is heard, and by cutting it, Wordsworth to this extent drew back from the poetry of relationships. But also to be considered is the poet's decision to extend the poem temporally, to say what happened next. The poem in this version breaks out of the arrested moment of panic and tells us that time and the lover moved on; he arrived at the cottage and spent a while as part of his love-making confiding his experience to the living girl he had come to see. It then takes the further step of showing that still more time has passed and other things, notably Lucy's death, have happened.

The stress therefore falls on the passage of time; we are aware of a sequence of events, and the poem is given a pronounced narrative bias. This is strengthened in the original version

---

[2] *The Poetical Works of William Wordsworth* (1944), ii, p. 472. Quotations are taken from this edition.

because the first verse of the poem as published does not appear
there. Wordsworth prefers a brisker opening which, ballad-like,
carries the seeds of the pathos:

> Once when my love was strong and gay
> And like a rose in June . . .

His initial conception seems to have been to rely on narrative
to bring out a poignant contrast between present and past. His
second thoughts alter this drastically. He cuts the final stanza
and adds at the beginning,

> Strange fits of passion have I known:
> And I will dare to tell,
> But in the Lover's ear alone,
> What once to me befell.

The new first line gives the measure of what is changed in the
poem and directs attention to what is now its focal point, the
sudden premonition of grief. The psychological phenomenon as
such has become central, and the love story itself has ceased to
control the organisation of the poem. The lyric has turned into
a concentrated rendering of a peculiar state of consciousness
and a record of the involuntary workings of the mind. It loses
nothing in poignancy, nor in its implications about the lover
and Lucy's fate, but in the final version it compresses narrative
into situation and subdues even the latter to the psychological
purpose.

The variations in this lyric present a diagram of a poet
gravitating towards his own heart's events. Wordsworth's venture into the poetry of relationships shows it remaining for him
a branch of the egotistical sublime, with the one reacting mind
of paramount importance, as the removal of Lucy's 'laughter
light' also emphasises. But none the less the poem still depends
upon Lucy and upon her history. Wordsworth speaks as, not
merely to, the lover, and also as one recalling a specific occasion
because of its being part of a longer story from which it draws
its meaning. Narrative as an organising principle is denied yet
the poem's emotion continues to depend upon awareness of
what was and what in contrast is.

The work on this first lyric, then, is that of a poet orientating himself to deal, not with the sequence of facts, nor with their simpler pathos, but with the implications of being a lover, when a moment's 'strange fit' cannot be isolated from the whole import of another being's life and death.

~ 3 ~

Lucy's death is the event chosen by Wordsworth as the focal point of the poems, a death first involuntarily imagined and in the other lyrics, meditated on as an actuality. The dramatic force of 'Strange fits of passion' is enhanced by its juxtaposition with the other poems, and this is a pointer to the kind of unity the lyrics reveal—the additional perspectives they bring to each other.

A bias towards extreme emotion is not uncommon in the Romantic imagination and though it may be unexpected to include these lyrics in such a category, I think they qualify. They are poems where the most extreme event of a relationship —its ending—stands central. Wordsworth writes of the shattering of the lovers' shared experience, not of its growth and flowering. The shock of abrupt destruction vibrates in the lyrics, for all their gentleness and delicacy, and this shock amounts to an assault on the lover's own life. The poems show him gathering together what is left to him, assessing what survives, what is gone, what is changed. However quiet the tone, Wordsworth is dealing with a state of personal disintegration and it is from this angle that he explores the meaning of love. 'The difference to me' is the text, and the poems are repeated attempts to interpret that emotional knowledge.

The lyric in which this line occurs, 'She dwelt among the untrodden ways', stands second in all arrangements of the poems. It carries the fact that Lucy is dead as its climax:

> She lived unknown, and few could know
>     When Lucy ceased to be;
> But she is in her grave, and, oh,
>     The difference to me!

The lines face the anguished conditional of the previous poem —'If Lucy should be dead'—with the unequivocal 'she is in her grave'. But the lyric taken by itself is fraught with more than death acknowledged; it recalls the quality of Lucy's way of life as well as her beauty, and it implies the central place the lover occupied in that life. Lucy lived in seclusion where strangers did not come and where the devotion of this lover was a rare and outstanding occurrence in her limited circle. Wordsworth's choice of images is his estimate of the experience the lover has known, not just a tribute to her attractions:

> A violet by a mossy stone
> Half hidden from the eye!
> —Fair as a star when only one
> Is shining in the sky.

She can be characterised by the most unobtrusive and the most arresting of beauties, and by means of them the poet suggests that he was attuned to her quiet ways, responsive on her terms, as one who values the violet *in situ* must be, and that he was also aware of her as a dominant presence, the one light in his sky.

Simple though it is, therefore, this Lucy poem has a claim to belong to the poetry, not just of lyric lament, but of relationships too, for it places the lover as well as Lucy beside the springs of Dove and conveys something of the 'difference' he feels by showing he is bereft of one who valued him and who presided over his life, calming it by her unassertive mode of being.

When, like Mary Hutchinson, we turn directly to the lyric, 'I travelled among unknown men', the sense of exploring an emotional situation is strongly advanced. The third poem relates the lover's feeling to other allegiances in his life, and in its structure it shows how all find their centre in and take their value from this one ruling commitment. The poem begins 'among unknown men', emphasising loneliness, the absence of any bond or meaning in these encounters, and the contrasting awakening to conscious recognition of the appeal of the native place. But Lucy is the animating spirit—England is loved 'more and more' not for itself but because of its associations, intensified now because her death has brought the speaker a renewed and deeper loneliness:

> And thine too is the last green field
> That Lucy's eyes surveyed.

The poem finds a more oblique way of approaching the fact of Lucy's death, and from this, a way of discovering the emotional import: what he has lost is more clearly understood by what remains. The 'difference' has been more precisely plotted, operating in this poem not as an unformulated sense of pain, but as an awareness of changed consciousness.

A special vision emerges as a legacy of love and bereavement: the earth is not seen simply as itself but read as a history of that love. A map of personal emotion is superimposed on the green fields and the lover is guided to a grasp of his condition as the survivor. He is one who sees what Lucy saw. And a love for nature is so far humanised that the landscape is pressed towards the status of a symbol; but in this lyric it is no more than a pressure. Nature is still an experienced locality, even if specific identity is gone—we are no longer explicitly beside the springs of Dove. In 'Three years she grew in sun and shower', however, nature and Lucy are brought together far less literally to aid Wordsworth's continuing attempt to find ways of representing adequately what Lucy was to her lover, what her dying means, and how it is to be consolidated and also assessed.

In separating this lyric from its three predecessors and classifying it as a 'poem of the imagination', Wordsworth alerts us to its tactical divergence, and its greater ambition. Whereas the 'poems of the affections' could be so described, this lyric with its device of personified nature allows for implications outside their simplicities. The imaginative quality does not lie in the personification, but in what Wordsworth frees himself to suggest by means of it. He is able to open out his exploration of the three parties—Lucy, her lover and nature—into an imaginative presentation of their triangular relationship. Here he does not merely wish to say, the fields mean more to me because Lucy saw them: he is trying to understand the vision of love which fuses the beauty of place with that of person and makes bereavement a complex psychological experience.

A naivety induced by the speaking voice of nature is not altogether happily reconciled to my mind with either the moral subtleties or the physical variety which the poet also attributes to it. But the poem turns on the recognition that a special intuition of harmonious communion between humanity and nature 'has been' but 'never more will be'. In showing the intimacy of Lucy with her surroundings, their beauty informing her physical grace, and her sensibility in tune with the free life around her, the lover is indicating what he loved and what he perceived: Lucy as the perfect human product of nature's beneficent power. The poem's description of Lucy in terms of natural phenomena enacts that unity, and from this the lover's response to her and his feeling for nature merge as a single experience; he himself therefore shares in, is a part of, their unity of spirit. A triune partnership is celebrated as Nature says:

> 'The stars of midnight shall be clear
> To her; and she shall lean her ear
> In many a secret place
> Where rivulets dance their wayward round,
> And beauty born of murmuring sound
> Shall pass into her face.'

The poem's final verse implies that such perfection as Lucy's could reach its logical conclusion only in her death; but the lines do not go on to sustain the vision of Lucy, nature and lover still held in one close intimacy, although the potential for such a conclusion is there, since nature lives, containing Lucy, as it were. But the poem changes key here:

> She died and left to me
> This heath, this calm, and quiet scene;
> The memory of what has been,
> And never more will be.

Things fall apart in these lines. Not with obvious violence, for there is an impulse towards consolidation in the steadiness of the statements, but none the less decisively. Nature here is neither speaking spirit nor active power, but a passive scene. Lucy is dead; and the lover is aware of himself alone in an utterly changed universe. Where there was unity, now there is a sharp sense of separateness and even isolation. Loving Lucy fostered a vision which the loss of that love has broken. Words-worth reaches his furthest—his most Victorian—point of exploration in the lyrics so far in this attempt to focus the shock of loss and the resultant psychological dislocation which amounts to a dismantling of a whole world-picture. There is a starkness about the final lines of the poem which the muted tone should not disguise: the lines force the speaker back on himself and leave him in an entirely new situation, with the facts somehow to be organised in a personal universe whose governing centripetal compulsion is gone.

'The difference to me' is here discovered to be total. Or rather, the phrase can be revised simply but radically as 'I am different'. The final verse of 'Three years she grew' which establishes this discovery could, without undue straining, be read as the cue for the final lyric of the group, 'A slumber did my spirit seal'. What is re-enacted here is the shock of a collapsed vision. Wordsworth rehearses the psychological change yet again, but he achieves a lyric wholly individual in character, not a repetition but an extension of his explorations into love and loss. Where 'Three years she grew' worked explicitly, by amplifying illustration, this lyric is oblique and elliptical because it reduces simplicity of statement to an economy which strikes beyond clarity to suggest the profoundly inexplicable nature of what has occurred, both to Lucy and her lover:

> A slumber did my spirit seal;
> I had no human fears:
> She seemed a thing that could not feel
> The touch of earthly years.
>
> No motion has she now, no force;
> She neither hears nor sees;
> Rolled round in earth's diurnal course,
> With rocks, and stones, and trees.

At the heart of the lyric is the clash between its two quatrains. Tension is generated in several ways, to depict an awakening, not to human fears, but to human facts. The transition from trance-serenity to shock recalls 'Strange fits of passion', but here there is no conditional, but accomplished truth. The verses do not describe the event, they concentrate wholly on the inner experience of security overthrown and revealed as delusion. Lucy is felt to die in the poem as the harsh statement, 'No motion has she now, no force', cuts across the dream of her immunity. She is lost as a person, absorbed into an equally impersonal universe. The lover again is seeking to realise his isolation as a sentient being capable of utter disorientation amid indifferent and undeviating natural processes. The degree to which things were felt to be otherwise in the calm created by love is eloquently implied in the assault of the second stanza on the first.

Yet there is a network of correspondences uniting the two, as well as the clash between them. The lyric's power, and its enigmatic quality, depend upon the ambiguity. There is a sense in which the second stanza supports rather than destroys the first. In the lover's visionary detachment, Lucy was already one apart from humanity: his feelings towards her allowed such an unreality to possess him, and thus love itself is discovered to be ambiguous, at once cherishing and distancing the individual human person. Further, the second stanza from another angle offers the lover his dream come true: Lucy now is a thing that cannot feel 'the touch of earthly years'. She, and therefore he too, is removed from the necessity for human fears; loss is totally disruptive and yet it marks the end of the anguish living relationships promote. The lover is himself distanced from the full human state—and here the poem joins hands once more with its beginning. The vision of Lucy's mindless, mute association with 'rocks, and stones, and trees' looks back to the mysterious spirit-sealing slumber with a haunting intimation of peace and affinities faintly apprehended.

The shortest Lucy poem is the most highly charged, and it stands out for the richness and density of suggestion carried within its simple form and vocabulary. Wholly successful in itself, it has no need of the other four lyrics to assist its impact. But when it is read as the final member of a group of poems dealing with one situation, it shows Wordsworth not only sustaining his explorations but pursuing his theme to a point where its complexity has become apparent.

In so far as the Lucy poems stand in sequence and progress, this is their destination. Wordsworth feels his way from simple observations on what loving Lucy has meant to the recognition of his love as a key emotion determining his other relationships, and so to a more intensive reconnaissance of the change in himself and his world-picture. The poems carry him from one 'strange fit' to another; beginning with a spasm of the mind which alerts the lover to his vulnerability and the power of the bond which holds him, they end with an awakening from self-absence which reveals a complex psychology of love and bereavement. The finding and losing of self, the illusions and revelations inherent in deep commitment to another being are issues inseparable from the catastrophic event as it is repeatedly contemplated.

The autonomy of each poem must be respected, however, intimately linked though they are. Wordsworth's finely reticent artistry does not force the lyrics together nor impose any consistency of outlook on them. He is faithful to the shifting winds of feeling—this indeed is part of his perception—so that the same situation can be differently seen and so appraised more fully. No questions find answers, no conflict is resolved, no one poem supplants another.

In these five diverse yet single-centred intimations of grief, the need for a special approach to a poetry of relationships is acknowledged. What is required is a persistent working of the imagination rather than a climactic statement, an effort to capture not a moment of crisis but an intricate history of loving and grieving. Room is needed to handle the phenomenon of a lover's experience and to trace the variety of implication in it. Evolution, change, displacement of various kinds are to be coped with, so that narrative, refused and repressed as a sequence of events, is to be invoked as a psychological necessity if the realisation of 'difference' is to be poetically caught and investigated.

Lyrical triumphs in themselves, Wordsworth's Lucy poems are also, I am suggesting, momentous because they open up these emotional regions, where the individual's sense of himself is contingent upon his sense of another. Although Wordsworth ventures no further, it is possible to say that he acts as Moses to the Victorian poets, showing them their promised land. Or, to put it another way, the Lucy poems are Wordsworth's *In Memoriam*.

∽ 4 ∽

Referring to Byron's separation from his wife, Goethe remarked: 'in its circumstances and the mystery in which it is involved, it is so poetical, that if Lord Byron had invented it he could hardly have had a more fortunate subject for his genius'.[3] He became acquainted with Byron's work through two examples of the poet's response to this subject, *Fare Thee Well* and *A Sketch.*

His opinion has not found many supporters, for Byron's poems on his personal affairs at their crisis in 1816 are not among those regarded as exhibiting his genius at its best, whatever the swings of critical taste. But this area of Byron's work offers the most direct example of a Romantic attempt to create a poetry of relationships by handling a crisis not of death, but of breakdown. In the 1816 pieces Byron is finding out how far, and in what ways, his imagination can work on the subject. The view that his efforts range only from the inept to the unmemorable may indeed prove too hasty a judgment; while whatever the level of success, in the attempt to meet the situation poetically there is certainly much of interest, as Goethe predicted, and of relevance too to Victorian domestic poetry.

First of all, the contrasts with the Lucy poems are helpful in showing the alternatives of approach to such material. Byron writes out of an immediate unconsolidated experience of upheaval, while Wordsworth is not so prompted, although it may be, as Coleridge said in commenting on 'A slumber did my spirit seal', that he 'in some gloomier moment . . . had fancied the moment in which his Sister might die'.[4] But unlike Lucy, Lady Byron and Augusta are potent emotional presences in the poems, so that here, the actual pressures of relationships are experienced. Byron's involvement with his material is dramatic where Wordsworth's is lyrically reflective. The impulse of the Separation poems, like that of the Lucy group, is to

[3] *Letters and Journals*, ed. Prothero (1901), v, appendix II, 'Goethe and Byron', p. 508, quoted from G. Ticknor.
[4] Letter to Thomas Poole, 6 April 1799; *Collected Letters of Samuel Taylor Coleridge*, ed. E. L. Griggs (1956), i, p. 479.

assess the personal implications of emotional commitment, but Byron is trying to measure his situation as its tremors continue to assail him. His are seismological poems, not Wordsworthian plummet-soundings of an intensely imagined event.

If these 1816 poems are placed beside two others of the same period, they can all be seen to stand together as products of a persistent struggle to come to grips with the crisis precipitated by the separation. In *The Dream* Byron tries a less dramatic and more distanced approach to depict suffering and shock in love; here he is structurally more adventurous and the effort to master such experience creatively is more apparent. And in the third Canto of *Childe Harold*, turned to as a relief in the time of crisis, there is an attempt, not to eliminate the personal, but to bring it and the public themes together.

In the months from March to September 1816, therefore, Byron was engaged in a series of bids to find poetic ways of dealing with sudden and deep disturbance. From *Fare Thee Well* to *Childe Harold* III he invites attention as a precursor of Victorian poetic research into the shocks of broken bonds and the consequences of those which endure.

ᑳ 5 ᑳ

When he published *Fare Thee Well* in *Poems 1816*, Byron added Coleridge's lines on estrangement in *Christabel* as a motto to it. The contrast between his poem and its epigraph is striking. Coleridge sums up the lifelong effects of a quarrel which severed 'friends in youth':

> They stood aloof, the scars remaining,
> Like cliffs which had been rent asunder;
> A dreary sea now flows between,
> But neither heat, nor frost, nor thunder,
> Shall wholly do away, I ween,
> The marks of that which once hath been.

The image carries several ideas; intimation of the force of the initial upheaval is combined with acknowledgment both of its continuing influence and of the love which preceded it. The six lines consolidate a whole drama. But the poem they introduce

21

is on the contrary written in the midst of the eruption, the immediate recognition that 'every feeling hath been shaken'. Byron predicts the relevance of the *Christabel* image from the extreme pain of the moment. This is explicit in the poem itself:

> Yet, oh yet, thyself deceive not—
> Love may sink by slow decay,
> But by sudden wrench, believe not
> Hearts can thus be torn away:
> Still thine own its life retaineth—
> Still must mine though bleeding, beat;
> And the undying thought which paineth
> Is—that we no more may meet. [5]

He is attempting to assess and to realise what has happened. But the fact that he addresses himself to his wife and spells out in violent terms what she has done underlies that his poetic impulse is active as opposed to reflective, a dramatic engagement with the situation in its rawness:

> Though my many faults defaced me,
> Could no other arm be found,
> Than the one which once embraced me,
> To inflict a cureless wound?

The blow is repeatedly seen as lethal:

> Every feeling hath been shaken;
> Pride—which not a world could bow—
> Bows to thee—by thee forsaken,
> Even my soul forsakes me now.

'More than this I scarce can die': Lady Byron, in short, has committed murder.

The betrayed relationship removes from the poet a means by which he knew himself; a support has been torn away, and the shocked condition so apparent in the tone of the emphatic quatrains is rooted in this loss as well as in wounded love and pride. As in much of Byron's earlier work, the histrionic excess

[5] Quotations are taken from *The Works of Lord Byron*, ed. E. H. Coleridge (1898–1904), iii and iv, and for *Childe Harold*, ii.

should not obscure the point that the poem is impelled by a strong current of imaginative energy. Moore was right in his first opinion that the poem was 'showy',[6] but it is also urgent with the recognition that a brutally severed emotional bond is an assault on the identity of one who suffers it. The lines hint that Lady Byron too may feel this loss of something essential to her self-experience, but their nerve-centre is Byron's certainty that the blow has been mortal to him. The energy of *Fare Thee Well* is generated by fear.

Whether the poem exaggerates or records his reactions exactly, Byron divined the deeper psychological import of the situation, and all the poems arising out of the separation are attempts to articulate this aspect of the ordeal in particular. The power of relationships both as they destroy and as they rescue is his theme whenever he addresses his wife, his daughter or Augusta, and equally when he surveys the love of the Boy for one whose 'sighs were not for him' (*The Dream*).

Thus in the more bitterly accusing *Lines on Hearing that Lady Byron was Ill* (September 1816), he sees her as a 'moral Clytemnestra' and repeats that the fatal nature of the injury done to him lies in its being the work of such a hand. His sins might deserve punishment, but Heaven did not choose 'so near an instrument' to act as Nemesis. Describing his feelings 'in the after-silence on the shore', he stresses even more the close link between an awareness of death and the suffering he is undergoing. 'All is lost, except a little life'; and as 'the mind recoils Upon itself, and the wrecked heart lies cold', even that 'little life' sinks under the 'wish to be no more'.

'I have had many foes, but none like thee'. The charge is accurate as well as vindictive, for these poems reveal the unique power which one who stands in this kind of relation, wife to husband, can wield. Only such a bond can lead to such a fatal wounding. The contrast between the lines to Anabella and *A Sketch*, attacking the 'Iago' of the affair, Mrs Clermont, bear out this point. Byron here uses Pope's couplets and his technique of character-assassination to produce an extroverted piece, in comparison with the poems to Lady Byron, precise in its exposure of evil done:

[6] Quoted E. H. Coleridge, *Works*, iii, p. 531.

> Skilled by a touch to deepen Scandal's tints
> With all the kind mendacity of hints,
> While mingling truth with falsehood—sneers with smiles—
> A thread of candour with a web of wiles . . .

The lines move with the confidence of unequivocal hate; there is none of the brooding on the 'cureless wound' and the hand which struck the blow as in the other poems. Byron coldly wishes upon his victim, 'the strong curse of crushed affections', but it is only when addressing Lady Byron that he speaks out of the confused anguish of discovering that curse come upon him, with its menace to the suddenly isolated self.

❧ 6 ❧

Between April and July 1816 Byron wrote two sets of *Stanzas to Augusta*, the *Epistle to Augusta*, and the lines 'The castled Crag of Drachenfels' in *Childe Harold* III which are also addressed to her. Like the poems to Lady Byron, these lyrics are concerned with the function of an intimate relationship in the life of one who submits himself to this experience. They reiterate the same views but from the opposite pole of feeling: where Lady Byron is seen as an assailant, Augusta is hailed as the one being whose enduring love offers the poet something to rest on and cling to as a sustaining thought. In the 'deep midnight of the mind', she is the 'solitary star'; she stands 'a lovely tree' above his grave, emblem of 'fond fidelity' (April *Stanzas*). The July *Stanzas* repeat the gratitude for her constancy, the imagery pointing to its life-giving effects:

> In the Desert a fountain is springing,
>   In the wide waste there still is a tree,
> And a bird in the solitude singing,
>   Which speaks to my spirit of *Thee*.

Neither poem rises to lyrical eloquence, but both are emphatic in their avowal that the only bulwark for the shocked mind is the knowledge that one heart 'can feel—but will not move'.

There are contrasts between the two which add dramatically to their point. In the April *Stanzas*, the emblem of a tree shading a monument is typical of the poet's view of his situation. He is dead to feeling, able only to acknowledge the protective gesture which outfaces his misery. In the July poem, on the other hand, emotion is more positive. Love is once more influential, encouraging reciprocal feeling. Travelling away from Augusta he finds the idea of her arouses resistance to pain: 'They may torture, but shall not subdue me; 'Tis of *Thee* that I think—not of them'. She is a saving, vivifying power, drawing forth a response.

In the *Epistle to Augusta* there is a continuity of theme, but the change of tone and mood is considerable. The poem offers further evidence that Byron was trying to consolidate the 'shipwreck', encouraged by the influence of a love which defied it. Shared experience with Augusta, common memories of earlier times and places, can be recalled without the feeling that all is gone, and so he is able to survey his past and present self steadily rather than desperately. The final verse of the *Epistle* epitomises the sentiment which makes the whole poem possible:

> For thee, my own sweet sister, in thy heart
> I know myself secure, as thou in mine;
> We were and are—I am, even as thou art—
> Beings who ne'er each other can resign;
> It is the same, together or apart,
> From Life's commencement to its slow decline
> We are entwined—let Death come slow or fast,
> The tie which bound the first endures the last!

This is the stabilising thought, assuring the poet that he can find himself 'secure' in another, mirrored in her being and therefore sustained in his own. On the strength of it he can review his sufferings in a more stoical manner, admit responsibility for them, and survey his situation against the scale of 'Kingdoms and Empires' and the quiet of nature. The third Canto of *Childe Harold* is miniatured here, and the *Epistle* helps to show that Byron's pausing in that Canto to address a lyric to Augusta is no digression.

The *Epistle to Augusta* is a return to normal consciousness; it is sober and meditative where the *Stanzas* were high-pitched, circumstantial where they relied on rhetorical figures and stock gestures. Grave but tender in tone, it conveys in its voice and its movement the trust and sense of anchorage from which it springs. The three Augusta poems, therefore, show a process of revival and recovery of self. Starting from passive gratitude that one relationship has survived, the poet then grasps it as a lifeline and so begins to retrieve his identity. The *Epistle*, with its references to Newstead and the past, shows him once more in possession of himself, saved from the maelstrom and able to take his bearings. Pain has schooled him, 'a strange quiet' has come upon him, but in Augusta he finds a way of bringing all his experience into focus.

∽ 7 ∽

The poems to Lady Byron and Augusta show that the individual can find himself destroyed or revived by the agency of others. That this was a serious issue to Byron's imagination as well as in his personal life at this time is borne out by another poem of the Diodati period, *The Dream*. Here he emphasises the negative side—the high price of broken ties and the torment occasioned by the rejection of love. But this poem is more ambitious, in scope and technique.

The failed marriage is only obliquely approached; it is seen in a context of the poet's earlier experience which, with its aftermath, is the emotional centre of the poem. Byron goes back to his first rebuff and recalls his youthful hurt at Mary Chaworth's lack of response to his passion. He then shows how this remained disturbing, turning the Boy into the Wanderer, and in later life erupting to play its part in the present misery. This is an interesting attempt to handle a psychological history: *The Dream* aims to bring out the pattern of cross-reference in the emotional crises of life, so that their formative influence is suggested and their permanent presence in the mind is demonstrated.

The power of a serious relationship is not exhausted when the association dissolves, the poem shows, for it never really ceases to exist. Byron implies that Mary, 'the Lady of his love' was herself haunted by the past, although she 'had loved him not'. Her latest descent into wretchedness and finally 'frenzy' is traced, its causes unknown, but involving disillusion, for she too was disappointed in marriage. So the poem reflects on 'the doom of these two creatures', the penalties of strong feeling for others and the entanglement of emotion old with emotion new.

By using the device of a dream, Byron frees himself from story-telling obligations, and is able to concentrate attention on the high moments of feeling, the logic of the inner narrative. The poem is divided into sections, each one presenting a tableau or dramatic scene, and each introduced and dismissed by the line 'A change came o'er the spirit of my dream'. Byron prefaces the scenes with a comment on the capacity of dreams to 'shake us with the vision that's gone by' and, more than this, to 'curdle a long life into one hour'; thus the emotional unity of the ensuing sections is prepared for. The dreamer feels the Boy's agony of unrequited love as it was, and he also knows the permanence of the wound. The poem adds the pain of hindsight to its dramatic submission to each moment. 'Long life' is indeed concentrated into 'one hour'. The change from scene to scene makes the psychological point clear: the Boy in love; the Boy desperate at the parting in the 'antique Oratory'; the Wanderer on his Eastern travels, no longer 'like what he had been'; the wedding day when the Oratory scene—'the day, the hour, the sunshine and the shade'—suddenly bursts once more upon the groom; and the later miseries for both 'maiden' and 'youth'.

*The Dream* is searching for a poetic technique and a structure which will render an emotional history accessible and expose its pattern. Its ambition is to be saluted even if its success is only partial. It is a prophetic experiment, and a moving one, despite its limitations: if Wordsworth looks on to *In Memoriam*, and does so with great tact and delicacy of touch, it is not too far-fetched a tribute to Byron here, I think, to claim that he is the only Romantic who, however crudely, anticipates *Maud*.

∽ 8 ∽

To include Canto III of *Childe Harold* as one of the 'domestic pieces' of 1816 may seem to lower its dignity. It is of course a work of more moment and far more range than the poems so far discussed. But it was written as a response to the pain of the

27

time, and the fact that the result is such an emphatically public poetry is of considerable interest from my present point of view. The incorporating of the poet's state of heart into a survey of Europe's history and topography—and vice versa—shows Byron's imagination fully roused to grapple with the implications of the shock he has suffered. His attempt to bring together personal relationships and the European scene is a move of consequence. It breaks away from the convention of handling personal predicaments lyrically, and asserts the legitimacy of exploring them in a broader context, which in its turn may be illuminated by the personal situation. *Childe Harold* offers a freedom and establishes an ambition which Victorian poets— while not discarding lyric expression—are able to accept and emulate in ways distinctively their own.

Byron has more often been censured for vulgarity than complimented for blazing imaginative trails, however. Arnold's phrase, 'the pageant of his bleeding heart', has been taken as an appropriate summary of *Childe Harold*, especially Canto III, and interpreted as a negative judgment. Certainly it suggests the Canto's far from reticent presentation of injured love and pride and its refusal to suffer in an undertone. But it can persuade us wrongly to assume that Byron is merely indulging in an empty display and so to underestimate his poetic seriousness. There is more to consider, first in Byron's judgment that he can —indeed must—proclaim a drama of relationships in conjunction with a vision of Europe, and secondly in his management of the Canto so that it encompasses both without fatal fractures in tone or incongruity of scale.

The Canto is framed by stanzas addressed to his daughter Ada; it pauses on the banks of the Rhine to greet and pay tribute to Augusta. The rift with Lady Byron is bitterly present in both utterances, and the poet's attempts to adjust to his situation as an exile from relationships in which he felt himself fulfilled can be distinguished here as a leading emotion of the Canto. 'This was in my nature' (cxvi), and because the expression of such feelings as parental tenderness is denied him, he has lost himself and stands in urgent need of a recovery of confidence. To see him as merely parading his private life or sulking in public is to miss the crisis of identity which grips him and also the degree to which this stimulated him as a poet. It is not a question of ludicrously inflating a domestic quarrel to the dimensions of the Pilgrimage. The extremity of the personal predicament is such that it can only be explored and assessed in a large context which can absorb, control and also provide correlatives for it.

The Canto is keenly aware of destructive human passion, whether this is a matter of warring nations or family hostilities. It is also preoccupied with what happens to, and what characterises, the isolated spirit—'all unquiet things' (xliii) who take the Napoleonic path and dominate rather than mingle with their fellows. Against their bleak and turbulent careers Byron sets such stories as the efforts of a daughter to save her father in Roman Europe, and her dying with him: 'these are deeds which should not pass away' (lxvii).[7] And in meditating on the 'great minds' who invite disaster on themselves and others, he says that some, like Rousseau, turn to a compensatory relationship with nature as a 'refuge from the worldly shocks' (xcix) and a way of transcending the personal isolation which the failure of human affections engenders. It is impossible to separate the strands of Canto III into personal feeling and public commentary. The joy in the Alpine scenery, the studies of tyrants and wars, the aloof spirits and the loving hearts of history are all part of his research into his own nature, its capacities and need for love, its pain and its resources when forced back on itself alone.

Rhetorical enlargement promotes the unity of theme and emotion. 'My daughter' is hailed as the 'Sky—Mountains—River—Winds—Lake—Lightnings!' (xcvi) are hailed; she is grandly seen as 'the child of Love' though 'born in bitterness' and 'nurtured in Convulsion' (cxviii), but so regarded, she takes her place more appropriately as part of the whole Canto's vision as it strives to cope with convulsion, personal and Napoleonic, and to evaluate the ties of love. The lyrical voice still has a place, however. When the Canto pauses by the Rhine

---

[7] The story is an invention of the sixteenth century; but Byron, believing it, remarks in his note: 'These are the names and actions which ought not to perish, and to which we turn with a true and healthy tenderness, from the . . . confused mass of conquests and battles . . .' *Works*, ii, p. 299.

to address Augusta, the tone changes to intimacy, but the themes are crystallised rather than set aside. The lyric, following stanza lv, can be seen as a moment of balance where, as in the other poems to Augusta, the value of reliable love is felt and rested upon. A shared experience is a richer experience—such is the simple statement here; the riverscape would be a 'double joy' in her company:

> But one thing want these banks of Rhine,
> Thy gentle hand to clasp in mine!

An unremarkable lyrical sentiment in itself, it takes on eloquence from its context and in its turn sums up precisely the nature of the burden carried by the Canto—that of love prized but removed out of reach.

Canto III of *Childe Harold* presents on a European stage the plight of the individual at once severed from and branded by his intimate associates. I would suggest again that Byron makes a *Maud* conceivable: here, in the scale of this Canto and its rhetorical attack, for instance, there are opportunities for a way of approaching a poetry of relationships which Tennyson is able to develop and exploit. *Childe Harold*, with the other 1816 poems, plays from this point of view a pioneer role.

### ✍ 9 ✍

Together, the Lucy poems and Byron's domestic pieces suggest the common ground and also the range and variety which a poetry of relationships permits. They prepare for the ambition of Victorian work and they plot some of its emotional epicentres. Both poets are moved by the sudden collapse of their world-view, created and sustained as it was, they discover, by the agency of others. For Wordsworth, death, for Byron, breakdown, but for both a calamity which their poems seek to evaluate and in some sense repair. The feeling of assault on the personality, of violence perpetrated, is not a surprising theme in Romantic work which is so often rooted in a crisis of identity, but it emphasises the fundamentals which are tapped by introspective poets who attempt to portray the grief of loss—in itself of course a poetic commonplace at all periods. Anticipated here are the exploratory energies of Victorians drawn to such material, although the later poets do not always need the incentive of crisis to embark on their effort to appreciate the implications of intimacy.

Neither Wordsworth nor Byron regards his situation as static or comprised of a single mood. The device of a group of lyrics is the outcome of a conviction that only multiple statements can hope to net the complexity of feeling; in Byron this is a comparatively fortuitous and improvised discovery, while the Lucy poems are sensitively designed to reveal it. Wordsworth subtly uses the group to convey the shifts of feeling which may seem to amount to an evolving assessment of the initial grief or may remain for the reader simply a record of fluctuation. The options are open, but the principle of seeing this kind of subject as fluid is established, together with the need for forms and structures which can cope with instability. Byron's set of stanzas to Augusta with much less artistry endorses the point that change and the assimilation of it is an essential feature of this poetry, while in *The Dream* and *Childe Harold* III, his sense of psychological history gives rise to work which begins more boldly to extend the poetic possibilities.

Byron's dramatic gestures are far from Wordsworth's muted, lyrically intense soliloquies on Lucy's ceasing to be. But there are Victorian ears to hear and understand each voice; and a vigorous line of Victorian poems which testifies to the significance of both Romantic excursions into a province otherwise left to await that later occupation.

# II

# 'The Fates, It Is Clear, Are Against Us'

## Arnold: the Marguerite Poems;
## Clough: *Amours de Voyage*

∽ I ∽

To begin with poems which concern themselves with the retreat from, and even the impossibility of, relationships may appear a curious policy in a study which purports to demonstrate the peculiar prestige and compulsion of the theme in Victorian work. But Arnold and Clough both acknowledge that intimate emotional encounters can be crucial and formative—it could be said this is what the lover of Marguerite, and Claude in his half-pursuit of Mary Trevellyn, are afraid of. For their poems of abortive relationships the two poets draw on the same expectations as are found elsewhere—Arnold lyrically, Clough ironically—and the urgency of their interest in non-commitment serves to highlight the general Victorian assent to commitment as a leading poetic preoccupation. The tragedy and comedy of hesitation and refusal can only be appreciated in an imaginative climate where avowal and its consequences are accepted as worthy of serious exploration.

The great contrast between Clough and Arnold in handling their common theme is already hinted here, and it provides a further reason for beginning with these poems. They help to establish one of the most impressive features of Victorian poetry inspired by relationships—its range. For Arnold, the traumas of disengagement, or engagement, are paramount; for Clough, the spectacle of his hero's temperament tripping up impulses towards engagement is at once sad and near-ridiculous. It oversimplifies to say that Clough is the more detached sophisticate, Arnold the more involved romantic, but the distinction serves as a useful pointer to the general diversity of stance, where there is no orthodoxy of presentation any more than there is uniformity of feeling.

No approach is typical, so none is deviant. But in turning from Arnold to *Amours de Voyage*, it is possible to see the differences as a move from an inherited Romanticism towards a more completely autonomous Victorian poetry. Broadly, where Arnold accepts an idea and an ideal of love and records the anguish of finding it unrealisable, Clough sees Claude's predicament as one generated entirely by his individual temperament. Love in *Amours de Voyage* is not regarded as a quality somehow independent of those who experience it, a vision to which they may or may not do justice, but as an event wholly subject to the responsive chemistry of two people when they meet, and only to be defined in terms of what follows from the encounter. Arnold can and does lament the impossibility of ideal love as well as his separation from Marguerite; Clough is intent on the snail-horn sensitivities of the tentative Claude, and what is lost finally is not Love, but the experience that might have been—Claude and Mary.

Such an emphasis on the particularities of specific pairings, the individuality of the participants, is a vital element in Victorian poems of relationships. Intimate feeling is contingent not absolute—and indeed, even in the Marguerite poems, this is recognised if only as part of the pain. Clough and a reluctant Arnold both show emotion historically, extended in time and to be understood in terms of temporality and its implications. Substance and structure alike are affected by this vision, and a closer study of first the Marguerite group and then *Amours de Voyage* will help to demonstrate how.

శ 2 శ

If the Marguerite poems are compared with the lyrics on Lucy, Arnold's work can be seen more clearly as transitional in the move from Romantic to Victorian. Like Wordsworth's, the poems may be taken singly as self-contained lyrics; but like the Lucy set, they relate to and affect each other as the products of a sustained concern with one theme. In preparing new editions of his work, Arnold 'added to and subtracted from'[1] the group as it had first appeared in 1853 under the title *Switzerland*, but he remained conscious of it as a group. The connection may be loose but it exists, as may be said of Wordsworth's lyrics. But here the two poets begin to draw apart.

Wordsworth meditates on one phenomenon, the death of Lucy; he circles round, changing the angle only. The impulse is consolidatory as the poet regards an accomplished fact. Lucy's death is the fixed point and he locates his own position in relation to it. Arnold's poems, on the other hand, do not circle round one centre, nor repeatedly rehearse one situation. They trace an emotional crisis as it approaches, breaks and recedes. They are poems moving from stage to stage, each offering a distinct moment of feeling with its place in the progression. This in short is a lyrical group which admits sequence, and takes movement and change as fundamentals. As has been indicated, Arnold does not go so far as to integrate his lyrics into a unified structure, but he shows the potential for development in this direction.

Lucy dies; and Wordsworth writes of Lucy dead. Arnold parts from Marguerite and writes of that separation, but he writes also of meeting her for the first time; of returning to her a year later; of a temporary parting; of the aftermath of leaving her; and adds another poem ten years later. Thus the eight lyrics covering the Switzerland experience range from *A Memory Picture* in the autumn of 1848 to *The Terrace at Berne*, composed in 1863 after his visit in 1859. For Arnold the psychological action involves not just the climax, or anti-climax, of the affair, but a much wider time-span. The emotional meaning begins with the first encounter and only ends— if at all—with memory's epitaph, years afterwards. He therefore displays, in a fairly primitive form, the Victorian sense of process, the perception that feeling is not exclusively a matter of the electrifying instant, but something which matures and declines in the slow working of hours and days. But he combines realism of this sort with a more heady yearning for love in its ideal character and so is not fully committed to the temporal, a

[1] K. Allott, *The Poems of Matthew Arnold* (Longmans Annotated English Poets, 1965), p. 115. Quotations are taken from this edition.

34

reservation which has much to do with the negative emphasis of the sequence.

∽ 3 ∽

> Ere the parting hour go by,
> Quick, thy tablets, Memory!

From the first, Arnold's poetic response to Marguerite registers passing time as a feature in his emotion. *A Memory Picture* was written after the initial meeting at Thun in 1848 and it shows Arnold moved as much by the thought of the coming year apart and by apprehension about reunion as he is by the immediate pang of separation. Time and the power of time is admitted as a threat to lovers, and hence an element of losing struggle—the moment against the years—is present in the lyrics from the beginning, seeming to be a strong incentive to their composition. In a note for this poem, Arnold summarises: 'Thun and vividness of sight and memory compared: sight would be less precious if memory could equally realize for us.'[2]

The poem's original title, *To my Friends, who ridiculed a tender Leave-taking*, together with its dashing trochaic couplets, would seem to indicate something of the posing gallant in Arnold's mood, yet this is undermined throughout by a fevered urgency which is fed by the suggestion of tension between the lovers:

> Marguerite says: 'As last year went,
> So the coming year'll be spent;
> Some day next year, I shall be,
> Entering heedless, kissed by thee.'
> Ah, I hope!—yet, once away,
> What may chain us, who can say?

In these lines provokingly unromantic, Marguerite is throughout a teasing presence. Her changes of mood and paradoxes of character—the 'arch' chin and the 'frank' eyes—are part of the poem's dynamic, and part too of its desperation. She is a person not just a presence, and her independent reactions carry *A Memory Picture* away from Lucy whose laughter was ruled poetically out of order, and into the Victorian sphere of relationships between individuals who differ from each other.

[2] Allott, p. 107.

Arnold's whole effort in the poem is to deny its assertion that 'clear impression' dies to 'dim remembrance'. He is trying to arrest the vision of a girl in a 'lilac kerchief', inducing the poem to refute what it says: 'Time's current strong Leaves us fixed to nothing long.' The moment is the more to be clutched at because it is felt to be vulnerable, destined not merely to fade but to be followed by others which may well alter its significance. Marguerite as a timeless loved object may survive by means of this verse photograph though ironically what the poem finally conveys is the sense of a difficult, dissolving relationship.

In its tensions and cross-currents, *A Memory Picture* stands as a prophetic beginning to the group. The poem of reunion, *Meeting*, condenses the same issues into its four quatrains. Arnold returning seems to find his fears dispelled, the girl he left 'unaltered with the year'. At least he can claim her to be so by listing the reassuringly familiar attributes of soft hair 'and those sweet eyes of blue'. But then the poem recoils abruptly in its tracks. The agitation of the first lyric reappears as the moment is menaced, this time by his own inability to accept it. It cannot be isolated, it must have consequences—its happiness demands a sequel in the form of a commitment to Marguerite which will turn the perfect moment into a union of two lives, the timeless into time. Arnold's immediate awareness that the meeting is conditioned by what it leads to, and by all that he and Marguerite are, turns the poem from a simple gesture of love into a dramatic lyric of rejection:

> Again I spring to make my choice;
> Again in tones of ire
> I hear a God's tremendous voice:
> 'Be counselled, and retire.'

The God's domicile is clearly Arnold's own heart, and here he emerges as an individual made up of contradictory impulses, as Marguerite did in the previous poem. The model of the lover hailing his unchanged beloved is superseded by the reality of a human situation. Arnold finds himself in the grip of an emotion involving choice and action, and one confusing to him because it springs from his temperament meeting Marguerite's, not

36

from two characterless beings in a state called Love, as the first two stanzas dream. This is history not romance.

There is an evasive uneasiness in Arnold's attempt to see his conflict as an act in a cosmic drama, which he can complain about but which he is doomed to suffer as a helpless victim. The desire to avoid responsibility, and to be excused his drawing back, by denying that the situation is really self-created, is obliquely betrayed in the rather petulant final lines—'let the peaceful be!'—and the poem as a whole shies away from what its two unreconciled halves show. It does not come to grips with the difficulties of loving, once the owner of the 'sweet eyes of blue' and he who beholds them have become two individuals.

To turn to *Parting* immediately after this poem is to find Arnold as it were admitting these weaknesses, and in impatient reaction writing a full dramatisation of his dilemma and the tensions of a love affair begot upon impossibility. The change to a formally unsettled and emotionally far more fluid and candid utterance is an interesting sign of Arnold's divided imagination as it responds, now faintly, now warmly, to the task of plotting experience as it is.

The poem falls into two sections. The first acts out in contrasting rhythms the contrary desires which tear the poet apart and the second, in more sober quatrains, announces and perhaps rationalises the conclusion he has reached. Within *Parting*, therefore, there is movement, a change of stance, a new situation arrived at. It is the one poem which displays intentionally in its structure the impulse which brings the whole set into being, that is, to trace feeling as it grows, clarifies and becomes action. *Parting* records the experience of drowning into crisis and struggling out again to decision, and in registering the price of a negative decision, it touches a nerve of the century's imaginative concern with relationships. Setting the values of the solitary man against participation in another life, Arnold resists with passion the adventure which his fellow poets are so ready to accept as their theme; but his very dwelling on withdrawal is a measure of the allure he also feels. To record the agony of saying no, is to admit the theme's power no less than those who deal with the joys and agonies of saying yes.

37

Where *A Memory Picture* sought to regard poetry as a preservative, a way of holding firm a vision which life would dissolve, *Parting* sees it as an instrument for drawing the graph of living, and therefore passing, moments. The poem conveys mounting tension and the growing awareness of clashing impulses which cancel each other out, until one prevails and forces the poem to alter its tone and adjust itself to accommodate the voice of explanation after the surge and counter-surge of feeling. Waiting in a room with storm-winds at the window and Marguerite approaching the door, the poet's situation offers him a dramatic symbol of his emotional battle, and he is carried to a resolution of the struggle because he is able to recognise this. The real bias of his mind is made clear to him as he takes the step from actuality to symbol.

Hearing the wind, and feeling its force within himself, Arnold follows it to its destination, and as the verse changes from description to the imagined scene of 'cold, distant' mountains, the latter at once become the magnet of desire:

> How deep is their stillness!
> Ah, would I were there!

Nature's turbulence is not incompatible with nature's peace; human love is different. Arnold's wish that it were not so, and that loving could be a less disturbing condition—not just a storm-wind—is apparent as the voice of Marguerite is heard on the stair. The images he uses to describe that voice are both taken from calm, unruffled nature: the dawn music of a 'wet bird-haunted English lawn' and the 'upland clearness' of 'some sun-flecked mountain-brook'. But as she comes into the room, the 'rushing winds' again return to possess his consciousness, and now the urge to retreat from such passion reaches its crisis.

He counters the desire roused by her 'lovely lips' and the challenging proximity of her personality by desperately fleeing again in his mind to the lonely hillside, where he can find the relief of 'no life but, at moments The mountain-bee's hum'. Here the psychological drama of *Parting* reaches its resolution, because in the second imaginative flight to the mountains, he has chosen to reject living passion for the undemanding repose and impersonal energies of nature. Abruptly the poem changes level, translating what has just been lived through into the reasoning of the rational mind:

> In the void air, towards thee,
>   My stretched arms are cast;
> But a sea rolls between us—
>   Our different past!

More particularly, Marguerite has received other lovers. The poetry is weaker in these final verses, but the statements made are more than evasive excuses. The 'different past' is a formidable concept in Arnold's struggle throughout the Marguerite poems to confront, and to escape, the temporal realities in an experience of love. The constancy and predictability of nature offers an easier kind of loving because it does not subject the lover to the problems of humans who meet each other with histories behind and within them. In *Parting* Arnold reveals the contrast and the dismay it engenders:

> Far, far from each other
>   Our spirits have grown;
> And what heart knows another?
>   Ah! who knows his own?

Human relationships are frightening because they involve two different individuals who grow, change and refuse to be as stably reassuring as pictures or mountains. And so, paradoxically, these attempted relationships increase awareness of isolation. The mortal millions live alone and this is never more apparent than when two of them fall in love. Better then to retreat to nature and declare such solitude inevitable. The price of trying to adjust to time, circumstance and difference is for Arnold too high.

∽ 4 ∽

*Parting* therefore leads on directly to the lyric *Isolation. To Marguerite*, and its successor, *To Marguerite—Continued*. In the three poems, experience evolves into a melancholy philosophy in which Arnold finds relief and justification for his recoil from the attempt at loving intimacy. *Parting* dramatises the conflict of the solitary man swept by passion, and moves on to declare the incompatibility of the lovers; *To Marguerite—Continued* deepens and extends that rather tetchy insight into an unresentful but stoically sad vision of human islands washed by the dividing sea. *Isolation* stands as the lyric of transition, taking up the assertion that hearts are ignorant of each other and elaborating this into a larger mistrust of the venture from solitude, so moving into the broader concept of an inevitable loneliness. Where *Parting* catches the turmoil of crisis and the later poem distances the personal, this lyric retains the immediate situation but contemplates rather than relives it.

The angle has changed somewhat. Here the obstacle is not so much Marguerite's 'different past' as her indifferent present. He leaves her not because of past history but because she has not kept faith since their meeting. But the undercurrents are not affected by this firmer allotment of blame. The lover wakes from his dream of a perfect harmony of feeling to discover the reality, 'The heart can bind itself alone'. The ideal is set against the harsher human facts and, though Arnold accepts that the ideal was an illusion, he recoils into solitude as a refuge from the shock of the discovery. His next step, that all loving is but a 'dream' of union, seems at once to ennoble his situation by universalising it and to betray a still bitter, even vengeful, rationalisation of his wounded feelings.

The flight to nature and solitude is idealised here, replacing the lost ideal of romantic love. The 'lonely heart' is the superior heart, it seems. Bidding farewell to the attempt at loving, the poet soliloquises:

> . . . and thou, thou lonely heart,
> Which never yet without remorse
> Even for a moment didst depart
> From thy remote and spheréd course
> To haunt the place where passions reign—
> Back to thy solitude again!

Arnold retreats because passion is unreliable, painful, capable of deceiving, rather than because it is all illusion. *Isolation* in the bias of its vocabulary makes this clear. Arnold's creative power is kindled by the decree he exalts as a truth: 'Thou hast been, shalt be, art, alone'. This is clear-cut, an absolute, unaffected by the agitation which is the consequence of trying to live as if passion could be worth the losing struggle to achieve its essentially limited rewards.

Arnold chooses here to remain the poet of no compromise, inhabiting a poetic country which, if lonely, is both safe and calm. Sorrowfully he contemplates man's separation from man, yet he prefers this as a theme to the messy confusions which arise because people are unable to love each other serenely in the way they may commune with 'unmating things'. Reciprocal love is impossible, says Arnold, a dream at best; what he means is, I discover it is an experience of trial and error, contingent, temporal, beset by quirks of personality and circumstance, and I cannot bear such an incarnation. He rejects what is to so many of his contemporaries the source of inspiration.

The ideal dream of love can in fact be preserved by this strategy of withdrawing into a stoical despair. *To Marguerite— Continued* illustrates this, and the very assurance of Arnold's success here emphasises how congenial such a vision is to his imagination. The emotion of longing and desire for contact is intensely indulged, allowed full expression because there is no risk that it can break out of the astutely selected imagery Arnold finds for it. The islands are indisputably separate in the salt estranging sea, and they are safe, as it were, in the geographical guarantee of this symbol. A single continent can be dreamt of, music can cross the straits: harmony if unattainable can be believed in, and the poem is not in danger of having to allow for a more complex situation.

It is almost complacently insistent that the islands cannot challenge the inevitable:

> Who ordered, that their longing's fire
> Should be, as soon as kindled, cooled?
> Who renders vain their deep desire?—
> A God, a God their severance ruled!
> And bade betwixt their shores to be
> The unplumbed, salt, estranging sea!

As in *Meeting*, the God's authority rests in Arnold's determination that his own bias of mind shall be deified into an absolute. The poem succeeds in transmuting the refugee panic of *Parting* and *Isolation* into a dignified statement on humanity's lot, and its symbolism both controls and liberates the ruling idea. But I think Arnold miscalculates in trying to literalise and elevate his motivation by postulating the activities of 'a God'. By dropping from imaginative suggestion to rhetorical assertion, he betrays his anxiety that the situation shall be agreed by all to be the destiny of man, useless to question. The fine recovery in the last line makes the lapse the more regrettable—and the more revealing.

૭ 5 ૭

*To Marguerite—Continued* is the one lyric of the Switzerland series which stands clear and complete as a satisfying poem. It is also the only one where immediate emotional circumstance precipitates but does not feature in the lyric, and this is a significant pointer to Arnold's uneasiness with the material of relationships. He is most poetically at home when he is denying the possibility of the latter. But, as the poems already looked at show, he is drawn to try his hand at charting the history of his encounter with another person, and these efforts shadow forth the potential of such a poetry. Imperfect though they are, flawed in diction, tone and structure, their roughness itself indicates that this theme is demanding, its unfixed nature setting technical problems, its complexities refusing to be smoothed away by routine approaches to form or image or states of feeling. Isolation may be beautifully conveyed by allowing one symbol to grow and flower; but human conjunction or attempted conjunction is less amenable to such treatment. There is more to be assimilated.

*A Farewell* illustrates this. Typically it is a poem of withdrawal, but Arnold here is trying to deal with his particular tangled situation, admitting indeed that such situations can exist notwithstanding his vision of islands, and also that they take their character from the individuals concerned. To sum up in one generalising symbol is therefore impossible, however attractive such clarifying simplicity might be. Even here, though, the instinct to scramble back from complicated actuality is apparent: Arnold's poetic movement is one with his psychological mistrust of sexual turmoil. *A Farewell* begins by vividly recreating a reunion with Marguerite, but it ends in a stained-glass vision of a celestial relationship remarkably indistinguishable from the serene joys of solitude amid unchanging nature:

> How sweet, unreached by earthly jars,
> My sister! to maintain with thee
> The hush among the shining stars,
> The calm upon the moonlit sea!

Arnold's predilection for peace and quiet imposes an ending remote from the 'earthly jars' which otherwise, in their disturbing joy and pain, form the substance of the poem. The attempt to combine his customary retreat to nature with a conventional piety of heavenly rest is not happy, and there is a banality about this section of *A Farewell* which emphasises by contrast the strong pulse-beat of an occasion relived at the poem's beginning:

> The poplar avenue was passed,
> And the roofed bridge that spans the stream;
> Up the steep street I hurried fast,
> Led by thy taper's starlike beam.

These opening stanzas are bent on repossessing the experience as it was, and on tracing how the moment 'locked in each other's arms' turned into cooler response and then into the decision to part. The middle verses are occupied with an effort to explain why the affair could not work, oscillating between theories on the different needs of men and women and analysis of the poet's own temperament, restless and partly feminine.

The two stages, emotion recreated at its height and in its ebb, followed by the attempt to diagnose the failure, are sharply opposed to the anonymous, haloed figures with which the poem ends. At the outset, passion and its dependence for survival on character, the adjustment of two people to each other, is acknowledged; then all is put aside to celebrate a state of being where none of it need apply. Arnold again renounces the poetry of relationships and substitutes statues for people as the price he is prepared to pay for the reassurance of the eternal shining stars in place of the taper's temporal invitation.

As a whole, *A Farewell* is an equivocal poem. It never rises to eloquence after the opening verses, but it works away at trying to probe the dynamics of personality as a means of understanding the comings and goings of love, only to end with what is virtually a judgment against expending imaginative energy on such emotional dramas. History is to be transcended, its personal unpredictability neutralised by a fixed vision of humanity's fate. But history is none the less uncomfortably there.

Such is the conflict of Arnold's Switzerland poems. The ironic confusions of his position are further exposed—without irony—in the brief lyric, *Absence*. This poem betrays Arnold's sense that life carries him on rather than proceeds under his control, even though he interprets it as a ceaseless struggle to follow an appointed direction and reach 'the light', the mastery of fate, emotion and temperament. The poem, like the group as a whole, seems merely to suffer mixed attitudes and to reveal them involuntarily rather than to recognise and exploit contradictions, a passivity which reduces the poetic achievement. Here it leads the reader into a confusion similar to Arnold's, as the statements and images fail either to knit together or to generate any tension of opposed forces.

But what can be gathered from the *Absence* stanzas is the nature of the maze he wanders in. If Marguerite could be forgotten by an act of will, this would be a sign of progress in the struggle towards the light; but she and the light too grow dim simply because of the accumulating trivia of the 'passing day', and nothing can be done about it. Yet struggle is still insisted on, and Marguerite's role in it is far from clear: is the passion for her an enemy to be fought, or the one comfort and encouragement helping him on to a goal which then disowns her? The poem ends at an impasse, which is only half-acknowledged:

> I struggle towards the light; and ye,
> Once-longed-for storms of love!
> If with the light ye cannot be,
> I bear that ye remove.

44

> I struggle towards the light—but oh,
> While yet the night is chill,
> Upon time's barren, stormy flow,
> Stay with me, Marguerite, still!

The formula seems to be: passionate love may ease us amid time's storms, but eternity or true spiritual freedom will rescue us from love too. Arnold basically seeks, as always, escape from disturbance, and the enriching aspects of love are set against its frightening, explosive character. The beginning of the poem, however, where Marguerite is recalled by 'this fair stranger's eyes of grey', puts the stress on the accidents of life, the fortuitous spark which ignites a fire, and so shows his imagination responding to what it clearly fears and flees from.

## ᔑ 6 ᔑ

If there were any doubt that Arnold was poetically drawn to work with, as well as against, the awareness of time as emotion's element, *The Terrace at Berne* would dispel it. This poem records the disturbance of returning ten years afterwards to the scene of the abortive affair and, rather than recalling what was, it takes the passage 'through the crucible of time' as its theme and speculates on what may have happened to Marguerite in the interim. Where, at the beginning, *A Memory Picture* sought to fix the moment, this valediction to the Thun experience refuses to enlist poetry for that idealistic purpose. Indeed it swings at first to the other extreme, melodramatically putting down the stirrings of romantic sentiment:

> Doth riotous laughter now replace
> Thy smile; and rouge, with stony glare,
> Thy cheek's soft hue . . .
>
> Or is it over?—art thou dead?

But romantic regret, the dream of a special bond, reawakens at the idea of her death—could Marguerite die, 'and I not know?' This too is put down with a realism now less hysterical. Arnold looks life in the eye as an experience of temporality:

45

> Or shall I find thee still, but changed,
> But not the Marguerite of thy prime?
> With all thy being re-arranged,
> Passed through the crucible of time;
>
> With spirit vanished, beauty waned,
> And hardly yet a glance, a tone,
> A gesture—anything—retained
> Of all that was my Marguerite's own?

Yet, finally, Arnold turns sharply away from contemplating what may have happened and withdraws, as he did from the emotion itself, to his austere vision of inevitable human isolation. Speculations are futile, so is the attempt to translate them into fact by actually looking for Marguerite: 'I will not know'. Better, he says, to accept the transience of such experience as destined in the nature of things. We are,

> Like driftwood spars, which meet and pass
> Upon the boundless ocean-plain . . .

The substitution of drifting flotsam for the islands of *To Marguerite—Continued* is at least a concession to the possibility of relationships, however impermanent, and the poem as a whole moves towards the pathos of such a fate and away from the absolute tragedy of the islands' eternal separateness. None the less, it still affirms that Arnold chooses in the end a poetry which rests in its sense of regret for an ideal of love and union which cannot be, and not one which will face the world of flux and flow as its *raison d'être*. 'I will not know', he says, not 'I cannot', and his imagination invokes his god of separation rather than pursues the implications of a possible second stage to a relationship between people who, having once loved each other and parted, have changed and grown older. This is not his theme, though he has been roused to write ten stanzas which show it potentially active within him, before he retreats to the sad yet safe certainty that life decrees, 'Marguerite I shall see no more'.

*The Terrace at Berne* takes its place as a lyric typical of the Marguerite set in its half-recognition of time as the human element, of relationships evolving and devolving, and its rejec-

tion of any close engagement with such issues. As a postscript
to the group, briefly included in it by Arnold, *A Dream* confirms
the bias of his imagination. He sees himself sailing swiftly along
the river of life—'a green Alpine stream'; momentarily, Marguerite appears on a balcony, waving eagerly to him, but the
boat, hesitating only an instant, is carried by the 'loud thunder-
ing' river towards its ocean destination. Thus, vividly aware of
the flow of life, Arnold sees it as a force compelling separation.

Yet the poet who laments love as a hopeless dream writes
lyric after lyric tracing the history of his retreat to this position.
The Switzerland poems—and *Faded Leaves* too—exemplify the
tension of love's impossibility meeting with its indisputable
actuality as an emotional experience, unsatisfactory and complex, demanding acknowledgment if only by precipitate flight
and further avowals of man's essential loneliness. Romantic
love dies in Arnold's lyrics, and the realism of the Victorian
approach to the heart's events struggles to be born.

૭ 7 ૭

What is suffered in Arnold is exploited by Clough. The confusions, rationalisations and equivocations which dominate the
Switzerland lyrics are controlled and used in *Amours de Voyage*
(1849), being recognised for what they are in the creation of
Claude. Arnold provides a barometric record of his feeling and
his recoil from feeling; Clough reads the barometer.

Clough is in creative command; his hero undergoes the
panics and alarms of the situation, and the poem thrives on the
irony of the contrast. The poet sets up the love affair for Claude
to knock down, and in this deliberate journey to nowhere,
Clough is able to display his appreciation of the poetic consequences of recognising love as a theme, not in its ideal dress
as an eternal verity—or impossibility—but as its tragi-comic,
earthly, nineteenth-century self. Love here is a matter of two
people with well-defined characteristics, meeting at a particular
place and time, and in the company of others. Emotion is not
isolated but firmly set within a social context—family, friends
and public events—which is influential in determining its
course.

47

Tiresias-like, Clough presides over the cat's-cradle of correspondence which brings out these points; he witnesses all and invites the reader to do likewise. The letters pass from Claude to Eustace, from Georgina to Louisa, Mary to Miss Roper, and only the reader and the poet can recognise the ironies of the diagram they draw. The more Claude struggles to disengage himself, to declare relationships a bore, dispensable, doomed to disappointment, the more clearly does the poem demonstrate that the repercussions of even such a grudging emotional response are far-reaching. The richness of relationships as a poetic theme is convincingly and entertainingly displayed in the failure of Claude and Mary to reach each other.

There are no letters between the two of them; when she writes to him, it miscarries. But the awareness and influence of each on the other is at the centre of all the letters from all the correspondents, so that we experience both the power of the feeling and its impotence. The arrangement of the letters is so skilful that the frustration of what is potentially possible is structurally demonstrated. The rising curve of feeling in Claude never quite meets the equivalent phase in Mary: he grows warm and Mary reports on him coolly; but when he hesitates, she, though warming herself, 'neither will help nor dismiss him' (II.viii.236).[3] The lack of precipitation in both characters is clear from the start, and Clough brilliantly shows how the source of the attraction, an affinity of temperament, contains within it the obstacles which doom the two of them to a game of blind man's buff.

In Canto III, Claude's retreat calls forth Mary's strongest admission of feeling and begins her active spell of pursuit, while he philosophises on 'mild monastic faces in quiet collegiate cloisters' (ix.182). But then: '*hang* this thinking' (x.207)—and he becomes resolute, pursuing and admitting his eagerness, as she falters into doubt and vexation (IV). Canto V opens with Mary momentarily restored to hope and candidly declaring how 'exceedingly happy' (i.14) she is to know he has followed; the next letter records Claude's weariness at failure and shows

---

[3] Quotations are taken from *The Poems of Arthur Hugh Clough*, ed. A. L. P. Norrington (Oxford University Press, 1968). Canto, Letter and line numbers are given.

him on the brink of inaction again. For the rest of the Canto he argues himself away from further effort, and misery: 'After all, do I know that I really cared so about her?' (viii.156). He renounces the whole episode, as she, reading his nature and betraying her sympathy with it, also submits, 'although in a different manner' (xi.215). This conclusion is the nearest they come to a chord of feeling.

The accidents of altered plans and switched destinations merely abet this irony of love unable to commit itself and speak out. They symbolise the odds of the game when two people attempt the difficult task, as Clough sees it, of manoeuvring their lives into intimacy and, in the touch of farce the mishaps bring to the story, they emphasise his appreciation of the part played by fate in such encounters. A fate not seen as some chill ultimate law of the universe like Arnold's 'God', but simply as the caprice of circumstance, ridiculous as well as frustrating. Clough as poet does not shrink from any of the difficulties of relationships, either those inherent in character or accidental; on the contrary, though his hero gives up, they are Clough's inspiration and his theme.

### ✍ 8 ✍

Claude loves and fails in love because he is Claude, the year is 1849 and he is in Rome, and because travellers change their minds; he also loves and fails because Mary is Mary and subject to the same twists of social and political behaviour. *Amours de Voyage* exploits these facts of life and, if its main achievement is the creation of Claude, the strategy of this creation is only to be grasped when the full use of context—and especially of Mary— is realised. Claude lives in the poem not just in Clough's masterly management of his self-revealing letters to Eustace, but in the poet's refusal to confine the poem to the one letter-writer or the one angle.

Even while Claude rejoices to Eustace at the 'blessing' it is to be alone in Italy, free from social pressures, he is already laying himself open to them once more—'we turn like fools to the English' (I.i.28, 32). His self-consciousness is of a kind— poetically, a Victorian kind, it may be noted—which is

49

susceptible to what 'others suppose one' (31). He mocks this sensitivity when he meditates on the 'curious work' of re-entering society:

> Do I look like that? you think me that: then I *am* that.
> (iv.86)

The paradox is that this is true, and yet instead of revealing Claude as an entirely negative person, the poem shows him to be ruled by a strong regard for his inviolate self as well. The tension creates the drama, and it is only made clear by the presence of the other letter-writers, or off-stage persons, whom Clough shows as influences upon his hero. Claude is to a degree what George Vernon, Louisa, the senior Trevellyns or Miss Roper think he is; more nearly, he is Eustace's friend, a personality made to the expectations of that correspondent's view of him; and most intimately, he is what Mary sees and loves. Claude responds to the latter half willingly, acknowledging the validity of her Claude, but also with alarm, for living in terms of another person's vision when that person is important to him has its terrors and is an ordeal for a personality such as his.

To have his intentions questioned is also a shock for him because he is forced to see himself as the Trevellyn circle does, in the conventional role of suitor. As he admits to Eustace, he has become what they are prepared to welcome from the first uneasy days when he adjusted himself to their company, and here, the social logic of his behaviour reaches its destined end. But his dialogue with Mary is proceeding on quite a different level, a wavering, tentative discovery of each other and a slow, experimental testing of the possibility of their developing a joint identity. This delicate process collides brutally with the simple black and white assumptions of the family, and Clough demonstrates the extent of the hurt done to Claude by revealing it retrospectively and showing the effects obliquely, as the stampeded lover retreats to his philosophic citadels (III.iv, vi).

The cross-cutting from Claude's letters to those of the girls, and the contrasts within the sisters', dramatise such psychological crises. Thus the brash Georgina, in a postscript:

Mr Claude, you must know, is behaving a little bit better;
He and Papa are great friends; but he really is too *shilly-
    shally,*—
So unlike George! Yet I hope that the matter is going on
    fairly.
I shall, however, get George, before he goes, to say
    something.
Dearest Louise, how delightful to bring young people
    together!

(II.xv.336–40)

Mary has just offered her own postscript answer to the
question of the state of their relationship:

All I can say for myself is, alas! that he rather repels me.
There! I think him agreeable, but also a little repulsive.

(xv.331–2)

Clearly this last is a voice Claude will understand—dry,
detached, subtly discriminating, and the slangy crudities of
Georgina are doubly exposed by the complex alliance between
the other two, which Clough—master of tone and verbal
shading—implies in the very caution of Mary's reaction.

Mary's presence in the poem as a separate personality,
recognisable in her style of speech, is an essential feature of it.
In Arnold's struggles, some suggestion of Marguerite emerged,
faint but distinct: she exerted pressure in the lyrics sexually and
personally. But the poems could not accommodate her or release
her as an independent voice; Arnold's formal diction inhibited
her individuality, and his own, with its lack of dramatic or
colloquial flexibility. Here, however, through Clough's bolder
linguistic freedom and his ability to convey temperament by
verbal inflection and turns of phrase, Mary is realised as the one
person who could impinge upon Claude and attract him in a
deeply disturbing way. Clough is showing that it takes two
individuals for a love affair, two minds and two temperaments
whose components may or may not mix. The pull of Mary on
Claude is felt in the poem as she exerts it, not exclusively
through his reactions; and likewise his impact on her. The
remarks of each about the other, with their adroitly suggested

51

blend of perception, misunderstanding, appreciation and disappointment, display the necessary ambiguities of a relationship of ambiguous people, who find 'agreeable' what also 'repels' them.

As Mary makes this cool yet interested remark, indeed, Claude is writing:

Ah, and I feel too, Eustace, she cares not a tittle about me!
(Care about me, indeed! and do I really expect it?)
But my manner offends; my ways are wholly repugnant;
Every word I utter estranges, hurts, and repels her;
Every moment of bliss that I gain, in her exquisite presence,
Slowly, surely, withdraws her, removes her, and severs her
     from me . . .
Not that I mind very much! Why should I? I am not in love . . .
                                        (II.xiv.298–303, 306)

The magnetism operating between them positively and negatively is perfectly shown here, as it is later when each waits on the other and attraction risks being cancelled by repulsion. Mary observes:

            He thinks that women should woo him;
Yet, if a girl should do so, would be but alarmed and
     disgusted.
She that should love him must look for small love in return,—
     like the ivy
On the stone wall, must expect but a rigid and niggard
     support, and
E'en to get that must go searching all round with her humble
     embraces.
                                        (III.i.35–9)

So each is gradually created in the mind of the other; Mary's final submission to their failure is ironically the ultimate testimony to this consummation, the complete grasp of the other person's nature: 'Oh, and you see I know so exactly how he would take it' (V.xi.210). This sympathy only finds its fulfilment in the certainty that there is to be no fulfilment, and the letters in which they meet so closely yet all the time bypass each other carry the ironies and the sadness into the poem's structure, as well as underlining them linguistically.

Claude in Canto III (vi–vii) muses loftily on the idea of 'juxtaposition' as an accident of the universe, but *Amours de Voyage* takes it seriously, both by analysing its consequences and by using it as a far from accidental strategy of organisation. The poem's whole design, depicting Mary as well as Claude and each through the other, shows how juxtaposition can lead to 'affinity' (III.vii.151) and what ensues from this—not necessarily a simple progress to the wedding bells society expects, but an intricate figure of advance and retreat. Clough shows that what is involved is learning the nature of two persons, oneself and the other, and possibly remaining with this as the sole prize of the experience: not because we are inexorably enisled in the sea of life, but because juxtaposition is only the preliminary to a delicate transaction whose negotiations may succeed, but are highly vulnerable to the moods, shynesses, or uncertainties of the parties endeavouring to conduct them. No perverse 'God' need be postulated here; the poem is Clough's challenge to Arnold's absolute, impersonal excuse for failure between lovers.

৩ 9 ৩

Clough does not concentrate exclusively on character, however. As I have said, he sees his people caught in the web of circumstance and fortuitous events and, in this sense, fate and its decrees are admitted to his as to Arnold's universe. Had the Trevellyns been confined to Rome by the siege, juxtaposition might of itself have brought the affair to a head; had the French not been threatening the city at all, the fellow-tourists could have worked out their relationship at their own pace. But the situation was just ominous enough to suggest the prudence of speedy departure for Florence, and not ominous enough to prevent that departure: so Claude was forced to a resolution—to go with them—and had it killed by Vernon, who took leaving as an excuse to drop alarming hints about 'intentions'. History to this extent interferes with the natural and devious rhythms of the heart's events.

Yet Clough is not constrained to prove that there is no hope for personal initiatives. His tone about fate is not tragic. Rather he demonstrates that these are the forces human affairs must acknowledge as part of the gamble of existence; public tangles with private, and sometimes chances to thwart it, but there is no malice aforethought and no rule that it must be so. As the interplay between Claude and history shows, the former is not merely subject to events: Clough is arrested by the spectacle of the individual reacting to the situation he finds himself in, and being roused by it, whether it is as dramatic an occasion as a city under siege, or whether it is as unremarkable as his meeting a particular person. When both kinds of experience come together as they did for Claude in Rome in 1849, Clough finds his poem in the resultant patterning. The checks and balances, the influence of one set of events on the other as they converge in the mind of Claude; how Claude comes to learn more of his own nature through his vulnerability and his resistance to what assails him: these are the aspects which move Clough. It is a vision of living as in a sense makeshift, the observable laws being those of flux and change; interaction with other people and unpredictable circumstance are seen as the norm of significant personal experience. Arnold flies to the Alpine peaks or to his island to find his soul, but Clough rejects the absolute, whether as blessing or curse, and accepts man as an emotional, contingent being whose home is history.

Claude at every point challenges any assumptions of fixed rules for living. Whether he resists the Trevellyn view of conventional behaviour or meditates on the proposition 'dulce et decorum est pro patria mori' (II.ii), he sets up attitudes personal to himself. The moment as a unique complex of individual feeling and specific event provides its own criteria; it is not to be assessed by an appeal to some immutable standard supposed to be permanently applicable. Claude evaluates situations in the light of what he is, and discovers what he is by every situation in which he finds himself placed, from meeting Mary Trevellyn to hearing the French are at the gates.

This is Claude's freedom. Reacting to the particular situation, he is able to decide it is not for him sweet and decorous to die for a cause. Such views identify him, but so too does his vulnerability to the particular and to the accidental. In his pursuit of the Trevellyns through northern Italy, for instance, there is a subtle kind of collaboration between Claude's temperament and the bad luck of the chase. Clough almost caricatures the portrayal of the desperate lover foiled at every turn by the caprice of chance. But each time Claude is frustrated it becomes that much more probable that he will abandon his quest. He is not defeated by fortune, but by the fact that fortune conspires with the reluctance to woo which Mary saw as part of his nature. Thus the twists of circumstance cannot be taken as evidence for the god who keeps asunder—they are only decisive in conjunction with Claude's character. Once more, the stress for Clough falls on the interaction between the person as he is and what happens to him day by day.

∽ 10 ∽

Claude, in finding and losing 'a single small chit of a girl' (V.vi.116) is profoundly affected. He is worked on emotionally and changed, and at the same time he is clearly faced with his own unchangeable characteristics. In showing this, Clough accepts the theme of relationships, even abortive ones, as material offering promising poetic opportunities. But he does so without the connivance of his hero. Claude's nature includes the Arnold-instinct, as it may be called; like Marguerite's lover, he too feels the call to a philosophy of solitude and contemplation beyond the human world. There is the same fear of passionate involvement:

I do not like being moved: for the will is excited; and action
Is a most dangerous thing . . .
(II.xi.272-3)

It 'simply disturbs, unsettles, and makes you uneasy' (267). And even the less alarming kind of feeling that 'fixes and holds you' (268) could only be acceptable because it is an 'ad-interim solace and pleasure' (III.vi.143), and there is another vision which transcends it—the 'perfect and absolute something' (144), beyond life, where the relieved male spirit can slough off temporal pastimes and its female companion who, she must realise, was 'but for a space' (143) and not for eternity.

55

Although this is Claude trying to argue himself out of the love he is even then acknowledging in the misery of knowing Mary gone to Florence, his yearning for a 'freer and larger existence' (123) is a genuine part of his nature and the equivalent of Arnold's desire to flee to a solitary and timeless Alpine world. Claude's ideal seems to be a relationship which confirms rather than threatens his sense of separateness and leaves him quite free. One of his most vigorous outbursts concerns the idea of 'obligation' towards another person. It is, he insists, a 'terrible word':

> But, oh, great Heavens, I repel it!
> Oh, I cancel, reject, disavow, and repudiate wholly
> Every debt of this kind, disclaim every claim, and dishonour,
> Yea, my own heart's own writing, my soul's own signature! Ah,
>     no!
> I will be free in this; you shall not, none shall, bind me.
>
>                (III.ix.190–5)

Mary's attraction was precisely that she exerted no pressure:

> No, my friend, if you wish to be told, it was this above all
>     things,
> This that charmed me, ah, yes, even this, that she held me
>     to nothing.
>
>                (196–7)

'*She* spoke not of obligations' (205)—though as the reader knows, she read Claude's aversion to them more shrewdly than he does himself.

By showing Claude weakly grateful that he was not brought to the point of taking any responsibility for his pleasure in Mary's company, Clough shows that such responsibility is a necessary condition for the growth of intimacy. To evade it is to lose the rewards of greater commitment. At the same time, in allowing his hero to appreciate that freedom and reticence are values of importance, permitting each person to remain independent and unpressured, Clough is touching on another aspect of relationships which has its positive place in other poetry of the age besides his own.

Using Claude's reluctance to the full, therefore, *Amours de*

*Voyage* probes various aspects of what takes place when one individual tries, if only half-heartedly, to enter the life of another, and the poem seeks to suggest what is at stake in such encounters. Clough does not shirk or mock the instinct which fears violation, but neither does he deny the potential enrichment if the solitary becomes the shared life. The sharp frustration of the poem's ending, as the disappointed letters tail off into resigned silence, brings out Clough's evaluation forcefully enough. By taking us through all the nuances of this tentative association, and offering us only what we must feel is a spoilt equation, he makes a point strongly complimentary to relationships out of the very sadness of these ruins.

Arnold, declaring relationships impossible, none the less traced the story of the disappointing love which led him to that conclusion, finding in its failure a theme demanding an extended exploration. He therefore reluctantly joins the much more willing Clough in investigating love as a phenomenon of time and the individual. One despite himself, and one wholly acquiescent, they are both moved to write their commentaries affirming Claude's observation, 'It is a curious history, this' (V.viii.171)—and the phrase might be applied equally well to all the Victorian poems of relationships which the Switzerland lyrics and *Amours de Voyage*, somewhat perversely, yet effectively, introduce.

III

# 'Till All My Widowed Race Be Run'

## Patmore: Odes of Bereavement;
## Tennyson: *In Memoriam*

﹏ I ﹏

In discussing Wordsworth's Lucy poems, I saw them as evidence
of a Romantic tendency to choose the moment of extremity as
that yielding the most illumination. Lucy dead brought
Wordsworth to his evaluation of what her life meant to him,
and each poem dealt in some way with the idea of her being
gone, taking this as a fixed centre. When Victorian poets
follow the Romantic lead and approach a relationship from its
terminal point, they agree with Wordsworth that the event
demands repeated scrutiny if its emotional significance is to
be adequately charted. But for them the fact of death cannot
be isolated, fixed, or in any way lifted out of time; it is to be
faced and assessed in the context of the shared experiences
which preceded it and the varying perspectives of the days and
years which follow.

Patmore says of the manner of his wife's dying, 'It was not
like your great and gracious ways'; memory of what was is
central to all his estimates of the difference her death has made
to him, and the successive odes acknowledge both the changing
nature of grief and the effects of this on her posthumous survival
within him. Similarly with Tennyson: *In Memoriam* is aptly
titled, for it is a poem where remembering the dead recreates
Hallam alive, so that Tennyson understands his loss in the context of a still-developing relationship, though this does not
remove the bitter certainty of absence. Thus the Victorian poets
see the one event as part of a tissue of experience which continues to grow as the new situation is gradually absorbed.

Beginning as a series of separate lyrics, *In Memoriam* ended

58

as a unified long poem, a development which occurred because Tennyson accepted time as his element and used it—as sequence, as cyclic pattern, as memory—to aid his understanding of the calamity of death. The lyrics cohere into an enactment of grief as it gropes from day to day and discovers its position by relating past to present and sensing the difference between yesterday's pain and today's. In Patmore likewise, the state of the widowed soul can only be defined by historical research, less ambitious than Tennyson's, but just as aware that emotional amputation is not a confined shock but a prolonged and complex ordeal. To both poets, the business of the imagination is to trace an evolution of feeling, not simply to set a single blow in accurate perspective.

What Wordsworth merely hints at, these poets seize on as their proper material. The lover of Lucy felt that his reading of the universe was changed by her fate. Though the lyrics make no dramatic play with this aspect, they do suggest that bereavement can precipitate a crisis of myth. Loss calls into question explanations of the universe, challenges their adequacy, perhaps exposes their complacencies or confusions. Latent in the Lucy poems, these pressures are openly recognised by the Victorians as central. Tennyson without Hallam is prey to a vision of a mindless universe more hostile to human life than Wordsworth's diurnal course. His poem fights out the conflict between values introduced and supported by love and the proposition that, because death is an incontrovertible fact, these are null and void. He is a battleground for two states of feeling, on the one side his crippling grief, and on the other his growing confidence that love survives the loss of its object. His whole reading of life depends on the outcome of his struggle to discover the true character of relationship: if commitment to another is simply cancelled by the accidents of physical existence, then there is no significance or real identity; but if the sharing of love generates an experience which maintains its vitality despite bodily separation, then the individual and the life he lives make emotional sense. This is to translate the issues into a more clear-cut argument than the poem offers—its strength lies in its fidelity to the slow, wavering and obscure way in which feeling fights its wars. But what is brought out in such a summary is the

59

inextricable dependence of Tennyson's larger vision on his immediate involvement with one other person. His poem only exists because this is so.

For Patmore, the issue of meaning in life is less desperate, but equally, it is centred on the values of a deep relationship. Assured in his religious outlook, Patmore none the less prizes intimate love as the keystone of his system. Keystone and touchstone, for the odes of bereavement show him testing his view of ultimate spiritual happiness against the experience of earthly loving, its gifts, the anguish of parting and the idea of reunion. *Tristitia*, for instance, evaluates heaven and hell in terms of the attitudes of the lovers towards each other should they be destined for an eternity of separation. Patmore is moved to assess his position in the shock of a loss which, though it does not raise the spectre of complete pointlessness, does impinge upon the fundamentals of his beliefs. As with Tennyson, his psychological enquiry into what loving means is acute, and each poet is able to review and develop his myth of the universe by the creative sensitivity he brings to that enquiry.

In going beyond Wordsworth, the Victorian poets expose themselves to risks Lucy's poet never ran. Death for them is not an accomplished event to which a dignified timeless monument may be erected, but is to be confronted as a temporal fact—as the act of dying, something which happens cruelly on a particular day. The deathbed, the funeral, and the days which follow them come into their own in the mid-century poetry of mourning, and sentimentality or worse obviously becomes a threat. But Tennyson and Patmore find their own dignity of bearing, in both senses, as they patiently and receptively follow the course of grief wherever it leads them.

လ 2 လ

The poems of Patmore which I am grouping as his 'odes of bereavement' appeared together in the first volume of *The Unknown Eros* (1877). Seven of them stand in sequence: *The Day After Tomorrow*, *Tristitia*, *The Azalea*, *Departure*, *Eurydice*, *The Toys*, *Tired Memory*; two more, '*If I Were Dead*' and *A Farewell*, follow them, with political odes interspersed.

Commentators do not agree on the extent to which these are poems inspired by the death of Emily Patmore, the poet's first wife. Frederick Page argues for a close connection between them and *The Angel in the House*, seeing some of the odes as dramatic poems spoken by characters from the long poem, while J. C. Reid, without rejecting this view entirely, stresses their source in Patmore's personal experience.[1] Page's argument is a pertinent reminder that Patmore is a poet extensively concerned with the theme of marital intimacy, and that the odes belong to a larger context, notably *The Angel in the House*, the other odes in *The Unknown Eros* volumes, and the aphoristic prose in *The Rod, the Root and the Flower*. I shall take account of this wider vision in discussing *The Angel in the House* in Chapter V; but Reid's view of the nine as a clearly identifiable group concerned with a crisis in a specific relationship[2] is more immediately helpful. The link with *In Memoriam* is clearer from this angle, and it encourages appreciation of the odes as a set of poems individually rich and mutually illuminating.

Patmore considered the final arrangement of *The Unknown Eros* volumes with care, and it is unmistakably apparent that the poems beginning at *The Day After Tomorrow* and ending at *A Farewell* are connected contributions to the study of a single evolving experience. They form a series of responses and adjustments to the death of a beloved partner, the nature and import of the living relationship being scrutinised as an essential part of that adjustment. Two time-schemes are apparent: one, the history of the event and its aftermath, the dying and the time following, and secondly, the psychological time interwoven with the former but not confined to it, creating its own past and future. Framed within two poems on heavenly reunion, the odes pass through the complexities of grief, in all its guilt, memory and longing, and finally, they face the different pain begotten by time: the tiring of memory and the turning away to life again.

The view of ultimate reunion is itself modified by the intervening phases of sorrow, and the contrasts of emphasis between the first poem of the group and the last help to make clear how

---

[1] See J. C. Reid, *The Mind and Art of Coventry Patmore* (1957), pp. 282–3.
[2] Reid, p. 287.

far Patmore's sense of relationship, its meaning and value, depends on his openness to psychological truth and his acknowledgment that it is a changing truth. The poems draw much of their strength from their steady and uncensored regard for what takes place in the heart as it endeavours to consolidate affliction. Patmore's subtle powers of language and structure are both exercised to full advantage as he defies conventional pieties and sets aside all platitudes of grief, religious or social.

꩜ 3 ꩜

*The Day After Tomorrow* sees death only as the first stage in an already familiar rhythm of parting followed by reunion. The grief of separation is almost wholly subordinated to the anticipatory delight of its being over. Its duration, being measurable, is manageable and the days alone are simply the stepping stones to the renewed intimacy, a bliss known already but this time to find its endless perfection:

> One day's controlled hope, and then one more,
> And on the third our lives shall be fulfill'd!
> Yet all has been before . . .
> It all has been before,
> And yet out lives shall now be first fulfill'd,
> And into their summ'd sweetness fall distill'd
> One sweet drop more;
> One sweet drop more, in absolute increase
> Of unrelapsing peace.[3]

The poem suggests that love in its earthly and heavenly character is a seamless garment. 'Has all not been before?' is its key question, and the answering assertion, 'It all has been before', punctuates the ode and gives it shape. Patmore's use of repetition as an organising principle is always subtle, and here the homing back to the same phrases, charged each time with more implication, works in active conspiracy with his theme. The rhythm and quality of earthly emotional experience establishes the reading of eternity and the poem's structure carries that idea in its wave-like advance from, and return to,

[3] Quotations are taken from *The Poems of Coventry Patmore*, ed. F. Page (1949).

this base of feeling. The poem stresses assured continuity and at the same time its wave-movement mounts until the climax of the fulfilment, towards which each reunion has been tending, is reached. Heaven's consummation—blending a dynamic love with the repose of complete realisation—is outside human experience, but only the one logical step beyond it. The relationship over the years contains the promise of the final sustained intimacy in each rehearsal of that reunion.

The rehearsals form the passionate centre of the poem. The remembered meetings are relived and because of Patmore's sensitivity to their psychological complexities, they become also the anticipated crowning encounter. In the finely tuned response of each to the other, an embrace of body and spirit is suggested. As the lovers take hands—'Palm placed in palm, twin smiles, and words astray'—Patmore communicates fully the eager physical commotion of the moment, but he frames his extended portrayal of it within a question whose climax is 'calm', not passion's agitation. The incongruity is only apparent; the conjunction of the two and the authoritative way it is managed is crucial to the ode, and takes us deeply into Patmore's concept of relationship and its revelations:

> But shall I not, with ne'er a sign, perceive,
> Whilst her sweet hands I hold,
> The myriad threads and meshes manifold
> Which Love shall round her weave:
> The pulse in that vein making alien pause
> And varying beats from this;
> Down each long finger felt, a differing strand
> Of silvery welcome bland;
> And in her breezy palm
> And silken wrist,
> Beneath the touch of my like numerous bliss
> Complexly kiss'd,
> A diverse and distinguishable calm?

The blending of irregularity with steadiness which marks Patmore's metrical practice in his odes is perfectly fitted to convey the emotion caught in these lines. The passage is at once uneven with the pressure of excited feeling and controlled to a pace of dignity by the use of lines of varying length, which are to be regularised by pauses extending the short phrases to the same duration as the longer lines. The eye as well as the voice can grasp this combination of urgency and order, and it collaborates with the syntactical movement in holding off and building up the climax. Patmore's skill in leading to and achieving a climax which is felt as such, yet, in proving to be the word 'calm', comes as a surprise, is masterly. The lines epitomise his idea of love as an overwhelming attractive energy which conjures self out of self, yet is entirely compatible with a deep peace, a perfect self-possession reached only by the complete response to the other person.

The richly disruptive excitement and displacement of mind and body is suggested by the vocabulary of this climactic passage also. Love is felt with an immediacy of sensation which is at the same time elusive, as much spirit as body—a 'silvery' welcome from flesh and blood fingers, a 'breezy palm' and 'silken wrist'. And then, against this blissful but mysterious confusion, comes the precision and clarity of the calm, 'diverse and distinguishable'; distinct, that is, from the other sensations, unmistakable as a separate element, yet part too of the total experience, generated by what goes before.

Love is indeed properly characterised here as a web of 'myriad threads', and the whole poem insists, structurally and in all it says, that the calm of love is nowhere hostile to its passion, though 'unrestful rapture' is transcended. Patmore is concerned with

> The peace that should pertain,
> To him who does by her attraction move.

The idea is fundamental to his poetry, as *The Angel in the House* will show, but in this ode, where the separation of death gives intensity to the assessment of what united love means, it is hailed explicitly as the peak or apotheosis of the experience. 'Honied peace' is the security—or eternity—of love, and impatient desire wrongs it. It is also the freedom of love, a state of fulfilment which respects and confirms the lovers as autonomous beings despite their surrender to each other. Union is no destructive collision or confounding of the two natures; attraction defines and completes the individual, it does not annihilate him.

The ode which Patmore places first in his poems of mourning therefore stands as an affirmation not a lament. The values of love as they have been discovered in the rhythms of living are felt to be invincible, immune to death. In the revelatory moments it has already temporally given, love has offered its surety for the eternal, the 'absolute increase of unrelapsing peace'. There is no sense of rupture in death: what 'has been before' must be again, and more intensely so. Everything in the poem moves it forward to reunion as a destined goal; the 'heaving Sea'—to Arnold, cold symbol of estrangement—at first is seen ''twixt her and me', but it becomes a sea which 'separatest not dear heart from heart'. A poem of assured and 'controlled hope', it draws its nourishment from vivid memory and uses history as a pledge for what—on the third day—must be. Its faith in resurrection is inseparable from its experience of love.

But such a mood of 'golden patience' based on the best that has been is the prelude to grief, not the bypassing of it. Patmore's arrangement of the poems is shrewd here. *The Day After Tomorrow*, while possessing its own validity as a piece of emotional logic, is to be seen as the argument of the heart still numb to its loss. The pain is not yet recognised, the living presence of the beloved, so triumphantly established in the poem, is still more real than her absence. As we turn from this ode to *Tristitia*, *The Azalea* and their successors, the Victorian fidelity to the temporal stages and processes of feeling is demonstrated. Without diminishing the passion of remembered love, which remains the point of reference, Patmore moves in to the nerve-centre of bereavement and entertains to the full the various implications, spiritual and psychological. The confidence and simple certainties of the reunion ode are cut away. The bereaved self must speak as such in order to assess the phenomenon of loving relationship.

∽ 4 ∽

In *Tristitia* it begins to do so, though the change of stance is neither extreme nor abrupt. Husband addresses wife, there is an assurance of direct contact in the poem's opening,—'Darling, with hearts conjoin'd in such a peace'—and the whole can be taken first of all as a poem expressing the deep security of the years of communion and wonder at intimacy's continued growth. The more striking is it, therefore, that the ode develops into a vision of eternal separation. Instead of the euphoric conviction of a shared heaven in *The Day After Tomorrow*, *Tristitia* contemplates the prospect of divided destinies because of the poet's possible banishment from 'God's perfect bliss'. His plea, which is the core of the ode, is for her never to be 'dis-heaven'd' by grieving over his fate. The knowledge that her bliss was less than absolute would be the one anguish which would bury him in the remoter circles of hell, 'beyond just doom' and all relief.

Love here is still located on the spiritual plane, finding its definition by being associated with a Christian view of death. But now, this outlook itself permits the idea of dying as parting and loss to enter the poet's consciousness, whereas in *The Day After Tomorrow*, such misery was excluded. In other words, as well as heaven, hell is now needed to cover the experience and the evaluation of it. A step towards exploring earthly grief has been taken though the metaphysical situation remains central.

By means of the latter and the paradoxes it is felt to engender, Patmore acknowledges some of the moral tensions and insights of an intense partnership. His explanation of the reason for his possible damnation is revealing:

> If thou alone should'st win
> God's perfect bliss,
> And I, beguiled by gracious-seeming sin,
> Say, loving too much thee,
> Love's last goal miss . . .

These lines are fraught with contradictory values, and the ode admits that there can be division and rivalry between what is given in human love and what is due to God—striving 'the creature more than God to please'. Love, that is, is seen to involve snares as well as sweetness; the indulgence of it is not to be automatically or romantically equated with a state of highest good. It can on the contrary be a kind of selfishness.

66

The ode pursues this moral idea, pondering on God's relationship with the damned. This is not a digression into Patmore's theological interests but an organic extension of his attempt to clarify what, at its purest and richest, loving does require. In hell, God is found 'as a true but quite estranged Friend', still working with a kind of divine courtesy to alleviate the pain of those who deny him:

> Yea, in the worst
> And from His Face most wilfully accurst
> Of souls in vain redeem'd,
> He does with potions of oblivion kill
> Remorse of the lost Love that helps them still.

In the taut paradox of the final lines, Patmore holds like a poised wrestler the insight that love must be prepared to withdraw even the memory of its existence if that memory proves a source of suffering. In self-denial, almost perjury, love defines itself.

Meeting with this perception, Patmore's prayer that she forget him in heaven gathers urgency and takes on its full moral force, and the poem declares its acceptance of sacrifice —even extinction—as the ultimate token of a lover's commitment. The 'prime care' is 'thy happy state', even when it is admitted that the happy state may decree the freedom of the beloved to break all bonds between them. Hell's comfort lies in assent to this; its wretchedness in the spoiling of the other's heaven:

> It never could be anything but well,
> Nor from my soul, full of thy sanctity,
> Such pleasure die
> As the poor harlot's, in whose body stirs
> The innocent life that is and is not hers:
> Unless, alas, this fount of my relief
> By thy unheavenly grief
> Were closed.

*Tristitia*, fighting out its difficult argument, can seem a more stilted and ungainly poem than the passionately flowing, finely controlled ode which precedes it. But its own emotion is no less passionate though it cannot of its nature imitate the steady rhythms of assured feeling sustained there. Facing the idea of parting, the poem works out some of the implications of loving from this, finding the sentence of banishment only bearable in terms of its moral discoveries. Rising to a climactic cry, 'Promise me this!', the ode affirms the depths of love's trust and dependence even as it entreats the cancellation of such bonds as the ultimate expression of what lies still deeper—love's disinterestedness.

Without much pressing the ode yields further ironies. Hell and heaven are both seen more as states determined by the lovers' relationship than as those described by orthodox doctrine; Patmore is still committing his 'gracious-seeming sin' and putting the creature first. But this is in keeping with his whole attempt to use human love as a means of evaluation and definition, a policy which in turn illuminates that love. The poem is open to the reading, however, that the poet is in fact still seeking his own ends, for he is urging on his beloved the way to ensure less agony for him: selfishness is enmeshed even in the effort to make the most selfless gesture, it seems. Such a psychological truth would not be lost on Patmore. As later odes will show, he is alert to these complexities of feeling. He does not work on the point here, but it is not concealed, and *Tristitia* is a worthy introduction on this level to the themes of mixed responses in love and loss; it contributes also the first revelation of the lover's need to place himself at the bar of self-judgment and assess the morality of love's transactions. It modifies the previous ode by showing that to celebrate love's ecstasies is not enough.

∽ 5 ∽

Psychologically, as I have said, *Tristitia* also moves on in that it admits the idea of parting as a possibility of more moment and more permanence than *The Day After Tomorrow* allows. With the third ode of the group, *The Azalea*, the poet begins to grapple with the facts of death and grief. This poem conveys the shock of realisation, as it describes the lover's dream of loss fading into confused waking relief that it was a dream, and

then this too giving way to the surge of fully conscious recollection—the dream is the truth.

Patmore's sensitivity to the tides of consciousness and to all
the currents which determine emotional response are shown in
this ode. The varying rhymes and pulse of the lines keep pace
with the feeling throughout, letting it find its natural emphases
yet controlling it with an unobtrusive but firm rein:

> At dawn I dream'd, O God, that she was dead,
> And groan'd aloud upon my wretched bed,
> And waked, ah, God, and did not waken her,
> But lay, with eyes still closed,
> Perfectly bless'd in the delicious sphere
> By which I knew so well that she was near,
> My heart to speechless thankfulness composed.
> Till 'gan to stir
> A dizzy somewhat in my troubled head—
> It *was* the azalea's breath, and she *was* dead!

Patmore here is vulnerable to snap-judgments on Victorian
sentimentality. He is apparently falling willingly into black-
crêpe grief, indulging himself in the role of the bereaved
husband. But the automatic prejudice against the lines is un-
warranted. The subtlety of the whole movement and its tactical
shifts of language precludes the possibility that Patmore is
merely serving up the cliché of the mourning spouse. The most
extravagant and most obvious expression of feeling occurs in
the dream, and the ostentatious language here stands in deliberate contrast to the presentation of the gradual, blurred onset
of waking misery, with its culmination in cold statement, not
groans. The line, 'And waked, ah, God, and did not waken her'
is ironically-toned, already pregnant with what is to come, so
that 'ah, God' acts as dramatic punctuation, unlike the purely
exclamatory 'O God' two lines earlier. Both are therefore
functional devices, and in their contrast, they lead forward to
the psychological verisimilitude of 'A dizzy somewhat in my
troubled head', where there are no histrionics but the actual
elusive sensation of a dawning truth. Through this advance to
a more precisely notational vocabulary, Patmore shows that
the cutting edge of grief lies simply in the certainty of its

justification. Fantasy can afford to groan, but reality means slowly surfacing to know the burden of fact.

The poem centres on the sharp ironies which deepen the wound of realisation. The anguish of waking to find himself alone depends for Patmore on the security of habitual presence which has preceded it. Here as in the other odes he draws on the long time together, its quality and character, to convey what the sudden solitude means. *The Day After Tomorrow* built upon the rhythms of remembered reunions; *Tristitia* began its petition by recalling the past, 'our love's most happy track'; so in *The Azalea*, the flower whose breath symbolises her presence was reared by her. The ode begins:

> There, where the sun shines first
> Against our room,
> She train'd the gold Azalea, whose perfume
> She, Spring-like, from her breathing grace dispersed.
> Last night the delicate crests of saffron bloom,
> For this their dainty likeness watch'd and nurst,
> Were just at point to burst.

Patmore's management of the ironies in the flower symbol is as delicate as the 'crests of saffron bloom' themselves. Identified with her living quality, the expression of her individual essence, the azalea is also the means by which the absence of that personality is brought home. It grows during the poem, as it were, to open its buds and impose its own existence on the senses of the poet, forcing him to admit that azalea and wife are not indissolubly one, but distinct, and that the living 'breath' of the flower is to be sadly contrasted with the dead woman. Having been herself, the flower becomes her memorial. By breaking the symbolic union he has created, Patmore conveys the dislocation within himself; it is his first move towards assessing his loss.

Finally, the ode rests its case on the discord between the situation as it is, and her words written earlier, when a parting was 'till to-morrow eve', and 'well-paid', she said, 'with soon again to meet'. The pathos is left to make itself felt simply in the reported letter. There is no emotional gloss: the waking reality is now in possession of the poem, and this is enough to communicate the depth of the recognition that the present parting has no such speedy recompense to hope for. Compared with *The Day After Tomorrow*, the change in mood is eloquent. The letter echoes the sentiments which prevailed in that poem, where they brought assurance and a bulwark against loss, but here, by their placing, they reveal grief and the assent to grief.

Yet still in its final lines, *The Azalea* reiterates the value of the living relationship as it was, its intensity and its significance in transforming the lovers for each other. Her letter says:

> 'So, till to-morrow eve, my Own, adieu!
> Parting's well-paid with soon again to meet,
> Soon in your arms to feel so small and sweet,
> Sweet to myself that am so sweet to you!'

As Patmore begins to scrutinise his bereaved condition, he finds it enhances his awareness of all that has been, and the poems continue to explore the nature of intimacy the more fully as they penetrate to the heart of acknowledged loss.

## ⌁ 6 ⌁

Thus in *Departure*, where the moment of death is faced, that moment's special anguish is its apparent betrayal of the tender courtesy of love which characterised the shared life. One of Patmore's most moving poems, this ode simultaneously captures the harmony that was and the blunt truth that dying is neither 'great' nor 'gracious', but a discordant ending, unequivocally cruel and abrupt.

This summary helps to bring out how completely Patmore avoids the pitfalls of a subject which is notoriously a Victorian favourite: the deathbed scene. As in *The Azalea*, he refuses the clichés and instead reports the mixture of pain, terror and bewilderment in the situation with a poetic tact that does not vulgarise it. The note of reproach which is symptomatic of the shocked state of the survivor is admitted, but not allowed to coarsen into egotism, and is in fact inseparable from the poem's tribute to the dead wife. Patmore fuses the complex hurt of being mortally deprived with the revelation of the other person

which the mode of her dying has brought him. Many psychological strands are woven together, in short, but central to the
ode is a comfortless candour from which there is no defence.

Once more, the shaping and verbal patterning of the poem
help it to plot rather than succumb to feeling. If the opening is
compared with the closing lines, the collaboration of structure
and emotional meaning is clearly apparent. After a flash of
perception which contains the germ of the whole, *Departure*
moves into one of Patmore's beautifully managed extended
questions:

> It was not like your great and gracious ways!
> Do you, that have nought other to lament,
> Never, my Love, repent
> Of how, that July afternoon,
> You went,
> With sudden, unintelligible phrase,
> And frighten'd eye,
> Upon your journey of so many days,
> Without a single kiss, or a good-bye?

The anguish of both witness and victim are acknowledged here
and, worse, seen to be a different anguish: the 'frighten'd eye'
and 'unintelligible phrase' separate her from him before she is
physically gone, and the weight which falls on the shortest line,
'You went', preceding these phrases, emphasises this element of
the departure. The question, leading up to its own climax of
finality, expands the opening exclamation, allowing the facts
to carry the justification of that reproach—to which the poem
returns for its conclusion. But then it stands itself as realised
fact, a flat statement of what is known to be so:

> But all at once to leave me at the last,
> More at the wonder than the loss aghast,
> With huddled, unintelligible phrase,
> And frighten'd eye,
> And go your journey of all days
> With not one kiss, or a good-bye,
> And the only loveless look the look with
>     you pass'd:
> 'Twas all unlike your great and gracious ways.

When these lines are compared with the previous quotation, the repetition, amplification and verbal adjustments show Patmore circling within the experience yet at the same time moving forward in his ability to locate the nature of his pain. 'So many days' have become 'all days'; outrage and disbelief are now crystallised, the moment explicitly weighed against the lifetime: 'the only loveless look'. What began as bare revelation of bewildered hurt ends in the bare consolation of it.

But to juxtapose the beginning and end of the ode, though it displays Patmore's skill in exploiting structure, is to do violence to the poem's complete organisation. A Patmore ode is so firmly articulated that quotation does not serve him well; the lines extracted are always dependent on what follows and goes before. The final passage above, for instance, reveals itself in context to be the fulfilment of the middle section of the poem, referring back to the line, 'I knew, indeed, that you were parting soon', which introduces the depiction of the last minutes together. The pain of contrast is emphasised, as Patmore in this section conveys the communion which prevailed, unweakened and apparently unthreatened despite the knowledge of death's imminence, and then repeats the facts of the departure as they suddenly struck:

> I knew, indeed, that you were parting soon;
> And so we sate, within the low sun's rays,
> You whispering to me, for your voice was weak,
> Your harrowing praise.
> Well, it was well,
> To hear you such things speak . . .
> And it was like your great and gracious ways
> To turn your talk on daily things, my Dear,
> Lifting the luminous, pathetic lash
> To let the laughter flash,
> Whilst I drew near,
> Because you spoke so low that I could scarcely hear.
> But all at once to leave me at the last . . .

The positive version of the poem's opening and closing lines— 'And it was like your great and gracious ways'—coming here at the heart of the ode demonstrates a sure instinct of placing

73

which at once unifies the poem and ramifies its feeling. But the whole passage is one of subtle pointing. In its intimacy of tone and tenderness of detail, it establishes the values by which the discourtesy of the parting is to be measured. The final moments are tested against the history of a relationship whose hallmark has been an habitual appreciation of the quality of the other person—and that phenomenon of being 'Sweet to myself that am so sweet to you', as *The Azalea* put it. Thus the betrayal of the 'loveless look' is a double blow, the desolation that of losing the self who was loved as well as the beloved person. Again in *Departure*, therefore, Patmore's psychological divination is acute, and his reading of death depends on his reading of the shared life, with its gifts of love as they are discovered in the 'great and gracious ways' of daily intimacy.

&#8766; 7 &#8766;

The odes discussed so far show Patmore's grief coming down to earth and hitting it in the shock of that stranger's lack of leave-taking. In the remaining poems he is predominantly concerned with the aftermath of this rough lesson in realism. They are poems of 'a mortal sorrow'. Without losing hold of love as a centrally enriching experience, Patmore probes more searchingly into its human limits and limitations. He recognises its entanglement with guilt and failure, disappointment and in-adequacy, and he pursues the evolution of bereavement in a further demonstration that emotional commitment is not immune to time. Love has its history, and relationships their posthumous history too: there can be no simple enshrining of the living or the dead.

*Eurydice* marks the advent of disturbed self-criticism, a sense of moral failure which haunts the widower's mind. The change of tone is indicated in the poem's imagery. There is no fragrance of the azalea's breath here, but a deliberate ugliness in the choice of a slum setting where she is to be sought. Dream has become nightmare:

> I, dreaming, night by night, seek now to see,
> And, in a mortal sorrow, still pursue
> Thro' sordid streets and lanes

74

> And houses brown and bare
> And many a haggard stair
> Ochrous with ancient stains . . .

His love when found lies 'on pallet poor'. This kind of scene
and the coarser vocabulary it demands is so untypical of
Patmore's imagination that its presence here must be taken
seriously. It is a measure of the alienated condition the poem
tries to dramatise, a wretchedness composed not simply of grief
but of self-revulsion too. His normal range of image and symbol,
taken from his own style of living, would be false to this state
of mind. He searches therefore through 'hapless rooms',

> In whose unhaunted glooms
> Dead pauper generations, witless of the sun
> Their course have run . . .

This Hades is neither tragic nor awesome, nor is he an heroic
Orpheus. He fights his way to Eurydice through the squalid
landscape of his poverty as a lover, and knows he does so against
contrary impulses and resentments within himself:

> And ofttimes my pursuit
> Is check'd of its dear fruit
> By things brimful of hate, my kith and kin,
> Furious that I should keep
> Their forfeit power to weep . . .

Such are the constituents of an uncouth 'mortal sorrow'; the
vision of reunion is in keeping, and still uncompromisingly self-
accusing:

> But ever, at the last, my way I win
> To where, with perfectly sad patience, nurst
> By sorry comfort of assured worst,
> Ingrain'd in fretted cheek and lips that pine,
> On pallet poor
> Thou lyest, stricken sick,
> Beyond love's cure,
> By all the world's neglect, but chiefly mine.

Loved 'ev'n more than Heaven', yet she has suffered from his lack of complete commitment. Only when this failure has been faced can the dream finally soften to tears of gratitude, for having found, 'after exceeding ill, a little good':

> A little good
> Which, for the while,
> Fleets with the current sorrow of the blood,
> Though no good here has heart enough to smile.

The weary, dragging step of the one-syllable words in the flat observation of the final line sums up the new, heavily penitential mood of this ode, so remote from the euphoric buoyancy of *The Day After Tomorrow*. Hell is now located in the 'sordid streets' of the lover's consciousness, and bereavement is seen to involve a personal inquisition, with a verdict of guilty. There is suffering 'beyond love's cure' because love itself inflicts the wound; Orpheus does not merely lose, he drives away Eurydice.

～ 8 ～

Next to *Eurydice* in Patmore's arrangement of the odes stands *The Toys*. J. C. Reid rightly observes that in context the poem is less 'soft' than it might appear in isolation, but he emphasises the consolatory religious elements in it which perhaps weakens his point.[4] A poem using a domestic episode between father and child to illuminate the relationship between God and the poet, it is also one, I think, where the tensions of *Eurydice* are again fundamental. Touching and gentle in its compassion for the child's attempt to console himself, the poem none the less admits that bereavement teaches harsh lessons and confronts the mourner with unpalatable truths about himself. The opening lines are the key ones:

> My little Son, who look'd from thoughtful eyes
> And moved and spoke in quiet grown-up wise,
> Having my law the seventh time disobey'd,
> I struck him, and dismiss'd
> With hard words and unkiss'd,
> His Mother, who was patient, being dead.

[4] Reid, p. 288.

The final observation is not gratuitously added for the sake of pathos. Patmore the impatient is distressed not merely by his roughness with his son, but by behaviour which seems a betrayal of the mother too. The contrast between her great and gracious ways and his own lack of control is part of the poem's misery: his theme is still, as in *Eurydice*, the failures of his love. The separation from her now comes home to him most acutely on this moral plane; after the physical and emotional realisation, he faces the gulf which cuts him off even from the simple relief of untainted mourning. *The Toys* can best be understood, and best resists the charges of sentimentality, if it is seen in this light.

The note of moral accusation is implicit in the statement, 'Having my law the seventh time disobey'd', with its allusion to the gospel's injunction to forgive not seven provocations but seventy times seven. Patmore feels himself alienated from wife, child and Christ as well, and his description of his son's reflective quietness further implies a criticism of the irascible and far more childish father.

The prayer of the final section carries the weight of these perceptions and does not really alleviate the mood. God's right to chastise his erring children is accepted as wholly justified, and the hope that *his* love will prevail to stay his hand, and make him 'sorry for their childishness', is still a verdict against the moral stature of the human soul. 'How weakly understood, Thy great commanded good': this idea is as important in the poem as the plea for gentleness. Patmore's 'sad heart' is here facing the shortcomings of its claim to be a loving father and, more deeply, a loving and grieving husband. The commonplace episode tests him and finds him wanting. A poem in which the speaker painfully admits he is so much less than love would have him be cannot be dismissed as mawkish, and this ode, using its situation soberly and sensitively, takes its place as a valid if minor link in the chain of Patmore's study of bereavement.

ᗌ 9 ᗍ

The study returns to full power with the sustained psychological investigation of *Tired Memory*. The failures of loving, the refusal

of the spirit to rise to the insights love brings—these inadequacies are succeeded by the honest acknowledgment that love
and grief themselves can prove subject to time and the exigencies of human nature. Memory, in short, can tire. Yet at the
same time, the process of change is shown to be more subtle and
less dramatic than a simple cessation of feeling. What is discovered to be of the past nevertheless extends its influence into
the present.

*Tired Memory* brings together Patmore's emotional and moral
perceptions and takes the theme of bereavement forward to a
new phase, one where he experiences the stirring of a new love
from the ashes of the old. The phoenix suggestion conveys one
aspect of the ode's character, its demonstration of the close
relation between the death and birth of emotion, both in the
necessity of the death to bring about the birth, and in the new
emotion's likeness to what it replaces. But the poem stresses too
the tension of this particular sort of resurrection. A new ordeal
of self-questioning accompanies it. Part of the pain is the
admission that separation, at first not even conceivable, is now
a fact the mourner can willingly assent to in its inevitability.
In so doing, he is present at her deathbed once more, and this
time, he is an accomplice in her dying.

The poem traces the movement, devious as it is, from one
condition of grief to another and from one level of desire to
another. The development on which all depends is announced
in an opening where unflinching statement and 'stony' imagery
alike concede that grief, and death itself, change their nature
with time. Like all the odes, *Tired Memory* never gasps its
despair or its passion, being disciplined and controlled in its
emphasis by the patterning of long and short pauses, as is well
shown in these lines:

> The stony rock of death's insensibility
> Well'd yet awhile with honey of thy love
> And then was dry;
> Nor could thy picture, nor thine empty glove,
> Nor all thy kind, long letters, nor the band
> Which really spann'd
> Thy body chaste and warm,

Thenceforward move
Upon the stony rock their wearied charm.
At last, then, thou wast dead.

If *The Azalea* marked the first anguish of loss, these lines give
the measure of a discovery of death's finality which goes beyond
that grief. There, her letter lived and spoke as a poignant relic
of her presence; here such intimate mementos rouse no echoes.
Death has now become a matter of insensibility on both sides
and a more complete desolation than the earlier state, when to
weep over an empty glove was to retain the remembered contact of the hand. What was once no more than a three-day
parting promising rapturous reunion is now a 'stony rock'
which yields no hope either from memory or from love's faith
in its own invincibility.

'At last, then, thou wast dead': the conclusion seems to leave
no more to say, but Patmore sees it not as an ultimate statement, but as one inviting further enquiry. He goes on to diagnose this barren misery as being the sheer exhaustion of love
—itself a death: 'My heart was dead, Dead of devotion and
tired memory'. The paradox reveals Patmore's psychological
acumen, and shows him aware of the ironies as well as the
suffering in his bereft state. The more the widower grieves the
more likely he is to commit emotional suicide and, because of
this, to lose her in a second death which this time he has
himself inflicted. There is a tangle of guilt, love, and sorrow
here which Patmore refuses to simplify and in which he allows
fully for the way the one loved, in death no less than life, takes
over as well as depends on the lover's emotional resources. The
survival and death of one personality within another is a
subordinate but not a minor theme of this poem.

In the middle section, Patmore carries further his analytic
record of his efforts to defeat or come to terms with this experience of a second death. He reports on his bargaining with
God, taking up the hint in *Tristitia* that there can be conflict
between the love for the creature and that for the creator.
While clinging to his conviction that heaven for him must be
defined in terms of her presence, he reads the possibility of
divine censure in her complete withdrawal from him, and

so submits his will, in an Easter prayer of a somewhat equivocal nature:

'Though there is no intelligible rest,
In Earth or Heaven,
For me, but on her breast,
I yield her up, again to have her given,
Or not, as, Lord, Thou wilt, and that for aye.'

He is rewarded by a dream in which he possesses her 'with heretofore unknown reality of joy'. But there is no naivety in Patmore's survey of these prayers and answers to prayer. He knows that he is employing stratagems of dubious religious and moral character. 'None thrives for long upon the happiest dream', he drily observes, and describes his next step in the attempted bribery of God:

And fresh despair
Bade me seek round afresh for some extreme
Of unconceiv'd, interior sacrifice
Whereof the smoke might rise
To God, and 'mind him that one pray'd below.

This time, he bows absolutely to the Lord's 'strange will'. If his love has also been his pride and must be 'crucified', then,

I do submit, if I saw how, to bliss
Wherein She has no part.

The tension compressed in these words shows that basically he is unable to let go his faith that human love is inseparable from the greatest good; his submission is a betrayal, as well as the most extreme sacrifice he can make:

O, my most Dear,
Was't treason, as I fear?

He answers himself: 'I cannot see But faith was broken'. And he was taken precisely at his 'remorseless word'. His heart revives—but to 'bliss Wherein She has no part', in that he responds to a 'fair stranger', not the old passion. He has killed her once more. Yet it was discerning 'a strange grace of thee' which subtly affected his behaviour towards the new person, so that she responded. Patmore registers these intricacies with a verbal delicacy which is none the less capable of exposing the element of duplicity in the situation, as well as the irony of it as an answer to prayer.

Having in his exhaustion surrendered his first passion to be restored or for ever removed as the Lord willed, the result is a lightening of his own responsibility towards it, as it were. The vain striving to revive emotion ceases, and out of this relaxation, spontaneously fresh growths of feeling are made possible. But he suffers in the fear lest he has in effect betrayed, not only the old love, but the new also. The old both dies and lives in the new, and therefore neither woman survives or is discovered as herself. The end of the poem—still addressing the dead—leads to and does not resolve this further tension brought about by changing love. She, he says, is

> Thy Sister sweet,
> Who bade the wheels to stir
> Of sensitive delight in the poor brain,
> Dead of devotion and tired memory,
> So that I lived again,
> And, strange to aver,
> With no relapse into the void inane,
> For thee;
> But (treason was't?) for thee and also her.

*Tired Memory* exemplifies the Victorian acceptance of love as an experience to be defined in terms of specific relationships, and the history, actual and posthumous, of these relationships. In its faithful following of every twist and turn of the psyche, there is a refusal to smooth out either the living or the dead situation. The romantic ideals of union for ever and the religious version of this, the hope of eternity, are alike challenged by the actualities of psychological need, emotional capacity, and the straight facts of temporality. Loving is not made up of any single state of divine simplicity—as Arnold vainly wished —but, like the spiritual life, is composed of mixed human reactions, not all of them admirable, and including impulses to betray, reject, or behave equivocally towards God and the beloved.

In addressing his dead wife in an ode portraying his heart's involuntary movement towards a second marriage, Patmore

shows himself to be a poet who shirks nothing of the ironies of
love, and who accepts that the emotional life is never static.
Yet equally, it is not in his view merely a matter of moving
onward. The influence of past on present is crucial; the resilience of the heart is mysteriously connected with the intensity
of previous love and grief, while the intermingling of personalities does not cease with the physical end of one relationship.
The lover loves again because he has loved before, and what
he is, what he finds in the new person, depends upon that
earlier encounter.

↜ 10 ↝

The distance between *Tired Memory* and *The Day After Tomorrow*, or even *The Azalea*, is considerable. But as he passes from
the first flush of unassessed loss through the stages of acute grief
to its metamorphosis, Patmore does not discard any of the
stages as illusory or less valid than others. As I have just
indicated, he is concerned with a comprehensive rather than
sequential situation; the experience is the sum of all the shifts
of feeling, and the reading of bereavement is drawn from them
all. The final ode, *A Farewell*, must be set beside the first. In
their contrasted treatment of parting and ultimate reunion
they epitomise the evolution which has taken place, emphasising
the reorientation of attitude.

But before *A Farewell*, in '*If I Were Dead*', Patmore gives one
further sketch of the bereaved husband tormented by the
consciousness of failure and inadequate love, and feeling her
death as retribution as well as affliction. Remembering how
she would gently hint to him both that she might die and that
his love could seem casual—'If I were dead, you'd sometimes
say, Poor Child'—he realises how he wounded her, and faces
what he now knows: 'It is not true that Love will do no wrong'.
In his loneliness he fulfils her prophecy, but the phrase is
charged with the pain of guilt, and pity for her pain:

> And did you think, when you so cried and smiled,
> How I, in lonely nights, should lie awake,
> And of those words your full avengers make?
> Poor Child, poor Child!

82

Loving relationships are stripped of illusion here, as in *Eurydice*. Deprivation extends insight and sympathetic understanding: love does do wrong, and grief can perceive but not repair it. The poem ends by referring the fault to divine judgment; unless she is now richly recompensed for her grief, 'O God, have Thou *no* mercy upon me!' The sentence is clearly his own verdict on his conduct. Slight though the ode is, it helps to show that Patmore has no mercy on himself in the inquests on the morality of his love and his imperfect fulfilment of the role of lover.

The fact that after eight poems on the subject of bereavement Patmore can still offer, in *A Farewell*, a further poem on parting demonstrates how convinced he is that to be separated from a loved person is not a single event but a prolonged operation. Realising the severance takes time and poetry must follow suit. And only after all has taken its course is the moment of farewell reached, when

> With all my will, but much against my heart
> We two now part.
> My Very Dear,
> Our solace is, the sad road lies so clear.

This is the ode of consolidation, accepting life apart from her; its grief, like its hope, is controlled and seen in perspective —both of eternity and time. Where *The Day After Tomorrow* preserved its initial conviction that the time apart was insignificant and that the interim could be filled with anticipation, *A Farewell* can only work round tentatively to any concept of an ultimate return to each other. Beginning with the cautious observation, 'We will not say There's any hope, it is so far away', it moves hesitantly and obliquely forward, subtly deploying its negatives to reinforce its conditional syntax, and arrives at a muted climax of imagined meeting which depends entirely, as the tense phrasing shows, on the resolute acquiescence in the completeness of separation—'through faith of still averted feet'. Patmore's handling of this movement is one of the many structural triumphs of the odes. The extended pattern of rhyme and the finely modulated long sentence build up to the climax with just the right balance of restraint and momentum:

> We will not say
> There's any hope, it is so far away.
> But, O, my Best,
> When the one darling of our widowhead,
> The nursling Grief,
> Is dead,
> And no dews blur our eyes
> To see the peach-bloom come in evening skies,
> Perchance we may,
> Where now this night is day,
> And even through faith of still averted feet,
> Making full circle of our banishment,
> Amazed meet;
> The bitter journey to the bourne so sweet
> Seasoning the termless feast of our content
> With tears of recognition never dry.

The bliss of reunion, so absolute an ecstasy in *The Day After Tomorrow*, is here seen as a complex state, not cancelling but involving the remembered pain, and compelling a vigorously paradoxical mode of expression to flower in the last seven lines of the poem. This meeting is a new encounter, strange and utterly familiar, a 'recognition' which is at once recovery and discovery, containing the sorrow of full understanding as well as the heavenly content of restored communion. All the odes are implicit in Patmore's last word on the nature of separation and possible reunion. *A Farewell* confirms that the poet's faithful study of bereavement yields a developing lesson in the implications of loving, and an art which relays them eloquently.

### ꙮ II ꙮ

To turn from Patmore's odes to *In Memoriam* does not demand a great effort of adjustment, whatever the differences of scale, range and technique. Both poets feel that they have suffered, not merely loss, but a profound personal dislocation which

forces them to search out the meaning of their central relationship. Memory and its evidence is vital to both of them, and
with this goes a willingness to submit to time's shifting emotional
perspectives; Patmore and Tennyson accept the fluidity of
experience and use the concept of becoming as their guiding
inspiration.

Beside *In Memoriam*, Patmore's sequence of nine poems is a
miniature exposition of the notion that feeling is to be understood in evolutionary terms, but it helps us to appreciate what
takes place in the Victorian imagination when it is confronted
with the knowledge that Lucy has ceased to be. So aided, we
can approach *In Memoriam* as a poem which renders that
imagination fully articulate. By writing, first, a series of lyrics
with a common theme and contrasting shades of feeling,
Tennyson followed Wordsworth; by going on to see that there
could be more cohesion than this, simply because he 'had
written so many',[5] he took the decisive step into the long poem.
In so doing, he acknowledged the principle of change as an
essential to be worked with, but he also showed that such a
principle need not subvert the formal stabilities: it has its own
ways of establishing shape, structural relationships and an
overall unity.

Tennyson, that is, renews even as he challenges the tradition
of the long poem. When he works on his 'short swallow-flights
of song' to organise them into a single utterance, he creates a
wholly contemporary version of what began as epic story-
telling. Now the story-telling is concentrated on the interior
life, but it is close to its ancestry in that the concept of 'what
happens next' is important, for meaning to Tennyson is to be
located in the sensitive recognition of how feeling follows feeling.
But the complexities, as in sophisticated epic, go beyond the
sequential flow and its implications; the poet shows in the way
he finally groups the lyrics that the unity he sees involves the
repercussion and recoil of time present on time past and the
reverse. To experience consuming grief is not to plunge into
undifferentiated timeless misery, nor is it merely to drift

[5] *The Poems of Tennyson*, ed. C. Ricks (Longmans Annotated English Poets,
1969), p. 859, quoting Hallam Tennyson's *Memoir*. Quotations are taken from this
edition.

through a variety of reactions; it is to undergo a developing reappraisal of the entire being and the love it knew, and Tennyson, sharing this perception with his fellow poets, emphasises the dignity of such a saga of the spirit—the pilgrimage of a soul—by his reconstructive adaptation of a looser lyrical assembly into the unequivocally unified form of the long poem.

But he makes no concessions to that form. The lyric is not relinquished, revealing itself on the contrary to be the unit on which the whole depends. Tennyson, no less than Arnold or Patmore, needs flexibility. The sequence has become the single work, but the gaps, so to speak, are necessary parts of what is being said. By means of the pauses between lyrics, the poets dramatise the sensation of changing position; the fact that for Tennyson the pauses are within one poem heightens the interplay between the sense of a single evolving experience, and the multiple shades of feeling which demand distinct record if that evolution is to be grasped. By conceiving his long poem as a network, Tennyson accommodates an old form to new needs.

The retention of lyric units within a larger organisation also provides him with the means of preserving the impact of moment-to-moment feeling at the same time as he goes beyond that immediacy to present a total experience of far more intricacy than a simple chronology of transient moods. The poem is faithful to the uncertainty of any emotional progress as it is lived through, without forfeiting the ability to assess each moment in a context.

*In Memoriam*, then, forces us to revise but not at all to abandon our ideas on the expected unity of a long work. To deny that it possesses any coherence is to fail to perceive the elegy's place in a period of experimental concern with the poetic handling of experience, and to call it an anthology of emotions is to miss the spectacle of a mind remaking itself after shattering disorientation. Losing Hallam, Tennyson lost his magnetic pole, and his poem works to restore his sense of his position, using its grief to take its bearings, not merely stumbling from one moment's mourning to the next.

What is involved is a painful rebuilding of personal myth. When Tennyson includes lyrics on the religious or geological readings of life, he is not rambling into issues which are incongruous in a poem of requiem for a friend, nor is he striving misguidedly after philosophical prestige. It is all part of the reappraisal; the intellectual validity of the views expressed are less important than the self-searching and testing which they affirm. They are as pertinent to the bereaved state of mind as any of the lyrics mourning Hallam directly and, equally, they are integral to the study of the nature of love and the import of loving which is *In Memoriam's* governing preoccupation. Tennyson is not attempting to solve the universe but to grasp the phenomenon of loving as it occurs in his own consciousness, exerting an influence over all that he is.

The imagery of the poem is also related to the effort of self-definition and reconstructive understanding. Tennyson's comparisons of his state of mind with widows, young girls leaving home and similar vignettes of contemporary life have upset some of his readers. But such images show the poet placing his experience in a social context of suffering commonly encountered, the better to realise its fundamental character. He is writing neither sentimentally nor naively, and his imagination is working on a level deeper than the homosexual implication at which his critics, sorrowfully or excitedly, stop short. That Tennyson compares himself to a bereaved wife is of consequence because it helps him to evaluate and realise the self-commitment and communion of love: the sexual alignment is of no poetic significance. The juxtaposition of *In Memoriam* with Patmore's odes in this chapter underlines this point, and the two together direct attention to the priorities of Victorian research into intimate relationships and the emotional roots of personality.

A closer look at the poem, with Patmore's odes still in mind, will illustrate further how Tennyson brings to his theme the resources of the large-scale approach without losing the flexibility essential to a vision accepting change as its leading principle.

∽ 12 ∽

In Patmore's history of bereavement, an easy hope of reunion had to give way to the certainty of loss in order to acquire a more sober validity. To learn the implications of love it was necessary to learn the implications of bereavement. *In Memoriam* too has to discover and sound its grief, rehearse its various kinds of pain, and move from the confusion to the understanding of the bereaved self before it can assent to a temporal conclusion of the relationship, with the conviction that intimacy matures through such separation. The final expectation of reunion is not merely a glib assurance that all shall be well.

The first twenty or so lyrics of *In Memoriam* reveal the affinities with Patmore's sequence and the contrasts brought about by the differences of imaginative range, form, temperament and psychological need. These lyrics show Tennyson moving as it were from *The Day After Tomorrow* to *Departure*. From the first unreal half-awareness, he comes to face, not the deathbed itself—for the absence of such a possibility is part of the special situation of *In Memoriam*—but the burial of Hallam. Once this evidence of the reality, and finality, of the event has been assimilated, the process of adjustment and assessment can proceed more coherently. But the first uncertainties impel the poetry to try out the rhetoric of death—a preliminary with no parallel in Patmore.

Thus the first lyric, 'I held it truth, with him who sings', offers the conventional view, that loss can be seen in time to yield some benefit. This indeed is to be a thesis proved upon the pulses of the whole poem, but here it is rejected for the hollow comfort it is. Rather, 'Let Love clasp Grief lest both be drowned': Tennyson extravagantly embraces sorrow as a way of proving his love. The poetic and psychological weaknesses of this are apparent in the histrionic language, shown again in the opening and other parts of lyric III, where the first attempt to link grief with an idea of the universe is made:

> O Sorrow, cruel fellowship,
>   O Priestess in the vaults of Death,
>   O sweet and bitter in a breath
> What whispers from thy lying lip?
>
> 'The stars,' she whispers, 'blindly run;
>   A web is woven across the sky;
>   From out waste places comes a cry,
> And murmurs from the dying sun:

'And all the phantom, Nature, stands—
With all the music in her tone,
A hollow echo of my own,—
A hollow form with empty hands.'

And shall I take a thing so blind,
Embrace her as my natural good;
Or crush her, like a vice of blood,
Upon the threshold of the mind?

Tennyson's search for emotional reality, his uncertainty of what his response should be, is betrayed in the meretricious diction, and made explicit in the final verse. Other lyrics here pursue rather more soberly the same enquiry into a proper attitude: is the 'stubborn hardihood' (II) of the yew tree, intimate with death, a symbol to accept? Is it better to capitulate to grief as in sleep, or to rouse the will to resist—'Thou shalt not be the fool of loss' (IV)?

Tennyson, with a larger scale than Patmore, is able to show fully the confusion which overwhelms one thrown suddenly into this frightening state of bereavement. He has to try to find himself, to place himself in relation to what it seems possible, or what it seems conventional, to feel. Following this policy, he takes seriously the cliché that 'Loss is common to the race', even while he rejects its false consolation. In VI, he aligns his own situation with the father or mother whose son is killed, and with the young girl whose lover suffers some fatal accident. At first sight this lyric is one of the failures of the poem, betraying him into mawkish anecdote. Yet it is more ambitious and more valid in its effort than this. It certainly chooses illustrations of loss which are obvious in their pathos, but the announced theme of the lyric is death as a cliché of experience: Tennyson has himself acknowledged the element of easy tears, as it were, because this is part of his point. Life in its fundamental relationships is subject to the melodramatic visitations of death; death is not a theme reserved for high tragedy but a daily blow, often crassly timed and crude in its disregard for the desires and needs of love.

The lyric provides Tennyson with a way of facing the state of shock which, at this stage, is his most urgent difficulty. All the sketches of loss he gives turn upon the irony of its timing: the father drinks his son's health as the bullet is striking its victim, the mother prays for the safety of the sailor at the moment when,

> His heavy-shotted hammock-shroud
> Drops in his vast and wandering grave.

The girl is at the peak of excited anticipation as her lover dies. Even so was Tennyson's own unsuspecting state, 'expecting still his advent home'. The stress is on the clash of feeling with fact, the realisation that love neither protects, nor provides intuitions of disaster, but is vulnerable to the strokes of fate.

Although sometimes weaker in its language than the sea-burial lines quoted above would suggest, the lyric as a whole marks a step forward in the poem towards the reality of what is at once common to the race and uniquely bewildering, a crisis of feeling, to each bereaved person. Another and firmer step is taken in the following lyric, 'Dark house, by which once more I stand'. The first to locate grief in a specific setting, this lyric is the stronger for its ability to dramatise in particular terms what has so far been contemplated as a generality: the need to adjust to the event and to take stock of its implications. Capturing here the contrast of past and present feeling, using the characteristics of house, street, weather and time of day, Tennyson begins to experience imaginatively the import of the statement, 'he is not here', rather than merely make uncertain gestures towards the formal propositions of death, sorrow and love.

As Patmore moves to the deathbed as his way of engaging with fact, so Tennyson advances to the burial of Hallam. The lyrics use the body's voyage back to England (IX–XVII) as a means of tightening the hold on actuality, and of coping with the restlessness of mood which characterises this time. Because his imagination can seize the potential of an imagery of winds and calm, shifting tides and a burdened ship coming irrevocably nearer, Tennyson finds his way into the nature of his experience; he is able to admit even the oddity of grieving, and its many-sidedness, instead of trying to adapt his feelings to some stereotype which can be addressed as 'Sorrow'.

Thus in lyrics IX to XII, emotion is brought into focus by the contemplation of the homecoming ship. Wishing it a steady and a calm journey, Tennyson is able to regard his loss in a calming way his heart can tolerate: Arthur 'sleeps', and parting is faced but qualified—'whom I shall not see Till all my widowed race be run' (IX). But in X, the soothing quietness— both his own and Arthur's—is questioned, as the contrast between the ship's meaning for him and for others is sharply realised. To the poet it brings not a returning friend but a 'dark freight, a vanished life'. The preference for an earthly grave rather than sea-burial is recognised simply as the comfort of habit, more bearable than the thought that 'hands so often clasped in mine, Should toss with tangle and with shells', but essentially, no more than a way of fooling oneself:

> So bring him: we have idle dreams:
> This look of quiet flatters thus
> Our home-bred fancies . . .

The recoil of feeling here from IX to X, and the refusal to rest on euphemisms, or halt at any one stage of reaction, is typical of *In Memoriam*'s use of its lyric structure, and its readiness to acknowledge every quiver of the compass needle. XI, 'Calm is the morn . . .', gathers together the implications and the imagery of the two previous lyrics, revealing the ambiguities of such terms as calm and peaceful. Nature is serenely calm; but the inner lack of storm is 'a calm despair', and the stillness of Hallam likewise is a wholly negative state—'a dead calm'. The pun is exact and unequivocal.

From this confrontation with reality, arrived at by the full play of imagination on the initial idea of the calmly sailing ship, the grieving mind in XII gives vent to its anguish in a sudden recourse to a more nervous and tense imagery of flight. In the slow waiting for the ship's arrival, confusion about its cargo's meaning returns, and the mind breaks free to swoop and hover questioningly over it, abstracted from all else. The lyric captures well the restlessness, the effort to grapple with the facts combined with the need to wait upon time, the physical numbness, and the personal dizziness and dislocation of being:

> And forward dart again, and play
> About the prow, and back return
> To where the body sits, and learn
> That I have been an hour away.

Continuing to use the almost hypnotic idea of the approaching vessel, the next lyrics give Tennyson's version of Patmore's *Azalea* period. They convey the muddle of unassimilated emotions, the grief which is still able to disbelieve itself and be convinced of its illusory status by powerfully persuasive dreams or fancies, only to surge back again on a stronger tide of realisation. The link with Patmore is pointed by the analogy of XIII:

> Tears of a widower, when he sees
> A late-lost form that sleep reveals,
> And moves his doubtful arms, and feels
> Her place is empty, fall like these . . .

But it is the appreciation of mixed reactions which is the deeper poetic link. In the same lyric, Tennyson pursues the ambivalence. 'For now so strange do these things seem' that there are moods when the thought of the coming ship leaves him, not submerged in grief but able to contemplate it with detachment, aware of but not pierced by its import. Or he is able, as XIV shows, to imagine still the return of a living Hallam, simultaneously to be aware of his grief and of its unreality. If Arthur should walk down the gangway, 'Should strike a sudden hand in mine', if 'I perceived no touch of change',

> No hint of death in all his frame,
> But found him all in all the same,
> I should not feel it to be strange.

The oscillations of belief and disbelief, dream and rejection of dream, and the entwining of fantasy with fact, so that grief can be told to its cause: the state of mind is minutely recorded, unable as it is either to accept its knowledge as final or to escape what it knows.

Hallam is and is not yet dead. In its first movement, *In Memoriam* wrestles with the misery peculiar to this stage of bereavement, when every lyric is needed to convey the contradictions and sheer puzzlement of the time. The 'changeling' quality of sorrow (XVI) is the key idea; so it is throughout the poem, but here it possesses the special strain of a new discovery, the astonishment at a self no longer understood, at unsuspected capacities of feeling: 'Can calm despair and wild unrest Be tenants of a single breast?'

In the distraction of such questioning, Tennyson turns again in XVII to hail the ever-approaching ship as the one focal and hence clarifying point for his feelings. It brings home the truth to him, literally and symbolically. Yet here too the ambivalence remains, dominating the expression and structure of the lyric. The ship brings 'all I love'; but 'all I love' is not Hallam, only 'relics', 'The dust of him I shall not see Till all my widowed race be run'. The sombre notes are stronger than they were in IX—relics and dust speak plainly of death—but still the ideas of active love and potential reunion persist.

In the lyrics of burial, XVIII–XXI, grief takes on the more resigned note of accepted fact. The grave now provides a focus: ''Tis well; 'tis something' (XVIII), and tentative moves towards consolidation and assessment can begin. The nature of grief is now pondered—what it is to 'endure with pain'. Its varying intensity is soberly contemplated, from the deepest suffering which is wordless to the lesser which can be formulated. With perfect judgment of what is appropriate, lyric XIX converts the tidal flow of the Severn, past Hallam's grave, into an extended image which carries this idea most resonantly:

> There twice a day the Severn fills;
> The salt sea-water passes by,
> And hushes half the babbling Wye,
> And makes a silence in the hills.
>
> The Wye is hushed nor moved along,
> And hushed my deepest grief of all,
> When filled with tears that cannot fall,
> I brim with sorrow drowning song.
>
> The tide flows down, the wave again
> Is vocal in its wooded walls;
> My deeper anguish also falls,
> And I can speak a little then.

XX, by contrast, characterises the degrees of feeling in a social image, distinguishing the grief of servants losing a master from that of his children. The switch in tone, and some would say taste, in the two lyrics is abrupt, but Tennyson needs both to plot and define the nature of his loss as he is now able to face it: the image which is sensitive enough to capture the submerged rhythms of psychological distress and the image which is sufficiently public to relate his condition to the world around.

From this point the lyrics begin the task of extending their explorations. The opening stanza of lyric XXI announces that the theme is fully admitted, its burden accepted. Hallam is dead and buried; mourning can become creative:

> I sing to him that rests below,
>   And, since the grasses round me wave,
>   I take the grasses of the grave,
> And make them pipes whereon to blow.

### ✍ 13 ✍

In looking at the first twenty lyrics of *In Memoriam* in some detail, I have tried to demonstrate the scale on which Tennyson works and the resources he commands. The comparison with Patmore shows that, while the odes respond sensitively to the movements of feeling, they do not dwell on each nuance, nor trace the subtleties, nor handle the opportunities of imagery, with such a fine eye for change and ambivalence as Tennyson is encouraged to do by the multiplying of his lyric unit.

The importance of memory, and the way it is used, provides another point of comparison between the poets which again throws into relief the character of the long poem. Memory for each of them is at once a stabilising and a dynamic power of mind; it is also a symbol of time passing and a mode of defying transience. Patmore can shape an ode, and move from one to another, by means of these complexities. Tennyson finds in them further justification for his lyric flexibility allied with the sustained momentum and patterning of a long poem. What *In Memoriam* is able to do is gradually to reclaim Hallam, turning the dead friend into one who is revitalised through memory. Grief is slowly carried beyond itself to a point where remembered love becomes renewed experience, and loss is secondary to a sense of essential survival and the conviction of the 'bond which is to be'.

Tennyson has room to start from the doubt, does memory deceive:

> And was the day of my delight
> As pure and perfect as I say?
>
> (XXIV)

This begins his evaluation of love, for it was the emotion shared which eased and distinguished the years of friendship, he sees, not any absence of trouble during them. Given a view of all the past, those years would prove 'its richest field' (XLVI). Yet it takes the poem a long time to turn and contemplate that past as it was lived. Not until lyrics LXXXVII and LXXXIX, when the days at Cambridge and afternoons at Somersby are recalled in an attempt to recapture their atmosphere, does Tennyson feel himself able to resurrect the experience of love. He continually testifies to its richness in his reiteration of crippling loss, but there is a kind of selfishness in this condition which urges that attention shall remain fixed on grief itself rather than on the experiences without which it would not exist. Tennyson's struggle to release memory from this prohibition is one of the signs the poem gives of grief as a changing phenomenon, and one challenged by the restorative instincts of love. A decisive battle is fought in the poems on sleep, dreams and night-fantasies, lyrics LXVII to LXXI.

Dreams bring the first tentative assertion of Hallam as a living presence, but they and the night hours generally are haunted by the misery which denies that presence. Walking with Hallam in the dream does not dispel the sadness—it is transferred to him: 'I find a trouble in thine eye' (LXVIII). With the stringent emotional logic of dreams, Hallam mourns himself. But this means the past is not as it was. And in lyric LXX, the strain of trying to recall it faithfully is enacted, in the poet's effort simply to see Arthur's face:

95

> I cannot see the features right,
>     When on the gloom I strive to paint
>     The face I know . . .

Nightmare shapes and shadows intervene, until out of the failure comes a moment's victory—a clear vision to quiet the longing:

> And through a lattice on the soul
> Looks thy fair face and makes it still.

Gaining strength from this, LXXI records a significant night when sleep at last ceases to be the associate of grief and allies itself to life:

> Sleep, kinsman thou to death and trance
>     And madness, thou hast forged at last
>     A night-long Present of the Past
> In which we went through summer France.

A change of direction is won here, the first move towards a waking 'present of the past' being taken. The lyric registers the slackening of grief as a negative tyranny obstructing memory, lifting with the suggestion of 'summer France', to establish contact with brighter days, and expanding in its final verse to recall living scenes experienced together—'The cataract flashing from the bridge, The breaker breaking on the beach'.

The waning of overwhelming sorrow is itself a sadness as well as a creative step; *In Memoriam* is faithful to the one reaction as to the other, as the lyric of the second Christmas-time shows —'O last regret, regret can die' (LXXVIII). But the lyric distinguishes between enduring grief and the mere exhaustion of tears, dried with 'long use', and marks the arrival at the Patmorean milestone where mourning is ready to admit other kinds of feeling, and other kinds of contemplation of the dead not dissociated from the living. For Tennyson it is not so much the tiring of memory as the hint that memory can bring a revival of love by its own freer activity.

Memory as a source of strength when new life is balanced with old pain is the theme of LXXXV, one of the longer lyrics. While still oppressed by his loss, Tennyson emphasises here the sustaining role Hallam continues to play:

> Whatever way my days decline,
>   I felt and feel, though left alone,
>   His being working in mine own,
> The footsteps of his life in mine . . .

He is 'an image comforting the mind', retaining his unique place as the 'prime passion' of 'first friendship', yet now encouraging the resumption of other friendships 'for the years to come'. 'Love for him' has not 'drained' the poet's 'capabilities of love'. Thus as Patmore recognised the role played by his first wife in his choosing of a second, so Tennyson points to the inter-action between past and present love, the turning away which is at the same time a ratification of the previous experience and of its survival. Memory is not discredited or censored but puts off its black and begins to operate as a life-directing force.

Where Patmore finds this a moment of leave-taking as well as a final affirmation of enduring love, however, Tennyson is only at the threshold of further stages in the liberation of memory from mourning. This is the point in the poem where reminiscences of Hallam enter, not where they vanish. In a deliberate act of waking will, Tennyson recalls the times together in the Cambridge rooms, and Arthur at Somersby 'as he lay and read The Tuscan poets on the lawn' (LXXXIX). The past lives and to that extent Hallam is rescued from the tomb, but the vivid recollections also generate desire for contact once more, and so the poem, carried by the power of memory, moves on to conceive living contact as a possibility.

Tension mounts in XC as the longing dominates: 'Ah dear, but come thou back to me'. In XCI the cry is the same, 'Come, not in watches of the night, But where the sunbeam broodeth warm . . .'. Recoil, as ever, follows: 'I shall not see thee' (XCIII). But the impetus which unchecked memory has gathered is too strong. Lyric XCV brings the leap from remembered times together, recorded in old letters, to an actual moment when reunion is an experience:

> So word by word, and line by line,
>   The dead man touched me from the past,
>   And all at once it seemed at last
> The living soul was flashed on mine . . .

Where the verb 'flashing', used of the cataract in LXXI, signalled the first dynamic brightening of memory, here it carries the higher charge of lightning's energy, a contrast which sums up the psychological distance travelled in this section of the poem.

Once the ecstatic immediacy of the moment is passed, the poem continues its eddying, hesitant course. But the emphasis continues to show love's experiences as cause for hope rather than grief:

> Yet less of sorrow lives in me
> For days of happy commune dead;
> Less yearning for the friendship fled,
> Than some strong bond which is to be.
>
> (CXVI)

Love has consolidated grief, which brooded on 'A hand that can be clasped no more' (VII): 'And in my thoughts with scarce a sigh I take the pressure of thine hand' (CXIX). Tennyson's sensitivity in charting this process of change constitutes the achievement of *In Memoriam*, and his step by step demonstration of memory's role in the conflicts, and the dialogue, between love and the shock of loss is one impressive feature of that sensitivity.

### ◡ 14 ◡

In *Departure*, Patmore faced not just death but the moment of dying and the violation of personality which characterised the event. The poet discovered the menace of bereavement, not just its grief, as his identity suffered eclipse in the disintegration of hers. This is an area Tennyson also explores, again with contrasts of interpretation as well as scale.

The fate of the self in its sudden isolation concerns him throughout *In Memoriam*, and the struggle to restore Hallam in the mind, recognisable as the man who was loved, is the more urgent because it is not only Hallam who is feared lost. Tennyson searches for his own personality as he fights to retrieve his friend's, and the degree to which he depends on

Hallam to assure himself of his own being is a striking element in the poem from beginning to end. There are, moreover, two opposite kinds of dismay which the lyrics try to cope with: first, there is the simple absence of the defining power—Hallam who loved him is gone, Tennyson no longer knows or feels who he is; secondly, even at the times when faith in Hallam's continued existence burns bright, there is the other despair—Arthur is so changed from his earthly self, the man whose hand was clasped, that he cannot be conceived of as the friend whose sympathy supported the poet.

The first fear assails the earlier part of the poem and suffuses all its disorientated misery; the second persists longer. It underlies all the poems on reunion, whether dreamt of, longed for, trusted in, or firmly looked forward to. The lurking uneasiness of how recognisable Hallam may be is intimately related to the anxiety that, if he is changed, the past may still be lost, with all that this entails for any secure sense of personal continuity. 'I prosper, circled with thy voice', one of the last lyrics declares, and although the poem chooses finally to stress this assurance, the disquieting question still arises: 'What art thou then?' (CXXX). However splendid the visions of Hallam in the later stages of *In Memoriam*, I do not think it ever quite overcomes the fear of being permanently out of reach of that reassuring love which the earthly friendship brought as one of its chief gifts. There is a note of hysterical over-insistence, for example, in CXXIX: 'Mine, mine, for ever, ever mine', and insecure tension, rather than the enriching complexity brought to the heavenly vision of Patmore's *A Farewell*, in the recourse to paradox—

> Strange friend, past, present and to be;
> Loved deeplier, darklier understood . . .

At the least I think Tennyson's poems on the glorified Arthur yield some of the weakest poetry of *In Memoriam*, and this is partly because he is unable to place himself or feel himself defined in emotional contact with this being. Memories of Arthur as he was, and grief itself to some extent, act as mirrors in which the poet can read his own history and experience, and

the poem thrives on, and advances through, this self-encounter-
ing. And while he admits the fear that Hallam may no longer
be the person who loved him, the poetry does not falter; 'A
spectral doubt which makes me cold' (XLI) is a state of mind
miserable for Tennyson but good for his art. When the lyrics
ignore that fear, however, the pressure of Tennyson searching
for himself is lost; and that gone, the energy of the work is
extinguished. Imagining the spirit of Arthur simply to eulogise
it offers no reflection of Tennyson's own face and the lyrics
fall back on rhetoric.

The contrast is well shown in lyrics C to CIII. Here Tennyson
takes leave of Somersby and tells of a dream on the night before
going. First, in the lyrics recording the emotion of uprooting
himself from the place in which all his life has been passed,
feeling and locality are blended in his most assured and moving
manner. He sees how this blending will take place in the lives
of the new inhabitants as time builds up associations:

> And year by year the landscape grow
> Familiar to the stranger's child . . .
>
> (CI)

These lyrics are imbued with the poet's strong sense of self-
realisation. In this place he knows himself, it offers him a
tangible symbolism of his emotional history, stretching from
childhood memories to those of Hallam (CII), with a final
merging of all memories in a single poignant assertion of the
unity of feeling, and being, in this 'well-belovèd place'. 'Rival'
memories 'mix in one another's arms To one pure image of
regret'.

This true epiphany contrasts with the account of a dream-
epiphany which follows (CIII). The reunion with a Hallam
'thrice as large as man', with attendant wailing maidens, is
poetically strained and psychologically unconvincing, though
dream-states are used effectively in other lyrics. What is absent
here is that coming home to oneself which is a vital part of
Tennyson's love and grief, but not of his reunion visions. Again
there is a contrast with Patmore's eternity and the two who
meet 'With tears of recognition never dry'. *A Farewell* achieves
a more moving suggestion of self-fulfilment in and through the

other person than any of *In Memoriam*'s attempts to envisage the apotheosis of the self in reunited love.

## ᓚ 15 ᓚ

One further comparison with Patmore will serve to complete this study of the two poets in their handling of common material. Both in their bereavement discover that the myths by which they live cannot remain immune to the inquest which grief imposes. Patmore, while admitting clashes between earthly and spiritual values, found that his religious outlook met with and helped him to articulate his perceptions about love in its morality and its emotions; he also found that his love provided the religious world-picture with essential motivation and meaning. Such mutual validation is found in Tennyson too, but *In Memoriam* reaches it only after prolonged doubt and questioning.

What is shadowed in Patmore takes place in substance in *In Memoriam*, for external acknowledgment of a set of attitudes is transformed into a psychologically validated acceptance of their tenability—indeed of their necessity. The poem slowly learns to swim in the element of faith—not faith in a formal creed, but in love as it withstands the apparent finality of death. Tennyson gradually ventures to trust his own secular experience—'I have felt'—and to admit that this is all he can do. Feeling and fidelity to its evolutions offers the only way to sustain the religious vision, and in the event this fidelity is not just desperately shoring up the vision, but is almost compelling it into existence as an interpretation of what is proved upon the pulses of love.

But an alliance with the experience of love also occurs in an area apparently opposed to the religious. The poem's imaginative grasp of a universe forming itself over vast periods of geological time is also validated, not overthrown, by the fidelity to feeling Tennyson shows. The idea of process, change, a time-dependent creation is, again, proved on the pulses and so geology becomes a symbol for the workings of the inner life.

That Tennyson is powerfully moved by the geological

universe is apparent in the strength of such lines as those in
which he hears 'the sound of streams',

> . . . that swift or slow
> Draw down Aeonian hills, and sow
> The dust of continents to be . . .
>
> (XXXV)

Taking its cue from this slow and austere creativity, the poem
discovers that the emotional life too sows by degrees its future
continents, and that such a conspiracy with time brings about
its fulfilment rather than atrophies its nature. Love continues
to assert its survival, capable still of growth and stimulating
activity within the bereaved personality, as it challenges the
evidence of a broken relationship. Grief and loss themselves
prove, in their very strength, to be dynamic and changing
states, interacting with love and inseparable from it, yet subordinate to its refusal to accept despair as an ultimate. The
movement of love warring with loss is finely controlled and
revealed from lyric to lyric, so that the pains and toil of an
evolution are vividly lived through. Evolution itself evolves,
from nature's death-sentence into the agency of salvation:
'Ring out the old, ring in the new' (CVI). The hopeful religious
view thus joins hands with 'Aeonian music measuring out
The steps of Time' (XCV), and while the two are thus allied,
the poem remains vital. A decline of power is apparent in some
of the later sections, as I have said, but significantly this occurs
in lyrics which slacken the bond between heaven and earth,
trying to rise into a spiritual dimension where the workings of
time and the inner self no longer actively contribute to the
poetry or form part of the concept of Arthur alive.

Change, in short, becomes creative, and 'every thought
breaks out a rose' (CXXII), as *In Memoriam* submits to grief and
love as an historical experience. By lyric CXV, the seasonal
move from winter to spring can be identified with the inner
development:

> . . . and my regret
> Becomes an April violet,
> And buds and blossoms like the rest.

CXVI speaks of turning away from 'regret for buried time' and so leads in to the clarified vision of time's continuing positive role in CXVII, 'O days and hours, your work is this'. The joy of reunion will be proportionate to 'every grain of sand that runs'. CXVIII then moves from the personal affirmation of an evolving relationship which can absorb and transcend suffering to contemplate evolution as a general idea once more. Here too is the same sense of purposeful necessity, a progressive yet intensely purgatorial movement to higher concepts of life. In its image of the tempering of metal, the lyric brings together the cosmic with the individual perception. It sums up the emotional experience, and the imaginative response to it, which *In Memoriam* as a whole exemplifies:

> . . . life is not as idle ore,
>
> But iron dug from central gloom,
>     And heated hot with burning fears,
>     And dipt in baths of hissing tears,
> And battered with the shocks of doom
>
> To shape and use.

This sequence of lyrics late in the poem stands linked in the same subtle interrelationship as the first twenty analysed earlier, and so discussion circles round again to reiterate the fundamental point that Tennyson successfully brings together his apparently conflicting ideals of 'short swallow-flights of song' and a long poem. The two are reconciled, and shown to be actively collaborative, in the poet's commitment, shared with Patmore, to portraying the 'widowed race', not as a monotonous state of lament but as a course to be traced in all its twists and turns and all its revelations of changing landscapes and horizons.

What Patmore accepts as a principle energising a sensitive, subtle, interacting group of odes, Tennyson sees as demanding one unified act of imagination which will capture the hesitations, the detail and the recoil of emotional events, while sustaining the sense of their dependence for their full import on the developing and defining role of time.

Patmore knew and reviewed[6] *In Memoriam*. He was in fact

---

[6] In the *North British Review*, August 1850; see Reid, p. 194.

one of the poem's first readers, in 1849, when 'Mrs Patmore . . . copied it out for the press, and Tennyson gave her the original'.[7] It must therefore have been present with peculiar poignancy in Patmore's imagination twelve years later when his 'widowed race' began, and he too embarked on the further discovery of love by recording the history of grief.

[7] Ricks, *The Poems of Tennyson*, p. 856, quoting William Allingham's *Diary*.

# IV

# 'If I Be Dear to Someone Else'

## Meredith: *Modern Love*; Tennyson: *Maud*; Browning: *James Lee's Wife*

∽ I ∽

After the crises of bereavement, the more Byronic traumas of broken, doomed or tormented relationships. Here too the Victorian poets follow the Romantic lead in choosing the extreme situation for their assessments of love as it builds, and also threatens, the personality, and here too they extend their study over a period of time, tracing the unhappy history of these relationships as they unfold.

They are poems animated by fear and other distraught states of mind. Where *In Memoriam* and Patmore's odes were convinced of love as a shared reality, and took stock of their deprivation in the light of this, these poems are founded upon no such certainty. At the least they question the endurance or success of a close relationship, and they can be forced to face the doubt of the genuine existence of such an experience. The conditional, 'if I be dear', looms large. Yet at the same time the poems admit having at any rate assumed that felicity, in the strained voices of their speakers, who are all depicted in the throes of severance from love. The speakers fear they are become mad, corrupted, annihilated, or simply strangers to themselves as a consequence of an intense association which is suddenly torn from them, or in some way ends badly. There is vigorous reappraisal, arising out of a keen appreciation of the hurt one person may do another because of the disarming which love induces; the vulnerability which is the price for love's seeming rewards preoccupies these poems. Love here is a matter of murderous and suicidal passions underlying what can prove to be a thin illusion of sweetness and light. The speakers fear themselves as well as for themselves.

If they were poems wholly of disillusion and repudiation, they would be other than they are. As Byron recoiled from one fatal love and turned for reassurance and reconstruction to another intimacy, so the Victorian poets, even in these poems where wounds are exposed, affirm that love can act as a healing as well as a destructive force. Dramatic tension is consequently high, and feeling is once more seen, as in the studies of grief, as fluctuating and conflicting to a degree which demands the resources of some kind of extended poem if it is to be faithfully mapped. Change is of the essence, 'seasons not eternities' the watchword for Meredith, Tennyson and Browning alike, as they wrestle with the mixed consequences of committing oneself to another.

Byron fired off his stanzas of pain and resentment at Lady Byron as the separation took its course; he addressed Augusta in successive lyrics as the various stages of this consolatory relationship became apparent. The sense of drama is high, because Lady Byron and Augusta seem presences active in the verse not just persons apostrophised. When, in the Victorian poems, the complexities are increased either by the merging of the two aspects of love—Lady Byron and Augusta—into one person, whose presence, again, is strongly felt, or by some other closer entanglement of the destructive with the positive, then the dynamic and dramatic pressures on the poetry are considerably increased. A loose sequence is inadequate, the drama decrees a flexible but unified structure, poems within a poem.

In the three works to be discussed here, the opportunities of such a structure are well understood. As in *In Memoriam*, 'swallow-flights' are used to catch immediate mood and the moment's insight; the larger context adds the time element, emphasises the way feeling grows out of feeling, and reveals the patterning as well as the flow of experience. But the structure also actively assists the dramatic tension so fundamental to these poems. Lyric clashes with lyric, sections criticise as well as reinforce each other, emotion is questioned or undercut by an abrupt change of stance. The threat of a disintegrated personality, the central fear, is eloquently suggested by the

juxtaposition of alien states of mind, the torment of such confusion is intimated in the restless shifts of form or the constantly checked and interrupted flow of feeling. At the same
time, as lyric follows lyric, section is added to section, the
cumulative tension is exploited, so that the structure conveys
the compulsion of the need to pursue and endure the experience
as time changes it and brings new kinds of pain to supplant or
redouble the old. Past contrasts with present, as it did in *In
Memoriam*, but in the poems of breakdown, the recognition of
the contrast is more cruel, near the nerve of the pain; the long
poem provides the poets with the means of making this, too,
dramatically clear.

The structure, offering these dramatic resources, also
stimulates an ironic approach. Tracing emotional clashes and
contrasts can generate a wry, disengaged awareness of the
vicissitudes of loving. The gulf between what was—or was
thought to be—and what is can be measured with a relish for
the spectacle of romanticism confounded; the juxtaposing of
one state of mind with its opposite can, similarly, prick preten-
sions. Meredith is the obvious example here, but neither
Browning nor Tennyson is wholly deaf to the ironies although
each attends so closely to the harrowing aspects of love. Conversely, Meredith does not exclude the force of the suffering in
admitting that it can be regarded critically, even cynically. All
three poems are the more interesting, in fact, because they combine different kinds of perception, in varying proportions certainly; but none of the poets ignores the point that his choice
of structure makes possible a wide range of tone.

Bereavement as a theme brought with it attendant risks, and
so does the material of these poems. Where sentimentality lay
in wait for Patmore and Tennyson as they mourned the dead,
melodrama threatens the poetry of love abused. Because the
situation is one of active collision and aggressive postures,
wounds given and received, the note can become shrill and the
emotion degenerate into uncontrolled display. The poets do
not so much avoid this danger as take it to themselves and make
the moment of hysteria, the exaggerated gesture or the loss of
self-control, part of their psychological portraits. The speakers
see themselves and the loved person as magnified by their

passions, and the poetry finds stratagems to convey this, including apparently crude devices such as a recourse to a rather gaudy kind of imagery, instances of which appear in all three poems. But feeling is not dishonoured by this readiness to acknowledge an element of excess within it: the poets admit and use melodrama, they do not succumb to it. This is another example of the Victorian capacity to redeem emotional cliché —the deathbed, the distracted lover—by accepting it as the starting point for imaginative exploration.

The characteristics of poetry which deals with the hazards, rewards, and illusory possibilities of thinking oneself dear to someone else all emerge the more emphatically when three examples are grouped together. But the grouping also reveals how much scope each poet found for his individual imagination in this theme, and the variety is as interesting as the common elements.

↶ 2 ↶

*Modern Love* even in its title makes a forceful contribution to this chapter. Ironically toned, it introduces an idea of love not as a vision set apart from time, place and society, but, on the contrary, to be characterised by these things. Borrowing an old device, the sonnet sequence, Meredith puts it to new uses, and the contrast with the assumptions of Elizabethan sequences is part of his point. The modern situation, if the poet is to cover it faithfully, needs an expansive treatment, not because the moods of the lover, from worship to despair, and his enthusiasm, demand it, but because a disintegrating relationship is the subject, and it is a process whose stages must be traced. Where the Petrarchan sonneteers began from the accepted premise that love was a phenomenon of enduring worth, recognisable as such whatever the price in pain, rage, desire or hopelessness, and despite the lack of active involvement by one party, Meredith starts from the denial that there is any such phenomenon over and above the relationship which creates it—or seems to do so. The Renaissance mistress provided the poet with the occasion for singing of Cupid's mischief and Venus's power —love was his subject more than she. But the Victorian depends entirely on being dear to someone else, the active coming together of two individuals, generating emotional consequences which can be called love but which are as mortal and unstable, as prone to change, as the persons themselves. As a value, love is inseparable from what it means, at any given moment, to them both. Meredith's interest is centred on this conditional character of love as a joint experience.

His is a drastic interpretation, highlighting the fortuitous, exposing the ephemeral aspects of 'being dear', while stressing the poisons which the experience leaves behind it. For him, it is not the lover who is variable in his response to a force which exists in itself as a constant, but rather love which is the inconstant:

> Prepare
> You lovers, to know Love a thing of moods:
> Not, like hard life, of laws . . .[1]

The peculiar tension of Meredith's sequence is hinted here. The sonnets are used to convey the unreliable and unpredictable nature of an emotional bond, and at the same time, the inevitability of decline which is inherent within this caprice. The lovers suffer not because love is a god demanding much, but because there is no god, or devil; only passions, whose consequences outlive themselves. The combination of the wholly transient with an abiding legacy, irresponsible impulses setting up an inescapable psychological chain-reaction, is sombre, dramatic, and ironic.

Meredith exploits the sequence to make it serve these ends. The fifty short fixed units give him room to tell the story of inexorable deterioration, full opportunity to show love as 'a thing of moods', and a means of enacting the varying shocks and assaults of the conflict. The movement through the sequence is balanced against the isolated emphasis of each sonnet; drama is persistently frozen into tableaux, and as persistently released. It is mistaken, I think, to see *Modern Love* as a nineteenth-century novel in verse, for the sonnets are not analogous to chapters, but units in a structure which relates parts to whole in a more complex way. Narrative is both promoted and

---

[1] Quotations are taken from *Selected Poetical Works of George Meredith*, ed. G. M. Trevelyan (1955).

resisted in order to focus the inner rather than the external action.

Meredith is particularly aware of the potential his form offers for changing the angle and so heightening the drama and the tension. One sonnet concentrates on the husband and his state of mind, the next places him in a direct encounter with his wife; a third distances the scene so that there is a stronger sense of the social context in which all is being played out, while in a fourth, the wife confronts the mistress. Thus the emotional action is seen from several vantage points, and Meredith holds firmly to the ironic detachment which this encourages even though he keeps the husband as the central consciousness in the poem. Indeed the recognition of ironies is to be taken as part of the psychological consequences for the latter. The shifting ground of *Modern Love* shows Meredith's appreciation of what emotional crisis means to a sophisticated consciousness: suffering which must watch itself and others suffer, adding the special bitterness of intellectual voyeurism to its pain. The misery is inseparable from a need to criticise, to mock, to dissect, with a third party's alertness to the absurdities involved.

The critical view which explains that in some sonnets the poet speaks, in others, the husband, may be nominally accurate, in that some are cast in the third person, some in the first. But the split into a 'narrator' and a character who is the husband is too superficial. Meredith shows that someone in this state of torment is at times in the centre of his suffering, at other times forced by it to regard himself objectively. 'He' in the poem is a deliberately ambiguous pronoun. It refers now to the husband, now to the wife's lover, and the reader's momentary uncertainty imitates the husband's wavering grasp of his own identity. There is the obvious irony: the husband was himself his wife's lover; now this is not his role—though it could be. But beyond this, the moments when the marriage is contemplated impersonally show a psychological distancing at an extreme point, where 'he' is indeed the man in the role the husband now takes but is alienated from himself by the shock of it. In the subjective, first-person sonnets, he shows an intellectual distancing as part of his nature; but in the third-person strategy, Meredith suggests there is a radical insecurity of self to be coped with as well as an ironic cast of mind. As Byron showed, the withdrawal of love undermines the personality to a murderous degree, and in some of *Modern Love*'s sonnets, 'I' becomes 'he' in a violent displacement of subjective feeling, the switch back again in other sonnets dramatising the vertigo of the experience.

Meredith thus seizes on the structural character of the sonnet sequence and finds in it ways the contemporary novel did not offer of revealing both a peculiarly self-possessed intellectual torment and the panic of a personality threatened with disintegration. Without the flexibility of the short juxtaposed units, the range would be curtailed, and also, the immediacy of the relationship itself would be less sharp and less claustrophobic. The pressure of the bond, even—or perhaps especially —in its demise, is a crippling feature of the situation for husband and wife, and their tension together and mutual awareness are well conveyed by the concentrated presentation of it in a mere sixteen lines. The poignancy and resentment in the contrasts between past and present are also brought out in their tangle of mixed sentiment by the sonnets' compression, and the sequence as a whole is able to show how the ruins of love are haunted by the ghosts of its heyday.

It is necessary I think to establish how much Meredith is using form and structure, and how ambitious his conception is, before looking at the sonnets themselves, for at first sight they can be disappointing. The strictures of Leavis on the 'flashiness' of the sequence, its 'vulgar cleverness working upon cheap emotion',[2] can seem very near the mark unless we are able to assess the poetry from a position which at least makes it imperative to ask whether cleverness is the limit of the poet's imagination, or cheap emotion its material. The tone and style of each sonnet must be assessed in context, for they play a precise part in conveying the full psychological repercussions of the breaking relationship. If the presentation of feeling, and the feeling itself, at times seem vulgarly exhibitionist, and I agree they do, this must be weighed against those aspects of the sequence which are the reverse of crude.

Meredith is not confined to crudity; rather he is aware that

[2] *New Bearings in English Poetry* (new edition, 1950), p. 21.

a degree of posturing, a theatricality of gesture, is a feature of the crisis he contemplates, where sophisticated perceptions are subjected to primitive emotional pressures. To capture this collision, he uses an exaggerated imagery, a style which combines the ironic with an excess of irony, to vulgarise rather than refine: 'we'll sit contentedly And eat our pot of honey on the grave' (XXIX). The husband maintains his sardonic detachment in such an image, but its over-emphasis betrays the decline of his personality, able to recognise and sustain itself only in a caricature of subtle sensibility. It is a nightmare distortion of himself the husband suffers; fundamentally intellectual, his way of envisaging his pain remains so, but his control is undermined. Assailed by destructive feeling, he registers this in ways which resemble the devices of fever-ridden minds, knowing themselves menaced but able to express this only in terms of monsters in the bedroom.

The first sonnet establishes such a mental situation. The husband, hearing his wife check her weeping as she senses he is awake, envisages the sobs as 'little gaping snakes, Dreadfully venomous to him'. Here is the half-mocking, intellectual reading; but at the same time, the image confesses the threat to himself which he feels to a demoralising degree: he must use a deliberately horrific emblem, rather than a subtly imaginative image to suggest its power. It is part of the husband's doom to be reduced to seeing himself and his pain in this melodramatic way. When there is vulgarity in the sonnets, it is inherent in Meredith's theme, not in the limitations of his 'clever' imagination; it shows the acuteness of his critique of this state of mind, not a poetic surrender to its symptoms.

∽ 3 ∽

Beginning with the two 'sculptured effigies' upon the 'marriage-tomb', the sequence then concentrates attention not on the death but on the dying. Meredith refuses to see the end of an affair as a clean severing stroke; emotional separation is to him a slow tearing apart, testifying to the deep roots of such unions in the difficulty and sense of violation which characterise the operation.

Each sonnet in the first ten catches the husband's strain. His clear understanding of the situation contends on the one hand wth sudden surges of debasing passions which threaten to engulf him and, on the other, with the social game of pretended normality which both partners play. Meredith depicts a mind lurching between bitter but controlled and honest contemplation of its plight and two kinds of self-betrayal—capitulation to the passions within, and the opposite alienation of civilised hypocrisy. The bewilderment is emphasised by the switches from third to first person and back again. In sonnet II, the distanced voice notes how the surface of pretence—'each wore a mask'—conspires to feed the fierce passions of resentment and hostility beneath, which in turn can only be checked by a further dissembling that leaves him all the more vulnerable, a 'shuddering heap of pain'. The phrase is sadistic in reducing personality to an anonymous tortured protoplasm. Immediately sonnet III speaks directly out of the consuming jealousy which is helping to bring about that anonymity. Here in the tones of rant is the destructive force at its work, sinking the sophisticated mind into its pit. The new lover shall be 'crushed until he cannot feel':

> But he is nothing:—nothing? Only mark
> The rich light striking out from her on him!
> Ha! what a sense it is when her eyes swim
> Across the man she singles, leaving dark
> All else! Lord God, who mad'st the thing so fair,
> See that I am drawn to her even now!
> It cannot be such harm on her cool brow
> To put a kiss? Yet if I meet him there!
> But she is mine! Ah, no! I know too well
> I claim a star whose light is overcast:
> I claim a phantom-woman in the Past.
> The hour has struck, though I heard not the bell!

The jerky rhythms and exclamations catch the hysteria which is replacing the individual who knew himself when her light shone on him.

IV confirms his eclipse with a return to the distanced, and

here more ironically reflective voice, admitting that all experience has 'suffered shipwreck with the ship', and life has become wholly negative with the loss of its central defining joy. Thus in three sonnets, a psychological state of some complexity has been established, and the extremes of cold and heat in the situation suggested.

The husband's dislocation is brought out strongly in sonnet VI, where the viewpoint continually shifts throughout the sixteen lines, so that an impression of confused unrest and instability is produced, together with, as always, the sharp awareness of what he suffers. The sonnet switches from his watching how 'his lips . . . meet her forehead' to articulate directly the inner jealousies which her self-conscious response releases: 'what's the name? The name, the name, the new name thou hast won?'. Then follows the taxing effort of restraint 'though the sting is dire' so that nothing is actually said, and finally the sonnet steps abruptly back and surveys the two of them:

> —Beneath the surface this, while by the fire
> They sat, she laughing at a quiet joke.

The outrageous incongruity between the surface role of married couple and the realities of estrangement beneath is emphasised by these lines, the double vision being the more tense because it occurs within the one unit.

From VII to X the sequence goes more deeply into the husband's fears. In confronting them he revises his concept of love, abandoning romance and the subtler illusions alike. Love, like people, is a 'thing of moods' because it is no more than the temporary disposition of those who are brought together by it. His route to this reading is the discovery that love rejected becomes distorted into a predatory and degrading force. What once was music now just as readily promotes discord. The 'wild beast' (IX) gains strength:

> I do not know myself without thee more:
> In this unholy battle I grow base.
>
> (VIII)

In sonnet IX there is a charged moment between them, sexual menace from him being met with seductive dissembling from her, leaving him helpless to harm or to forgive her—'And from her eyes, as from a poison-cup, He drank . . .'

From this climax, emphasised by the Jacobean flourish of the poison-cup, the tenth sonnet turns to face the facts of relationships. His crime was to assume a lifelong bond. Had he been willing to play a fairy-tale game of love, there might have been no disillusion, because there was no reality. But trying to live, not dream, love, he can only learn that there is no immunity from change, that love bears no magical powers to preserve what it initiates. This is the point of view the rest of the sequence accepts and shows being validated in the continuing history of the relationship. 'Seasons; not Eternities', says XIII, and yet the pain of disappointed expectation remains, and it is impossible to 'lose calmly Love's great bliss'. The capital letter persists and the memories of what has been support it, even while the past must be seen as illusion, thus undermining the sense of secure identity further: 'the mad Past, on which my foot is based' (XII).

These confusions—love so enriching, so ephemeral, so destructive—are aspects of the general ambivalence which characterises the story of the later stages in the relationship. Attention is drawn to a series of illuminating moments which plot the brutalising, sensitising, and always tormenting course of dying love as various little dramas are played out within the sixteen-line span. Three examples stand next to each other in sonnets XV to XVII, and the emotional point of each is sharpened by the juxtaposition. They move from the melodrama of a bedroom confrontation to the social game of dinner-party appearances, by way of a remembered episode from earlier days.

The husband's jealousy is depicted as he reads to his wife an old love letter from her to him, driving home his point by demonstration:

> I show another letter lately sent.
> The words are very like: the name is new.
>
> (XV)

He wakes her up to enact this scene, and her 'trembling' is shown without pity; the coarseness of his feeling informs the whole sonnet and its production in the theatrical sense. So XVI, with its tender recollection of the 'old shipwrecked days', is an abrupt change of tone, again with production and setting to match. In the firelight of a 'hushed' evening when they sat secure in their love, he affected a worldly wisdom: '"Ah, yes! Love dies!" I said: I never thought it less'. She sobbed, upset; he kissed the tears away. The sonnet ends: 'Now am I haunted by that taste! that sound!'

The survival in memory of a time when they were vulnerable to each other but protected by their mutual certainty of love comes as a check to the near-hate of XV. The present is the more cursed but the less ugly for the memory. His baseness is countered by his inability to reject the past as simply false. Yet this less soured admission of a sense of loss is immediately poisoned by XVII which shows, not the callousness of battle, but, equally corrupting, its hypocrisies. Acting their parts as host and hostess, they admire each other's skill at dissembling:

> With sparkling surface-eyes we ply the ball:
> It is in truth a most contagious game:
> HIDING THE SKELETON, shall be its name.

So good are they that they 'waken envy' and seem to epitomise the happy marriage. The note on which this sonnet ends shows Meredith deliberately using imagery which lowers the imaginative tone to convey the moral decline: 'Dear guests, you now have seen Love's corpse-light shine'. The sneer belongs to the speaker's world of XV, so that the extremes of the situation, its naked antagonism and its buried enmities, are seen to meet in one state of degradation. Against this, XVI stands as a buffer, though itself charged with disillusion.

By working with such dramas, Meredith reaches not only the husband's complex feelings but the wife's too. The dramatic presentation leaves no doubt of the pressure of each upon the other, the nerve of the situation being the intimate awareness which was the gift of love and which remains as a fine torment in love's withdrawal. The irony that the estrangement increases their sensitivity to each other is enacted in XXI, for instance,

where 'on the cedar-shadowed lawn' a friend talks to them of
his coming marriage. They bear the arrows of his enthusiasm
together, consciously and without wincing, until she faints—
implying pregnancy to the innocent friend—and in this
extremity, the husband feels her strain as his own. This sonnet
ends not with a cheapening image, but with compassionate
assent to their shared misery:

> When she wakes,
> She looks the star that thro' the cedar shakes:
> Her lost moist hand clings mortally to mine.

The sadness rather than the corruption of a broken bond is
shown here, with a weight of implication in the hands which
cling 'mortally' together. The temporality of love, Meredith's
theme, deepens its note in this line.

But it is equally part of his theme that the deeper notes and
the moments of understanding are merely brief visitations; the
prevailing state is one of severed communication which none
the less allows mute recriminations and encourages the art of
wounds dumbly administered—so the next sonnet turns on this
silence. He reads her mind still, but:

> She will not speak. I will not ask. We are
> League-sundered by the silent gulf between.
>                                            (XXII)

The silence is dignified, however, in comparison with the cal-
culated hostilities by which the husband more often carries on
his war. In XXV the innuendo in a discussion about a French
novel is clear to both sides, she declaring that the heroine's
choice of husband before lover is 'unnatural', he suavely
approving of one behaving 'like a proper wife' and insisting
maliciously, 'these things are life'. He adds, 'And life, some
think, is worthy of the Muse'—a motto for the sequence. When
in XXXIV the 'proper wife' reaches a pitch of misery which
impels her to attempt to speak, the cruelty of embittered love
is laid bare. Refusing to accept the openings he sees her offering,
the husband mocks her in stilted small-talk, blocking her confession:

I am not melted, and make no pretence.
With commonplace I freeze her, tongue and sense.

∽ 4 ∽

But the full measure of the process of debasement and hardening in the husband is revealed in the sonnets addressed not to his wife but to 'my Lady', his 'distraction'. There is a conscious acquiescence in the new character here, a swaggering display of grosser demands and lowered expectations. The references to the devil in the sonnets XXVII and XXVIII indicate how willing he is to see himself in such a mirror, with an unequivocal adoption of selfish motives as his standards and his bargaining position: 'No matter, so I taste forgetfulness'. The terms are cynically spelt out:

> O Lady, once I gave love: now I take!
> Lady, I must be flattered.

(XXVII)

That this is a strategy to salve wounded pride and self-esteem is spelt out in XXVIII. Playing 'the game of Sentiment', he demands her beauty for himself, and publicly so: 'For I must shine Envied,—I, lessened in my proper sight!' The pain of diminution feeds the fantasy of demonic stature, and makes him pathetic as well as ugly in his new conceit:

> I feel the promptings of Satanic power,
> While you do homage unto me alone.

Yet even here, when he is abandoned to a set of attitudes which seem more appropriate to the realities of loving as he now sees them than the old assumptions, the conflict is not over. Before the final shrug of the shoulders which accepts again the standards of expediency, sonnet XXIX admits the continuing pain of disappointed expectation: 'Something more than earth I cry for still'. Love had seemed to enhance the human situation, lifting it beyond mortality—Arnold's dream of a romantic ideal is resurrected, only half in mockery. The loss is real even if the earlier feeling was delusory:

A kiss is but a kiss now! and no wave
Of a great flood that whirls me to the sea.
But as you will! we'll sit contentedly,
And eat our pot of honey on the grave.

The sonnet is entirely in Meredith's idiom, but the conflict and
dilemma it conveys is central to the Victorian poetic imagination. The effort to reconcile value and experience, to find a
base for love on the shifting sands of life occupies all the poets
and poems in this study.

Sonnet XXX reverts to a cold assessment of how things are,
after the softening into regret. We are creatures of nature,
geared to seasons not eternities, and love only holds off our
appreciation of this for a little while, in its seductive warming
glow. Then 'we stand wakened, shivering from our dream'. Our
best course is to acquiesce in the situation, to live 'but with the
day' as 'scientific animals', knowing that this is our fate. The
poem ends: 'Lady, this is my sonnet to your eyes', a stroke of
Meredithian wit which kicks romance aside and brings to the
surface the cynicism latent in the previous lines. It is a brash
tactic but justifiable in its illustration that refinement is one
of the casualties in this revelation of a mauled sensibility.

When 'My Lady unto Madam makes her bow' (XXXVI),
the tone momentarily changes to one of social comedy. After a
sonnet probing, and appreciating, his wife's character, her
suffering and her power to wound, with an outraged protest at
the 'wedded lie' they live, the next stands back to survey the lie
in its guise of hypocritical game. The women fence with com-
pliments 'that hit with wondrous aim on the weak point'; the
conventions are at once scrupulously observed and turned to
weapons in the unspoken war. 'At the two I stand amazed'. But
he also participates in the same social rites, as the sequence
shows in other sonnets featuring the charades of house-parties,
with their chilling discrepancies between surface manners and
subterranean emotion. Thus in XXXVII, the 'quiet company'
awaits the dinner-bell 'in prae-digestive calm', sentimentally
enjoying the rising moon, as the husband, one of the party, far
from calmly hears 'the laugh of Madam' and sees his Lady
before him: 'Our tragedy, is it alive or dead?'

His confusion comes to a climax as his own emotions take him unawares, shattering the *modus vivendi* which had seemed a possible resolution. As his Lady and he arrive, in the moonlight, at something like an impulse of love, a harmony, or so at least he persuades himself, beyond the merely sensual refuge he demanded earlier—another couple appear:

> What two come here to mar this heavenly tune?
> A man is one: the woman bears my name,
> And honour. Their hands touch! Am I still tame?
> God, what a dancing spectre seems the moon!
>
> (XXXIX)

The reversion to cheapening exclamation provides an accurate notation of the plunge back into jealousy, the sick loss of balance, which the sight of his wife and her lover precipitates. The new silvery-moon sentiment is pale and unreal beside this rush of instinctive passion, and only the grating tone of the final line and its image could convey the psychological shock so faithfully. Meredith's is a strange poetry that succeeds by in a sense debasing itself.

Sonnet XL follows up this lurch of feeling, and brings forward the sense of disintegrated identity which haunts the whole sequence. 'Can I love one, And yet be jealous of another?' Love is now 'terrible', refusing to relinquish its territories even when assumed to be no longer in occupation. The sophisticated philosophies of its temporality are ironically set at nought by this persistent survival of some of love's characteristics. The result is a kind of paralysis, an abdication of the personality in the face of such a challenge to what had, it seemed, been painfully learnt about the necessarily ephemeral bonds between people:

> Helplessly afloat,
> I know not what I do, whereto I strive.
> The dread that my old love may be alive
> Has seized my nursling new love by the throat.

Despite the violence still registering in this last metaphor, the ten remaining sonnets trace with more compassion than bitterness the legacies of the 'old love' to the two it linked together—legacies they may well desire not to receive but which they cannot refuse. Love has its posthumous history in this situation, just as Patmore and Tennyson found in theirs. Coming together again, husband and wife are aware they have 'taken up a lifeless vow To rob a living passion' (XLI); nothing affirms the death of love more eloquently to them than their conspiracy to pretend it rekindled. This is a new twist to hypocrisy, sad rather than vicious, and it brings the husband to further insight as he 'digs Love's grave' (XLIII):

> . . . no morning can restore
> What we have forfeited. I see no sin:
> The wrong is mixed. In tragic life, God wot,
> No villain need be! Passions spin the plot:
> We are betrayed by what is false within.

But this verdict on breakdown is reached through only a part of the experience. 'Tragic life' offers no clean break even now. There are impulses still active between husband and wife, the sensitive chords of the relationship still vibrate, keeping them responsive, able to hurt and yet ease each other to a bewildering degree. He is moved by pity for her: she cannot accept it (XLIV); they feel a common need to speak openly and, in the very familiarity of such intimacy, find at once a new pain and a momentary peace: 'Love, that had robbed us of immortal things, This little moment mercifully gave' (XLVII).

Drinking 'the pure daylight of honest speech' proves a 'fatal draught' (XLVIII). Sonnets XLVIII and XLIX show an ambivalence of attitude which defeats the attempt either to renew or snap the threads of marriage. She in 'jealous devotion' plans to set the husband free once she knows of 'my lost Lady'. He reacts with admiration for the gesture, but sees it as wrong-headed. In both, the awareness of the other partner as a person is intensified, raised to a new perception by a plight mirroring their own. As they meet once more, there is a pathetic attempt to believe the love which initiated such sensitivity is still possible —that in their beginning can be their end:

> She took his hand, and walked with him, and seemed
> The wife he sought, though shadow-like and dry.
>                                                    (XLIX)

The exhaustion implicit in the images points on to the final act: she kills herself, prompted by love which is over. The paradox in which she proves its life as she acknowledges its passing is only the final enigma of a long review of love as a fragile but tenacious force. 'Thus piteously Love closed what he begat' (L): the end does depend on the beginning, for loving means living out a process of intricate involvement, following it through all shades of emotion and recognising them all as part of the one experience.

The bonds chafe, pinion, even strangle. In sophisticated relationships such as this one, they hurt too through attempts to scrutinise their nature; 'deep questioning' leads to suicide. Meredith's violent ending has been censured but it is the logical consummation of a relationship which is violent throughout. The theme of the sequence is the struggle in the snare, love as a trap. Desired for its most evanescent qualities, love becomes a power slowly destroying its own creation. A poem of psychological murder as well as suicide, its tone, language, imagery and structure are all exploited to convey a sense of assault and abuse. Mood cuts roughly across mood, debasement is enacted in the vocabulary, irony uses the bludgeon of cynicism not the rapier of detached wit. Of all the poems in this study, Meredith's makes the most unrelieved statement on the ugliness generated by a close relationship, and the peculiar agonies of its dying grip as it tightens its hold on the struggling psyche of each partner.

Stepping back into the impersonal voice at the last, sonnet L surveys 'the union of this ever-diverse pair' and asserts the inevitability of such catastrophe; the hopes lovers have must in the course of time fall foul of the double-edged reality that their union can outlive its origins but never forget them. The answers reached in *Modern Love* are not only dusty but brutal.

⌁ 5 ⌁

To love is to become more vulnerable. To be denied or torn away from love is to suffer a crisis of identity. From the angle of a highly sensitive and isolated personality, *Maud* explores these aspects of relationships, seeing the latter as dangerous enterprises whose moments of bliss heighten the risks and expose the lover as a helpless hostage to fortune. 'If I were dear to someone else', a proposition surveyed discouragingly enough in *Modern Love*, becomes in *Maud* an idea fraught with doom, either because it seems impossible or because it proves a reality. There is a more frantic beating of Meredith's ensnared falcon (L) here, a passionate rather than an intellectual immersion in the ordeal of desire, imagined union, transformed being, and broken dream. Maud's lover descends back into the pit, love having fleetingly offered him a hope of escape which in the event only emphasises his need while accomplishing nothing. Irony in Tennyson's poem is felt along the nerves rather than exhibited in caustic commentary, but it is central to its nature. The hero's outlook at the end of the poem is grimly consistent with his view at the beginning: life is a conflict against enemies, and an expectation of 'doom'. Such was the message symbolised originally by the 'dreadful hollow' which spoke to his obsessed mind of blood and death, and though there is a more extra-verted and positive flamboyance to the rhythms, imagery and sentiments of the final section, admitting a measure of recovery, the return to old conclusions is no more than disguised by a change of key. The anguish of *Maud* lies in the confirmation of a violent reading of life, for the hero's wild hope lay in a vision of something different being possible. But love brought great floods of unmanageable feeling, its peace was never more than transient and always threatened, while its only consummation was a climax of physical assault. *Maud* is founded on these desperate ironies and unrealised desires.

Tennyson said that the 'peculiarity' of *Maud* was that 'different phases of passion in one person take the place of different characters'.[3] It is a peculiarity showing the poem to be typical rather than unique in its time, however, though *Maud* is distinctive in the ambition and power with which it articulates its very Victorian vision. These poets were fascinated by the crowded hours of psychic living, the ceaseless change and persistently working forces of emotion, for ever composing and unravelling the patterns of the individual; and for Tennyson, the progression from one mood to another is the crux of his

[3] Quoted Ricks, *The Poems of Tennyson*, p. 1039.

interest in Maud's lover, at once a technical challenge and a psychological exploration. To do justice to the turbulent, undisciplined and hectic inner life, he calls on an extensive range of form, rhythm and tone: that he nevertheless keeps his poetic balance is a remarkable feat.

On the face of it he runs more risks than Meredith, who merely coarsened the tone, mainly through imagery, to plot the vulgarisation of a personality. Tennyson is essaying not the intellectual turned cynic, but the unstable, hysterical temperament pushed to an extreme of reaction, and he is adopting the same method of letting the character make his own poetry, as it were, to express this. Tennysonian lyricism is being asked to mirror extravagant, highly coloured emotion, unchecked by concepts of decorum. Maud's lover is consumed in his own fires, and he is to speak as one devoid of the restraints (or the poses) of self-criticism. Where *In Memoriam* found its inspiration and its ruling tone precisely in vigilant scrutiny and measurement of feeling, *Maud* deliberately rejects these subtleties in favour of submission to overwhelming emotion. Yet the poem is less open to the charge of tonal failures and a debasement of art than *Modern Love*.

Tennyson's poetic judgment and his resources are much greater than Meredith's, and he is able to dramatise passion at a histrionic pitch without losing his own verbal refinement. The voice is the voice of Maud's lover and simultaneously, that of Tennyson, but the two are not at odds—*Maud* gives authentic utterance to a dislocated personality without itself disintegrating. It is the success, but also the limitation, of *Modern Love* that it sets the reader's teeth on edge; the poetry, with the speaker, is undermined. But *Maud* offers the ease and assurance of fully poetic speech even while it convincingly transmits a wrecked personality stripped of such qualities.

The portrayal of the one personality in this way may 'take the place of different characters', but none the less Maud is an active presence in the poem. She gives it its title, and the speaker's dependency on her is its point. The 'someone else' in all these poems—'Madam' and James Lee as well as Maud—is shown as he or she lives in the mind of the one bound to them, but in *Maud*, this is observed as an obsessional condition.

Tennyson captures the lover's recreation of Maud from the dream of blissful possession to the despairing certainty of her inaccessibility. To complain that she remains unknown as an individual is beside the point, for she is not conceived as an independent figure with her own emotional angle on the events: Tennyson's interest lies in showing the way one person may come to live in terms of another, how love induces him to enthrone her within his mind and make over his world to her dominance.

This fealty can become ambivalent, Tennyson appreciates: the lover creates her arrogantly in the image of his needs even as he submits himself to her. The achievement of *Maud* is its portrayal of the extreme where the lover is at once prostrating himself to a self-invited tyranny and playing the tyrant himself. Violence, and violation, are inherent in his attitude, and the poem engages with the idea of love as potential disaster at a deep level. The actual route to calamity is less important than the frightening awareness that even requited love can be explosive as well as restorative. Husband and wife fall apart, love ends, in the other poems; here the very passion which is generated gives rise to an emotional drama as fatal in its consequences. Maud is her lover's doom because of the completeness with which she becomes his life.

He is left finally with the need to work out a new sense of himself in relation, not to Maud, but to society. He manoeuvres carefully and deliberately to associate himself with 'his kind'. There is a link here with Byron's inquest of 1816, as carried out in Canto III of *Childe Harold*, and comparing the two helps us to measure the change from Romantic to Victorian. Byron set his personal ordeal in the context of Europe's history, aligning his 'bleeding heart' with the fate of nations and connecting his domestic experiences of love, power and war, with those of wider renown. He dignifies and distances his sufferings by seeing himself amid the ruins of Europe, joining the afflicted and the lonely heroes through the ages. Man is thus, says *Childe Harold* grandly, and so am I.

When Maud's lover seeks to place himself in a reassuring context, to find out his affinities with the race, the impulse is the same but the outcome very different. Here there is no review of universal man but a commitment to a local war of the present moment and an assessment of the current state of one nation. Tennyson's vision is of the hour. He sees both the individual and history ruled by time and change, and his hero must read the nature of the moment his own society is passing through and adjust himself to it if he is to relate to the world outside himself. What was carved in marble for Byron is now writ in water. For the Victorian poet, history is now and in England, and it too has its psychology: to switch from a diseased inactivity to embrace a cause is recommended for the national as the individual malaise. Event has become feeling on all levels. Neither the moral difficulties of the aggressive end of *Maud* nor its ironies in the context of the whole poem should obscure these other implications which confirm that the Victorian vision is one of process and the inner consequences of action, bringing history into man rather than translating man into history.

### ᔑ 6 ᔑ

Throughout *Maud*, the social as well as the natural setting is more than a context. It is part of the hero's emotional life, conditioning his love and raising its temperature. Launched on an outburst of hate for the place where his father's body was found, the poem continues to feed on passions born in the past, involving as they do the iniquities of a Mammonite society, epitomised in the dealings of the people up at the Hall. Fulminating against the 'lust of gain', railing at the evil done to one family by another, the speaker may not seem like a man on the brink of overwhelming love. It is a strange beginning, looked at objectively, though to the modern reader this is less apparent, ready as we are to assume that a man's emotional history and all that contributes to it is a relevant starting point for an understanding of the climax of that history, his falling in love. But Tennyson's approach was a bold one, abandoning Romantic faith in the extra-temporal, self-sufficient, self-determining nature of a grand passion, to propose instead that the character of a love affair—and its doom—springs from seeds sown long before. All is relative, contingent, conditional.

The opening stanzas, so fraught with obsessional judgments,

desperate loneliness and expectations of disaster, prophesy the future. They pronounce sentence on the lovers even while the workmen are preparing the Hall for the still unseen 'singular beauty' of the adult Maud (1.I.xvii.67).[4] Love is longed for, but associated with the terrors of the past (1.I.xv); Maud is vividly remembered and already desired in fantasy, yet she belongs to the hated Hall and her coming is dreaded: 'My dreams are bad. She may bring me a curse.' (1.I.xix.73). The ambivalence is plain from the following sections II and III, where Tennyson brilliantly portrays the first stage of falling in love as it happens to this tormented personality—again, there is no suggestion of a universal phenomenon, but an emphatic demonstration that as the man is, so he falls. In II, the mixed reaction to Maud seen in her carriage includes explicit repudiation of any emotional commitment, disappointment that the sight of her did not hold out the hope of such a relationship, and the covert indication of the lack of truth in the claim to have 'escaped heart-free' from the encounter. The 'little touch of spleen' (1.II.87) which he confesses to is as much resentment at her failure to inspire him with recognisable passion immediately as it is indignation at her apparent hauteur. The ironies are clear as the image of her 'cold and clear-cut face' (1.II.78) is dwelt upon to a degree and in such detail that the birth of a new obsession can be witnessed in it.

This is recognised in III, where he describes how the face has haunted him 'half the night long',

> Growing and fading and growing upon me without a sound,
> Luminous, gemlike, ghostlike, deathlike . . .
>
> (1.III.94–5)

The sense of encroachment as her image recurs, and the knell beating in the repetition of the second line as it advances to 'deathlike' confirm the ominous disposition towards disaster which the poem has from the start underlined, and this section, where the power of Maud is first hypnotically exerted, ends with a sombre and repeated emphasis on death. The connection of dawning love with destruction is gloomily forged. Going

---

[4] Quotations are taken from *The Poems of Tennyson*, ed. Ricks; the figures indicate the Part, section, stanza, and line numbers of the poem.

restlessly down to his 'dark garden', he hears the tide as a 'shipwrecking roar', the shingle's sound as 'the scream of a maddened beach'; and walking in a 'wintry wind' until a 'ghastly glimmer' of day, he finds, 'The shining daffodil dead, and Orion low in his grave' (1.III.97–101). This passage exemplifies Tennyson's ability to give the speaker a style and a vocabulary—especially in his response to place and observed detail—which reveal the excess of his nature yet can also yield new imaginative perspectives, such as the linking of flower and constellation in the final line.

Structurally too, Tennyson conveys the erratic swaying to and fro of mood, with the strong cross-currents beneath. In IV, the section begins with a spring longing to be 'Like things of the season gay' (1.IV.i.104), obviously connecting this desire with love and the sight of Maud 'up in the high Hall-garden' (1.IV.ii.112), but it ends with panic-tinged retreat, a reversal of the hopeful imagery:

> And most of all would I flee from the cruel madness of love,
> The honey of poison-flowers and all the measureless ill.
>
> (1.IV.x.156–7)

And within a line, the poet conveys rejection which is simultaneously an admission of its opposite, the foreboding which is also the acknowledgment of an attractive and inevitable idea already becoming fact: Maud passes 'like a light'—'But sorrow seize me if ever that light be my leading star!' (1.IV.ii.112–13).

The section retreats from these unadmitted admissions to rail once more—'as my father raged'—at the 'little breed' (v.131) of men, and settles on a bearable goal, a state of 'passionless peace' (1.IV.ix.151). But the centre of the contradictory storms —now to succumb to desire, now to see love as madness, now to withdraw—is Maud, whose look of pride, as he reads it, stings him 'as she rode by on the moor' (1.IV.iii.116). The snub in answer to his bow excites all his feelings, confirming that she is his 'leading star', confirming that this means sorrow, warning that calm as an aspiration is gone irretrievably. The hate for the world likewise spills out because the Hall lady despises one who is 'nameless and poor' (1.IV.iii.119).

Love is playing and landing its fish. The anger and hostility of section IV shows how firmly fixed is the hook swallowed in II and III; then in V and VI comes the more yielding response to the line. To alter the metaphor, what begins to happen in these sections is a Pygmalion experience. Maud gradually changes from a coldly statuesque beauty to the living woman drawing love to her. Thus, in V she is actively present, heard as 'a voice by the cedar tree' (1.V.i.162), a 'wild voice pealing' (1.V.ii.174); the voice is 'beautiful' (1.V.iii.180), the face now not cold but 'exquisite' (1.V.ii.173). The 'sweetness' of the sound magnetises him (1.V.iii.185), bringing his first willing homage, but still he would distinguish, try to resist: it is her voice only, 'not her, who is neither courtly or kind, Not her, not her, but a voice' (1.V.iii.188–9). Repetition like this is a habit of the speaker's mind, and one which is taken full advantage of, rhythmically and verbally, for a variety of effects; here it hints clearly enough that he protests too much.

Immediately in VI, the psychological situation takes another turn, and Maud comes another step nearer, when the statement that she is neither courtly nor kind is proved wrong. Meeting him, she has behaved in a manner both kind and courtly—'she touched my hand with a smile so sweet' (1.VI.ii.201)—and the possibility that love might be mutual enters for the first time. The consequence is typical of this suspicious and frightened mind. Together with the confession that such a development could change his whole reading of life, the hero sets up agonised barriers of disbelief, alternative explanations of coquettish motive, or a plot by the 'curled Assyrian Bull', her brother, to win 'a wretched vote' (1.VI.vi.233, 245). The giddiness of desire to plunge into hope is exactly matched in this section by the morbidity of the hostile reactions. That hopes can be dashed is the keynote, illustrated by the weather; a sunset which promised a bright spring day yields only a 'wannish glare',

> And the budded peaks of the wood are bowed
> Caught and cuffed by the gale:
> I had fancied it would be fair.

(1.VI.i.193–5)

But a 'delicate spark' (1.VI.iii.204) has been struck, and the idea of transformation through loving, and being loved, is also

admitted and entertained. There is a sharpening of self-knowledge, and of time-consciousness, at this stage, which allows,
crucially, for the possibility of change and faces the horror of a
future offering only an intensified present: 'Ah what shall I be
at fifty . . . If I find the world so bitter When I am but twenty-
five?' (1.VI.v.220–3). The personality imprisoned within itself
can perhaps be released by the agency of love; but the signs
are clear also that one who is so vulnerable to another is threatened by this as much as by his suspicions. It is a precarious
universe when all depends on one woman's expression:

> Yet, if she were not a cheat,
> If Maud were all that she seemed,
> And her smile had all that I dreamed,
> Then the world were not so bitter
> But a smile could make it sweet.
>
> (1.VI.x.280–4)

After these skilful overtures, the poem moves rapidly into a
deeper crisis, 'the new strong wine of love' (1.IV.ix.271) proving
itself in the intoxication of jealousy. Tennyson plots the lover's
course with a fine sense of the disordered heart he is dealing
with, showing that in a violent temperament the violence is not
nullified by the growth of love, but transfers itself to the new
emotional environment and flourishes there, a plant still
poisonous. So, in VIII, Maud's love is believed in; in IX and X,
her lover is sick of 'a jealous dread' (1.X.i.330). VIII continues
to humanise Maud; she is contrasted to the angel 'carved in
stone' which weeps above her in church, for catching the hero's
eye, she 'suddenly, sweetly, strangely blushed'. The quickening
is matched by the response of his own body:

> And suddenly, sweetly my heart beat stronger
> And thicker . . .
>
> (1.VIII.304–9)

'It cannot be pride' in her, he is sure (1.VIII.313). Love is
tentatively becoming a dialogue, its exchanges spontaneous,
losing social formality.

But immediately the promise of developing intimacy is cut

across by the next lyric which describes a distant and receding glimpse of Maud, riding 'Over the dark moor land',

> Rapidly riding far away,
> She waved to me with her hand.
> There were two at her side . . .
>
> (1.IX.319–22)

The dark returns to his mind 'With no more hope of light' (1.IX.329). In X, all society is once more damned, its ugliness providing a context suitable for the 'new-made lord' who is wooing Maud, and for her who might receive him (1.X.i.332). In these terms jealousy finds its voice, despising its own rant and recognising that love reduced to expressing itself thus is only exacerbating not healing the state of self-division it had promised to cure. The sense of alienation—from society, from Maud, from self—is all one here, despairingly admitted:

> . . . splenetic, personal, base,
> A wounded thing with a rancorous cry,
> At war with myself and a wretched race,
> Sick, sick to the heart of life, am I.
>
> (1.X.ii.362–5)

The panic of self-hate can be heard in the whole of this section. In iii, he cries, 'Jealousy, down! cut off from the mind The bitter springs of anger and fear' (377–8), and calls for a national as well as a personal change of spirit, the connecting of the two looking forward to the end of the poem and illustrating that throughout, the state of society acts as a temperature chart on which the hero reads the report of his own disease.

This 'splenetic' section shows love, denied its fulfilment, ready to release its energies as hate. But out of the cry for a new spirit arises a fresh wave of positive feeling and love's role as a saving force is reasserted. XI and XII first pray for the blessing of knowing 'That there is one to love me' (1.XI.ii.408), and then rejoice at the meeting which seems to answer the prayer. Darkness fades, and the two lyrics stand as rehearsals for the greater ecstasies to come, when love is avowed and fully reciprocated. The extravagances of both, however, cast a shadow, amounting to prophecy in 'O let the solid ground'. If love once be known,

> Then let come what come may,
> What matter if I go mad,
> I shall have had my day.
>
> (1.XI.i.402–4)

There is no conception of love here as a life-long stabilising experience, a permanent antidote to the threat of disintegration. Rather it is envisaged as a necessarily brief moment of bliss, compensating in its intensity for its lack of durability. *Maud's* reading of love is a curious blend of faith in it as the one hope of rescue from isolation, acknowledgment of it as a passion frightening in its power, and conviction of its fundamental impotence to endure, or to change a doomed temperament. These are the complexities explored by way of the tonal contrasts in the poem's shifting 'phases', and they show how completely the emotion is to be identified with the nature of the one who is seized by it: to fall in love is to discover that nature, not to discard it for some special plane of being. And consequently what saves may also destroy.

Section XII hints at this. It is a simple, almost banal, set of quatrains marking a great event, Maud gathering lilies 'in our wood' (1.XII.ii.416). They were together, she was not proud, he kissed her hand, there was no rebuff. But the joy is extreme, that of one obsessed with its object not merely in love with it. The birds call her name, 'her feet have touched the meadows, And left the daisies rosy' (1.XII.vi.434–5): there is a note of fever and a vaunting of feeling which is very close to the expressions of spleen which precede and follow these lyrics— 'Go back, my lord, across the moor, You are not her darling' (1.XII.viii.442–3).

In fact, in the passages concerned with Maud's brother, XIII and elsewhere, the same sense of fanatical obsession is apparent as in the sections which brood on Maud as if his desires would consume her. The poem's oscillations, from Maud to her family and back again, reveal an ominous continuity as well as the swing from love to hate. The rapture at Maud's graciousness is the polar counterpart of the tirades directed at her supercilious brother with his 'stony British stare' (1.XIII.ii.465). He is the gorgon now, as Maud took that role at first; the feelings towards the two are intimately related. The lover recognises this, seeing that he regards the brother as scapegoat in order to preserve his faith in Maud's 'sweetness' (1.XIII.iii. 476). The family is tainted, Maud must be 'nothing akin' to such evil, and so 'the whole inherited sin' must be heaped 'all, all upon the brother' (1.XIII.iii.481, 484–6). And yet:

> Peace, angry spirit, and let him be!
> Has not his sister smiled on me?
> (1.XIII.iv.487–8)

But the impulse to encourage the light to dispel the dark fights all the time with the opposite tendency. XIV, encouraging love again as he haunts her garden and gazes at her rooms ends none the less in doubt, foreboding and dread. In the 'dim-gray dawn',

> . . . I looked, and round, all round the house I beheld
> The death-white curtain drawn;
> Felt a horror over me creep,
> Prickle my skin and catch my breath,
> Knew that the death-white curtain meant but sleep,
> Yet I shuddered and thought like a fool of the sleep of death.
> (1.XIV.iv.520–6)

This spasm is the recurring tic of his mind, the poem's deepest rhythm, a predilection towards disaster which love fights yet submits to, or even conspires with. The struggle is crystallised suddenly in XV, a pivotal section for all its brevity. The implications of loving are recognised here for what they are, and what they might be; the responsibilities of the condition, involving a new attitude towards the self, are contemplated:

> So dark a mind within me dwells,
>   And I make myself such evil cheer,
> That if *I* be dear to someone else,
>   Then someone else may have much to fear;
> But if *I* be dear to someone else,
>   Then I should be to myself more dear.

Shall I not take care of all that I think,
Yea even of wretched meat and drink,
If I be dear,
If I be dear to someone else.

(1.XV.527–36)

The tension and pathos of the speaker's state is finely evoked by Tennyson's subtle playing on the contrasts between the assertion of the first two lines and the hesitant, conditional, unsure logic of the rest. He uses the habitual repetitive speech to score the emotional rhythm of this mind as it tentatively formulates its hope. The intensity of the desire and the importance of it are revealed in the four reiterations, 'If I be dear', while the caution of these provisional statements is further stressed in the last two, where the weight falls on 'If' at the beginning of the lines. And the innate pessimism is exposed in the other emphasis—'If *I* be dear', with its implied disbelief in such a possibility. The only confidence in the lines is heard at the beginning, 'so dark a mind within me dwells': here is no self-doubt, only certainty. Thus the enormity of love's task is dramatised in the tone, emphases, syntax and rhythms of the lines as well as in their whole statement.

It is dismayingly typical of the speaker that his first unreserved admission that love can exert power should be on the negative side. Two people, he sees, may affect each other by 'being dear' to each other, but the likelihood is that his gloom will overshadow her. Only after this instinctive reading does he edge his way to further deductions which may be built on this same basis. She must be protected from such a fate; a sense of responsibility stirs, and he moves on to conceive that love as an influence may be applied to himself and, perhaps, beneficially. The effort of self-revision can be felt here as a brave hope, and a desperate one, all resting on that precarious conditional—'If I be dear, If I be dear to someone else'. The terrible dependency is one with the persistent implication that escape and change are not to be realised, though the craving for them is rendered the more urgent by the theory his heart has grasped, that they might be possible.

∽ 7 ∽

Section XV is exactly placed. Before it, the fluctuating lyrics show the dark mind gripped by love and experiencing the clash and tug of its unsettling revaluations, as it appears now a 'delicate spark Of glowing and growing light' (1.VI.iii.204–5), now a 'cruel madness' (1.IV.x.156). After it, the pace quickens to the climax of declaration, ecstasy and doom. The torment of the conditional has to be resolved. Its momentous nature having reached the point of articulation, then,

> . . . I must tell her before we part,
> I must tell her, or die.
>
> (1.XVI.iii.569–70)

The remaining sections of Part One, XVII to XXII, carry to its inevitable end the poem's study of love, calamitous not because it is refused, but because it is so entirely won. Were Maud still the statuesque beauty, to be resented as well as admired, the hero might remain much as he was; but the realisation that she too could love, could hold him dear, precipitates the fatal bid for a different destiny, which instead sweeps him on remorselessly to fulfil the potential of 'so dark a mind'. The chance of escape hurls him headlong into the prison he has dreaded, yet expected. These ironies charge the climactic lyrics the more because of the very euphoria to which the sections give full voice. Tennyson prepares for the collapse as the accepted lover is transformed into one who knows himself dear, and hence is the more completely and frighteningly dependent on Maud who has created this being; and at the same time, there is unmistakable evidence that the old mistrusting, doom-laden nature is still active, unable to believe the new dawn, his tensions only increased by its hallucinatory light. This strange condition, where all is changed and nothing is altered, is finely conveyed in the two sections, 'I have led her home' (XVIII) and 'Come into the garden' (XXII). Peaks of Tennyson's lyrical art, they are dramatic in their revelation that the poem's passionate arrival at such heights of love leaves it no other option than to plunge fatally down.

The elated babble of 'Go not, happy day' (XVII) immediately after 'I must tell her, or die', eloquently enacts the
onset of euphoria and at the same time serves as a reminder
of the voracity of this lover's need. The assumption that the
whole world will rejoice at the 'happy news' (1.XVII.585) is a
typical extravagance, carrying the convention of a lover's
egocentricity to a grotesque extreme. Grotesque too, and hinting at fever as well as sexual excitement, is the excessive 'rosi-
ness' of the lyric, Maud, sky, sea and earth being suffused with
one blush in a fantasy of universal betrothal. Maud loves him,
therefore he loves and is dear to the whole universe. The logic
is daunting.

But in XVIII, the same mood is more deeply experienced,
in its blessings of serenity and expanded sympathies, as well as
confirmed, more subtly, in its dangers—the shadow is here still.
Tennyson conveys all levels while sustaining the spell of
enchanted love in an aria of rapturous thanksgiving:

> I have led her home, my love, my only friend.
> There is none like her, none.
> And never yet so warmly ran my blood
> And sweetly, on and on
> Calming itself to the long-wished-for end,
> Full to the banks, close on the promised good.
>
> (1.XVIII.i.599–604)

Here the pulse-beat of the lines is ardent but steadier, emotion
flowing in a strong assured tide. The whole lyric is carried forward by long rolling sentences, travelling on from line to line
yet never impatient or incoherent, resting on the rhythmical
pattern and governed too by recurring phrases which here give
further stability. The movement is one with the heightened,
almost holy, ecstasy the words suggest, supporting the feeling
with its own feverless calm. This is the opposite of raging 'as my
father raged in his mood' (1.I.xiv.53), and the deeper current
of a passion whose froth alone featured in 'Go not, happy
day'.

Lying under the cedar, the lover endows the tree with
emotion and sees it in terms of Maud, yet uses it to expand his
vision of his own paradise by relating it to the first Eden. A freer

imagination works in these lines, one liberated not constricted and stifled in its obsession with Maud. The tree remains separate in its own personality but becomes the instrument for conveying the lover's exaltation:

> O, art thou sighing for Lebanon
> In the long breeze that streams to thy delicious East,
> Sighing for Lebanon,
> Dark cedar, though thy limbs have here increased,
> Upon a pastoral slope as fair,
> And looking to the South, and fed
> With honeyed rain and delicate air,
> And haunted by the starry head
> Of her whose gentle will has changed my fate,
> And made my life a perfumed altar-flame;
> And over whom thy darkness must have spread
> With such delight as theirs of old, thy great
> Forefathers of the thornless garden, there
> Shadowing the snow-limbed Eve from whom she came.
> (1.XVIII.iii.613–26)

By the end of the section, the whole cosmos like the 'honeyed rain and delicate air' seems returned to that initial harmony. First 'sad astrology'—that is modern astronomy—is defied. The stars which are 'innumerable, pitiless, passionless eyes' in their 'iron skies', with power in their 'cold fires' to convince man of his 'nothingness' (1.XVIII.iv.634–8) can also be, for all that, 'fair stars that crown a happy day' (628). Whatever their nature, it affords no threat: 'But now shine on, and what care I'—Maud cancels all menace (v.639). Finally, the rejection of an alien universe is explicit and total. There is a 'noiseless music' in the night and earth seems nearer the stars, so brilliantly they shine, in keeping with his own brighter fate: '*I* have climbed nearer out of lonely Hell'; all is one in sympathy and rejoicing, as the stronger, assertive rhythm of the two climactic lines emphasises:

> Beat, happy stars, timing with things below,
> Beat with my heart more blest than heart can tell . . .
> (1.XVIII.viii.675–80)

The earth is more itself, is known more intensely through the eyes of one released from the pit:

> A livelier emerald twinkles in the grass,
> A purer sapphire melts into the sea.
>
> (1.XVIII.vi.649–50)

Life is renewed to a pristine glory. All because of 'one simple girl' (v.643). The phrase admits the incongruity and the lyric is aware of the astonishing nature of the metamorphosis which has taken place. In this lies its first admission of vulnerability. One 'gentle will' has 'changed my fate' (iii.621), and here the extravagance is not in the tone, as is usual in the poem, but in the claim itself. It is the more striking, and points to the weakness of the personality believing it rather than affirms an incontrovertible truth. A certain fragility is suggested even as the words sing of joy, strength and enduring peace.

Even in the allusions to Eden and the bliss of heaven, it is apparent that tension is not dispelled, nor the disposition to envisage the worst really cured. For in both, the idea of paradise lost is inescapable. In stanza ii, Maud's door closes, and 'the gates of Heaven are closed, and she is gone' (610); the measure of dependence on Maud as salvation is given as much by the extreme image of banishment as by the lyrical joy which surrounds it in stanzas i and iii. 'There is none like her, none' (600), and the refrain sounds a warning as well as sings its panegyric. If she is lost, or such a loss is threatened, the last state will be worse than the first, for her power over his fate—heaven or hell—is absolute. The early introduction into the lyric of the idea of exclusion from heaven, together with that of the cedar sighing for an Eden which it, and Eve, lost, counterpoints the song of bliss in a subtle and disturbing way. Tennyson shows the ecstasy of mutual love declared, to be the very climate in which the seeds of disaster germinate. The poetry passes sentence even as it does full justice to the prisoner's certainty that he is free.

But the lover in himself shows his old forebodings and fears too. The lyric slides from its happy contemplation of a changed fate to the more equivocal, 'And do accept my madness' (v.642), and to thoughts of death and its close relation to love. Life cannot as it were live up to such devotion or express such commitment, and so to die for her would be logical:

> . . . for sullen-seeming Death may give
> More life to Love than is or ever was
> In our low world, where yet 'tis sweet to live.
>
> (1.XVIII.vi.644–6)

There is a hint here of the Romantic attitude: love fulfilling itself, not as a union of lives but as a moment's heroic gesture. But this is rejected as well as proposed; even this Victorian lover strives at this stage to see himself with a married future, Maud as 'My bride to be, my evermore delight' (viii.671). Yet thoughts of her remain stubbornly entangled with death. Maud asleep has 'given false death her hand' (viii.666), and her dreams might be menacing—sexually so, perhaps, is the innuendo of the prayer, 'May nothing there her maiden grace affright!' (viii.669). The lyric's tide of bliss then flows strongly back; hell fades away, the stars are bright. And even so, it ends not serenely but in apprehension:

> Beat, happy stars, timing with things below,
> Beat with my heart more blest than heart can tell,
> Blest, but for some dark undercurrent woe
> That seems to draw—but it shall not be so:
> Let all be well, be well.
>
> (1.XVIII.viii.679–83)

The nervous staccato pleading of the final line is far from the earlier legato and the assured march of 'Beat, happy stars', reasserting the old unchanged temperament, the more at risk now that it has a heaven to lose. The psychological patterning as revealed by Tennyson's technique is masterly in this lyric, making it at once the poem's high peak of love achieved and the confirmation of the inexorable progress of a doomed and desperate soul.

Section XIX prepares for the final movement in the relationship. The conflict between obdurate hate for Maud's brother and the desire to allow love for her to exorcise it, is central to a lyric which goes back over the past, Maud's and his own. The lyric insists throughout on the relevance of the past to the course of the relationship, and on the determining role of the two families. Maud was promised to him; the sentimental pledge by the fathers who 'betrothed us over their wine' (1.XIX. iv.722) is ironically set against the troubled attempt of their children to fulfil it, in the teeth of the subsequent family history of hate and ruin, which in the event was the earlier generation's real legacy.

Still the obsession with Maud's brother is recognised as the twin emotion in power to that aroused by Maud herself, and the resolve to bury 'All this dead body of hate' (x.780)—ominous image—because Maud finds him 'rough but kind' (vii.753), is hopelessly fragile beside the rest of the section which affirms, on the contrary, how active is the legacy of hate. Opening with the flat statement,

> Her brother is coming back tonight,
> Breaking up my dream of delight.
>
> (1.XIX.i.684–5)

the section ends in stubborn reiteration of the same belief. Hate is gone:

> I feel so free and so clear
> By the loss of that dead weight,
> That I should grow light-headed, I fear,
> Fantastically merry;
> But that her brother comes, like a blight
> On my fresh hope, to the Hall tonight.
>
> (1.XIX.x.781–6)

Hate is far from gone. The tone of XX reveals more symptoms of the fixed animosity which cannot rise above itself, but allows 'the Sultan' (i.790) to call the tune. XX is weakly derisory, pretending a superiority and a security of status in which the old resentments and the new are only too apparent. Tennyson brings a dramatic skill to his judgment of the right tone and rhythm for the speaker at this moment of approaching crisis. The verse is a jingle and its satire is childishly banal; the bondage of Maud's lover is never more betrayed than here where he asserts indifference to his ostracism:

But tomorrow, if we live,
Our ponderous squire will give
A grand political dinner . . .
A gathering of the Tory,
A dinner and then a dance
For the maids and marriage-makers,
And every eye but mine will glance
At Maud in all her glory.

For I am not invited
But, with the Sultan's pardon,
I am all as well delighted,
For I know her own rose-garden,
And mean to linger in it . . .

(1.XX.ii–iv.809–11, 819–28)

He claims his garden moment as the 'true lover' ready to pay homage to 'Queen Maud in all her splendour' (iv.832, 836). The title jars a little—she was a 'simple girl' recently—and there is an element of false display in this plan to prove she is his, not the Sultan's. War with the latter informs the lines as much as love for Maud, and the hope of her coming to him, the promise of patient waiting, are intense not relaxed. The mood to be so brilliantly communicated in 'Come into the garden' is already anticipated, in its vulnerability, its need, and in the double edge of its passion.

Even the garden-rose which floats its message of faith from Maud to her lover in XXI is a harbinger of distress as well as a pledge. To his eye as he finds it in the rivulet 'born at the Hall' (844), it looks 'lost in trouble' (841), unable to float on to the sea. The thirteen-line interlude swells expectation, stresses the longing, and darkens it: so the poem is brought precisely to the climax, its inevitably disastrous nature having been demonstrated and made steadily more certain from the first to the twenty-first section of Part One.

XXII is the lyric of consummation. But a consummation of hate not of love. Yet it is also the lyric of climactic love; the two go together, and this is the despair of *Maud*, as it runs its set course, towing its burden of past history as a ruinous handicap to its desires. 'If I be dear to someone else' is no

141

simple isolated emotional proposition, the poem declares, but one which can be cursed with terrible consequences if 'I' should happen to be the broken son of an embittered father and 'someone else' the daughter of his enemy. History is not mocked.

But this would not be so intolerable were the state of love not so nearly all that, at the great moments, it is felt to be. Section XXII is such a moment and the ecstasy and reward of it are not denied. Tennyson's tonal skill enables him to blend this joy with the fever which is the lover's besetting weakness, so that the final, fatal outcome is signalled in the lyric's whole evocation of positive and distorted passion.

Waiting in the garden, the lover exists in an utterly private world where the surroundings seem but an extension of his feelings, a communion which suggests the degree to which he has climbed out of 'lonely Hell'. The 'planet of Love' (ii.857) is on high and the cosmos is seen in terms of love; as in 'I have led her home', the state of alien loneliness is gone and the world-picture is transformed into one of sympathetic, paradisial response. Roses and lilies share every sensation of the waiting lover, Maud is the centre of all things. This lover who can say, 'the soul of the rose went into my blood' (vi.882) has changed greatly from the solitary who resented his inability to feel with the budding spring (1.IV), and the section, even before it is a lyric of passion, is an exultant hymn by one who has miraculously found himself and his place in the universe.

This is shown too by the new reading of the local landscape which he now proposes: 'the meadow your walks have left so sweet' (vii.888), 'our wood, that is dearer than all' (vi.887). The wood was a symbol of horror, now it is sanctified ground. But what is not changed is the temperament which interprets the world entirely in terms of itself and knows no detachment. Already, the dangerous edge is hinted; there is a fanaticism in the self-created harmony as there was in the self-created discord, and a claustrophobic closing-in on his own emotion. The lyric conveys this, while never losing its poetic balance, especially as it rises to an almost unbearable expectancy. The flowers cast off their reticence (previously they are only spoken to) to articulate his overwhelming desire:

She is coming, my dove, my dear;
  She is coming, my life, my fate;
The red rose cries, 'She is near, she is near;'
  And the white rose weeps, 'She is late;'
The larkspur listens, 'I hear, I hear;'
  And the lily whispers, 'I wait.'

(1.XXII.x.910–15)

They even catch his trick of repetition. What Tennyson
suggests here is an extreme beyond the joyous communion with
the universe which love has brought. The sensuous heightening
in which 'woodbine spices' (i.854) and all the fragrance of the
summer night mix with the music of 'flute, violin, bassoon'
(iii.863) creates a rapt harmony, but the speaking flowers
transgress its decorum: the lover is converting the universe
into his emotional lackey. *Alice* seems forestalled in grotesque
fantasy here. Tennyson's exploitation of the setting in this lyric
is therefore wonderfully rich, for he is able to show by means of
it both the promise love gives of transformed life, and the excess
such bounty inevitably results in for the stricken temperament.
  That the lyric should end in an explosive image is only to be
expected:

My dust would hear her and beat,
  Had I lain for a century dead;
Would start and tremble under her feet,
  And blossom in purple and red.

(1.XXII.xi.920–3)

It is logical that the sensations at the moment of Maud's
coming should be expressed in shades of blood and with over-
tones of death. Maud has indeed brought him violently to life
in the course of the poem; this is the atmosphere made familiar
throughout. And it is another unsurprising irony that the final
words of a lyric entirely given up to passion, testifying to the
victory of love over all other states, should be words erupting
with aggressive potency and carrying the sexual into macabre
implications. The lines seal the destiny of Maud's lover—
brought to life as he is, but blossoming with no new flower.
  The brother's insulting blow and the fatal duel which

143

followed it are narrated retrospectively, emphasising that such events are not the centre of attention, but only the seeds which grow in the mind of the hero. As the death of his father haunted and moulded him, conditioning his love as well as his hate, so this event takes root, and all that it means in loss and pain occupies the rest of the poem. But *Maud*'s chief concern is the ordained journey from the one event to the other; the links are stressed in the first section of Part Two, where the woodland once again becomes the setting for violence, and at the shot,

> . . . a million horrible bellowing echoes broke
> From the red-ribbed hollow behind the wood . . .
>
> (2.I.i.24–5)

Maud's landscape is invaded, the original reading has prevailed, yet without Maud and her alchemy, the past need never have led to more fatal consequences. Tennyson spends two-thirds of the poem on the evolution of the love affair because here the psychological traps are laid, ready to snap shut. What the lover is determines love's role, for it is not a divine visitation but an emotion which, once roused, must work with what it finds.

The disintegration and recovery of sanity is really the aftermath of a poem whose theme is the way such a crisis came about. Returned to a 'lonely Hell' worse than any before, the lover finds his memory haunted by the red-ribbed hollow and the Maud landscape of 'silent woody places' (2.IV.ii.146) together in a nightmarish intimacy. He wakes comfortless to 'shuddering dawn' (vii.192), his surroundings bearing no relation to any of his inner locality, so that the horror of separation and personal alienation are intensified. All is meaningless, the need to be dear to someone else discovered afresh as the only antidote to the panic of anonymous, estranged existence:

> And I loathe the squares and streets,
> And the faces that one meets,
> Hearts with no love for me . . .
>
> (2.IV.xiii.232–4)

The route to madness is marked out. It is the only refuge from the intolerable isolation, yet at the same time it is the destined outcome of the unbearable bliss of having known a heart with love for him—the loss is fatal because the gain was total. This poem of extremes shows how and where they meet.

Maud's garden too is now one with the hollow behind the wood. The roses look like blood, and to the sound of 'dancing music and flutes' (2.V.viii.314), a figure lies there with a 'hole in his side' (320), a 'second corpse' to join the first 'in the pit' (ix.326). This is the only fruit of love. The cry, 'why have they not buried me deep enough?' (xi.334) comes as a pitiful contrast to the end of Part One, where he declared that, however deeply he was buried, Maud's step would restore his life. Now, the plea is only to be removed from all fear of disturbance. Love is not able to save, there is no resurrection.

Part Three offers rescue of a kind. By finding some common ground with others, by looking out from himself, he establishes a working if not a loving relationship with humanity, and this, for such a man, is much. But taking the poem as a whole, it is no more than a disillusioned, compromise fate, for all that 'lawful war' is held to be 'scarcely even akin' to 'lawless' violence (2.V.x.332-3). Love promised transformation, and led only to death—and so it does still. There is no essential change at the end, only the confirmation that *Maud* is a poem about the power of love proving as shattering as it was ecstatic, and about the plight of a personality who cannot extricate the obsessions of love from those of hate. When 'to be dear to someone else' is so desperately craved as a life-line, it can tighten as a noose, and lead only to 'the doom assigned' (3.VI.v.59).

᮫ 8 ᮫

In *James Lee's Wife*, as in *Modern Love*, the failure of a relationship, not its frightening success, is the theme. It is a poem of shock and adjustment to shock, when love is discovered to be subject to time, likely either to go as it came or to remain with one partner as a dialogue suddenly reduced to soliloquy. This latter situation is Browning's particular concern, the predicament of such a deprivation and what it implies for the individual forced to revise her whole basis of life. The poem is one of shipwreck, but it is also a voyage of discovery, tentative but dogged, and leading to a personal apotheosis. The loss of love and the insights of loving are both explored and so, inseparably, is the sense of identity as it flowers and is sustained by a reciprocated relationship, and still painfully finds itself in the experience of the abandoned lover. Browning raises the proposition, 'If I were dear to someone else', to a new intensity of implication, in a tone less hysterical than *Maud*, less sardonic than *Modern Love*.

In the nine sections of *James Lee's Wife*, the speaker passes through a complex phase of experience, the psychological repercussions of a failing marriage being traced from the first fears to the accomplished separation. Browning is particularly acute in suggesting how experience is registered and passes into consciousness to become part of the recognised fabric of the self. And he is making the very Victorian point that the history of one individual in this way must also involve that of the other party in the relationship. On its publication in *Dramatis Personae* in 1864, the title was *James Lee*, and although the change four years later seems an obvious gain in accuracy, the poem *is* about James Lee, just as Maud is rightly the person named in Tennyson's poem. In fact the changed title emphasises rather than cancels the claim of the husband to be central, for his wife is only identifiable under his name. Maud's lover can only be described so; and the speaker here cannot be dissociated from her union with James Lee, even though their severance makes the occasion for the poem. The irony is closely linked to the theme of love, commitment to another, working as a self-defining agent.

*James Lee's Wife* readily joins the other poems in this chapter. As well as sharing themes and points of view with them, it can be classified with *Maud* as a lyrical monodrama,[5] exploiting the resources of flexible verse form and contrasting structures; and it was written soon after Browning enthusiastically acknowledged Meredith's gift of *Modern Love*—that is, within a few months of the latter's publication in April 1862.[6] Direct influences are not my concern, but it therefore seems reasonable to see *James Lee's Wife* in the context of Tennyson's and

[5] W. C. DeVane does so: *A Browning Handbook* (1955), p. 286.
[6] DeVane, p. 285.

Meredith's work, and to link it with the strong general trend of the mid-century imagination towards exploring relationships not as they might romantically be desired to be, but as they actually break or make the lives of those caught up in them.

But Browning's speaker is neither morbidly prone to obsessive passion, rooted in family history, like Maud's lover, nor attentive to the ironic comedy of manners like Meredith's protagonist. Conditioning by society is less crucial to Browning, as he deliberately chooses an isolated pair of 'people newly-married, trying to realize a dream of being sufficient to each other, in a foreign land'.[7] He sets up his experiment in perfect laboratory conditions: emotions are scrutinised and recorded in a kind of desert-island immunity from contamination. The Shelleyan ideal, it could also be called; but to the Victorian poet, it is no cue for celebrating a timeless rapture, merely the best situation in which the strengths, weaknesses and whole nature of a shared experience of love can be soberly assessed.

In accordance with this policy of stripping away to essentials, Browning also reduces events to the minimum. Tennyson and Meredith both retain an element of dramatic narrative, but Browning is concerned neither with intrigue nor action—simply with a relationship fading. In this sense the emotional fibre of *James Lee's Wife* is less coarse. More truly than Meredith's, this husband and wife can say, 'no villain need be'. All responsibility lies within the relationship itself; it destroys as it created, unprompted by incidentals or crises of circumstance or other people. In this poem, it is the more nakedly apparent that love is an earthly phenomenon, enriching, desirable, but adamantly subject to change and mortality, and the dispositions of those whom it draws together.

∽ 9 ∽

The first poem of the sequence, 'James Lee's Wife Speaks at the Window', sounds the notes of foreboding and predicts the crisis which is to develop. The rhyming words of the opening stanza chime with ominous emphasis:

[7] DeVane, p. 285.

> Ah, Love, but a day
>   And the world has changed!
> The sun's away,
>   And the bird estranged;
> The wind has dropped,
>   And the sky's deranged:
> Summer has stopped.[8]

Simple, even artless, though the lines seem, they carry the
particular fears of this woman in the extremes they hint at: the
weather change is a 'world' change; meaningful life ceases in
the season's passing—the bird 'estranged', a 'deranged' sky.
She reads a threat to life itself in the 'stopping' of summer, and
such a correspondence between the outer scene and the inner
predicament is maintained throughout the sequence, at once
fixing the emotion in a specific landscape and charging the
surroundings with the potency of symbol.

In the two remaining stanzas of the lyric, James Lee's wife
applies her intuition of nature's demise directly to the human
situation: 'Wilt thou change too?' Change can only be conceived
as disaster, and the assumption is already fatally made, that it
is possible. Browning implies the extent to which she is bringing
her fears into realisation. The anxiety, the impatience to be
reassured are revealed in stanza iii, and shown to be part of a
need for her own role to be known and secure, even to the point
of triteness, as the stock associations are made in a vocabulary
which this time is unparticularised:

> For the lake, its swan;
>   For the dell, its dove;
> And for thee—(oh, haste!)
>   Me, to bend above,
>   Me, to hold embraced.

Slight as a lyric, potent as a prelude, the stanzas express a
very Victorian sense of crisis, in that the idea of change is
central to the speaker's consciousness, but is one she is unable to
accept, desperately reaching for the Romantic view of love as

[8] Quotations are taken from *The Poems and Plays of Robert Browning*, Vol. II
1844-64 (Everyman's Library, 1906).

immutable, eternal, predictable as a value. Yet she knows it is not so: the lyric promises the conflict which the Victorian imagination found must be lived through, in any effort to come to terms with change as the element which both threatens and supports experience. *James Lee's Wife* is, on the one hand, a study of a rearguard action, as its speaker grieves over, and resists, the knowledge that change is inevitable, and on the other, a poem made out of Browning's own willing imaginative assent to the inevitable. He is fascinated by a changing emotional position as it is apparent even in one who pleads for permanence.

Thus the tone of the second lyric is already markedly different from the first. Where 'At the Window' begs for its apprehension to be proved wrong, 'By the Fireside' shows the idea of change fully in possession. Just as summer's stopping leads on to the need for a fire, so the emotional logic advances and the barely imaginable has become the admitted likelihood, an idea entertained in all its horror, as the imagery and the train of her musing makes clear. In the first line, Browning uses the setting to establish the sense of place and time, to remind us of the seasonal movement, and as an index to the emotional trend: 'Is all our fire of shipwreck wood?'

The keynote given, the pattern of association and symbol is prepared for: 'poor sailors took their chance; I take mine'. The readiness with which the speaker connects her life with the perilous voyaging of sailors is a mark of the deterioration in her mood and her rejection of comforting dreams. She now acknowledges that committing herself to love another person is a dangerous enterprise—not a cosy formula of 'dell' and 'dove'—and finds only irony in imagining sailors offshore envying their firelight, 'the warm safe house and happy freight' (ii). Weaned from that conventional interpretation of marriage, she betrays the degree to which her security is undermined by the vigorous imagery of corruption in stanza iii, as it grows from ironic comparison to a nightmare identification with the experience of decay. The dramatic loss of distance here at 'which crept' is masterly, and shows Browning alert as usual to the psychological leaps and twists which govern grammatical and all speech adjustments:

> For some ships, safe in port indeed,
>> Rot and rust,
>> Run to dust,
> All through worms i' the wood, which crept,
> Gnawed our hearts out while we slept:
>> That is worse.

The unexpectedness of the sudden realisation that her ship, whether in port or 'full-sail' on 'love's voyage' (iv), is unseaworthy combines in this lyric with the certainty that it is so, to evoke a mood where shock and fatalism meet. Hell has come upon her 'unawares'—the lyric's final word—but at the same time she is now 'watching the man' who has caused the situation, bringing the intensity of her feeling silently to bear on him. Browning suggests the changed atmosphere between them, in which she is steering the shipwreck course as well as he.

'In the Doorway', the third lyric, continues her reading of the elements of the autumn scene as a unanimous statement of impending doom. As examples have already shown, the skill with which Browning conveys the psychological state through the descriptive notation of detail (and sometimes through its absence or failure) is one of the achievements of *James Lee's Wife*, and is nowhere better demonstrated than here, from the simple opening:

> The swallow has set her six young on the rail,
> And looks sea-ward . . .

to the fig tree with its 'furled' leaves, and the vines:

> How the vines writhe in rows, each impaled on its stake!
> My heart shrivels up and my spirit shrinks curled.

> (ii)

This mode of speech, and mode of seeing, compares interestingly with the stylistic character-revelation of *Modern Love* and *Maud*. A personal stamp is similarly imposed on the words, images and scenes used. But the speech of James Lee's wife is less extreme in its idiosyncrasy, and she keeps her eye on the object even while she sees everywhere her own plight. Meredith's speaker reduced what he saw, annexing the properties of the outside world to his disillusion and tainting them with it—

'God, what a dancing spectre seems the moon!' Tennyson heightened rather than lowered his speaker's sense of the universe, but the hysteria of mind none the less enveloped the flowers of Maud's garden and the haunted woodland. Here, however, the emotional reading arises out of exact observation, rather than imposes itself upon what is seen. The vocabulary is first of all precisely descriptive and the shift to emotive terms —the wind's 'infinite wail' (i), the 'impaled' vines which 'writhe'—only intensifies that precision. Signs of storm are written in the look of the waves, 'in stripes like a snake, olive-pale To the leeward,—On the weather-side, black, spotted white with the wind'. The inference is then drawn, '"Good fortune departs, and disaster's behind"' (i), and this is just a more diagrammatic version of the lyric's whole method, as autumn's character, scrupulously noticed, yields its correspondences with the psychological season.

But the lyric also challenges that correspondence. Because the world outside is so sharply seen, because there is distance and objectivity, as well as relationship, the speaker can see herself as a separate being, and test the idea that her fate might be less inevitable than autumn's progress into winter. The last verse rounds on the readings of the previous stanzas, and brings a different tension and a different set of propositions to bear. Winter will come—

> But why must cold spread? but wherefore bring change
> >  To the spirit,
> God meant should mate his with an infinite range,
> >  And inherit
> His power to put life in the darkness and cold?

Love is here transferred from the natural cycle to a spiritual context. For the first time in the sequence, an opposition emerges between accepting change in emotional experience as inevitable, and denying that loving is subject to the laws of temporality. James Lee's wife begins to fight the evidence whose validity she feels, putting forward a view of love as a creatively dominant force; a view which is to be drawn on in the later lyrics, and brought into a more complex relation with the contrary implication, love as contingent, subordinate, tied

to the facts of mortality. This further development is hinted in
the tone of the lyric's final lines:

> Oh, live and love worthily, bear and be bold!
> Whom Summer made friends of, let Winter estrange!

The sudden lift of the jauntier rhythm comes as a response to
the new turn given to the lyric by its questioning finale; it is an
outbreak of sloganising confidence which seems to carry both
ironic and sincere encouragement to herself, an acceptance of
the worst which is at the same time defying its real power.

In this third lyric, Browning catches the process of articulation, the activity of a mind discovering its position and exploring
the possibilities in the attitudes it finds itself capable of holding,
especially as they arise in contradiction or rejoinder to each
other. The poet is demonstrating a creativity of change even as
his speaker sets her face against its negative threat. She is not
here the person who spoke 'at the window', nor yet 'by the
fireside'; but that person has brought into being the self-
challenging speaker 'in the doorway'. The relation of lyric to
lyric in this sequence is unique to Browning, though he shares
the dramatic clashes of mood and ironies of contrast common to
Meredith and Tennyson. Neither of their speakers goes through
a kind of birth, a journey to a state of full consciousness, in their
struggle with their predicament from lyric to lyric. This is the
experience of James Lee's wife.

In the fourth lyric, 'Along the Beach', the notion of love is
examined further and the ironies of relationships exposed from
several angles. The lyric has the pressure of the marriage within
it, for here James Lee is addressed, not merely in private
soliloquy, but directly as a listening and reacting presence
(though the poem may merely be a rehearsal in her mind).
Breakdown is dramatised, to extend the portrayal of the one
partner's forebodings. The first stanza is fraught with that
atmosphere of desperation which disguises itself as unemotional,
rational discussion, and which betrays the drying up of mutual
sympathy, the central failure discourse will never restore. The
low key and very simple words are perfectly judged after the
exclamatory climax of the third lyric, and the stanza moves
steadily to the revealing climax of its final question:

I will be quiet and talk with you,
And reason why you are wrong.
You wanted my love—is that much true?
And so I did love, so I do;
What has come of it all along?

The blank realisation that nothing has come of it informs the lyric. Its acknowledgment that love which joins can also put asunder by ceasing to be operative is an insight other Victorian poetry also bravely assimilates. But here a further discovery is made: love may well mean different things to different people. The shock of finding one's partner's interpretation to be incompatible with one's own can be as mortal a blow to the relationship as the withdrawal of feeling itself. 'Along the Beach' absorbs this shock and shows it to be suffered by James Lee as well as his wife.

'The man was my whole world' (vi): but the woman was a less comprehensive experience to him. After establishing her interpretation of loving, the lyric gives his point of view, refracted through her bitterness, confirming the hints in the previous lyrics that the very concentration of her devotion provokes the lack of response she dreads:

Yet this turns now to a fault—there! there!
That I do love, watch too long,
And wait too well, and weary and wear;
And 'tis all an old story, and my despair
Fit subject for some new song . . .

(vii)

The 'new song' ends the lyric, and offers James Lee's easier, less intense philosophy, ready to settle happily for seasons not eternities:

'How the light, light love, he has wings to fly
At suspicion of a bond:
My wisdom has bidden your pleasure good-bye,
Which will turn up next in a laughing eye,
And why should you look beyond?'

(viii)

153

The gulf between the two attitudes is emphasised by the vocabulary, opposing wisdom to pleasure, and the question, 'why should you look beyond?', clashing with its sombre counterpart in stanza i, 'what has come of it all along?' For him, the delights of the hour, while she must weigh the permanent values and meaning of the relationship.

How formidable the latter approach is, the rest of the lyric reveals, as it advances the wife's clarification of her attitude. She develops the idea launched defiantly in the preceding lyric, that love is a creative, transforming power, using active verbs and emphatic alliterative links to animate her belief:

> . . . love greatens and glorifies
> Till God's a-glow, to the loving eyes,
> In what was mere earth before.
>
> (ii)

A further step is taken as she makes it clear that such an idea of love is not at all incompatible with a realistic reading of the loved one's character. James Lee's wife had and has no illusions about James Lee:

> Do I wrong your weakness and call it worth?
> Expect all harvest, dread no dearth,
> Seal my sense up for your sake?
>
> Oh Love, Love, no Love! not so indeed!
> You were just weak earth, I knew:
> With much in you waste, with many a weed,
> And plenty of passions run to seed,
> But a little good grain too.
>
> (iii–iv)

Whether this is said to him or merely formulated in her mind, such a candid verdict carries the sequence on to a more difficult understanding of love's implications. Challenged equally are the romantic ideal and the 'light, light love' with 'wings to fly'. 'Such as you were, I took you for mine' (v): in this dry statement, Browning is showing that one experience of love can be a commitment to look on tempests and be never shaken; to accept the nature of the other, and neither to deny imperfections nor to abdicate when they are perceived.

She plots her position, therefore, more exactly and more profoundly at this stage, bringing the idea of unchanging love into contact, rather than collision, with assent to human fallibility. She is not simply opposing eternal to temporal. But none the less, a lyric which claims much for serious and responsible loving is also one which exposes the roots of this relationship's failure. Irony is active in the sheer discrepancy of the two points of view the lyric offers, and sympathy is not, I think, to be confined to the wife's attitude. Browning's imagery of weeds, passions 'run to seed', and the 'little good grain', confers so measured and merciless a judgment that it leaves James Lee no figleaf of self-esteem and causes the reader to flinch. The candour in this mode of loving renders its gaze unbearable to the recipient if he is unable to reciprocate in the same manner. A lighter emotion must retreat before it, for it will destroy even while it professes to accept him wholly. It sees too much. And the tone of the speaker here does not always clearly distinguish absolute love from disparagement: in 'such as you were, I took you for mine', he is judged more than he is accepted, and her disillusion at his failing her threatens her ambitious view of love unperturbed by inadequacies in its object. She is not above the battle, and her wounds accuse him though she tries to outface this harsh reality with a higher realism.

It is a complex lyric, depicting the predicament of different natures caught by love, only to be left floundering by what love demands of them. Neither can meet the other's interpretations of its requirements. She cannot be easy, nor he intense.

༄ 10 ༄

Some of the irony uncovered in lyric IV is absorbed into the little parable which is lyric V, 'On the Cliff'. Here, love is a phenomenon which momentarily visits the barren 'minds of men', and brings a grace and beauty not native to them, as the cricket and butterfly adorn the parched ground they settle on. James Lee's failed response, so acutely hurtful, is seen in a different light by the suggestion that love, of whatever duration, is a rare visitant, an involuntary bonus, to be wondered at but recognised as the foreign presence it is—as it settles 'unawares', so will it pass.

The deliberate construction of an allegory in which love is cast as the most ephemeral constituent of a scene otherwise 'burnt and bare' scarcely softens the earlier bitterness, though it gives James Lee a moment's glory, as it were, and absolves him from the expectation that he could offer more. A butterfly and a cricket, however splendidly accoutred, are flimsy emblems, and the rather heavily playful presentation of them —'No cricket, I'll say, But a warhorse, barded and chanfroned too' (iii)—looks back to the lack of sympathy with 'lightness' in IV. The disparity with her own love is implicit, directing the interpretation put on the incident of insects settling on rock and turf.

There is greater imaginative force to the contemplation of the latter. Barrenness is a more deeply realised condition than the nature of the creatures adorning it, and by this means too, the lyric advances the negative feelings in the situation, the shrivelling of her heart. The turf is 'dead to the roots, so deep was done The work of the summer sun' (i); the rock is 'baked dry', and extremes meet in one lifeless futility:

> . . . of a weed, of a shell, no trace;
> Sunshine outside, but ice at the core,
> Death's altar by the lone shore.

(ii)

Her defeat is mirrored here, as well as James Lee's inability to sustain love.

This habit of relating nature to the emotional life is ironically surveyed in lyric VI, 'Reading a Book, Under the Cliff'. Here too, change as an inescapable law of experience is once more faced, and further effort made to find a way of coping with it. The pain of this fact of life is unmitigated, but the lyric shows that assent to it, the attempted mastery of it, the struggle to take it fully into the reckoning, is a maturing procedure. Her original question, in lyric I, 'Wilt thou change too?', is discarded, in the certainty that time assigns its limits and 'Nothing can be as it has been before' (xiii). This is the 'old woe o' the world', the tune 'to whose rise and fall we live and die' (xiv).

Using his own lines from earlier years, 'Still ailing, Wind?', for the book in which she reads, Browning sets the 'young man's pride' in his grasp of life and art against her enforced interpretations of what the wind bemoans. The young poet's confident offer to articulate the griefs suggested to him in the wind's voice betrays his naivety and comfortable immunity from any true knowledge of what it must say. To him the world's failures and mistakes are 'merely examples for his sake' (vii), opportunities for him to display his sophistication while secure in the conviction that his own fate will be quite other:

> Oh, he knows what defeat means, and the rest!
> Himself the undefeated that shall be . . .
>
> (ix)

The stanzas describing the dying nun in the young man's verses (iv–v) reveal exactly that pleased relationship with his theme which Mrs Lee scorns here. Arresting detail—'her foot comes through The straw she shivers on'—becomes Gothic:

> Her shrunk lids open, her lean fingers shut
> Close, close, their sharp and livid nails indent
> The clammy palm . . .

The wind is not to be used as a cue for such fantasies; this is to caricature the relation between nature and the inner life. Browning sacrifices his own lines to expose the contrast between a young poet's self-indulgence and the sensitive reading of her emotional plight in this speaker's response to season, weather and wind. As the titles of the lyrics stress, she is living out her misery rooted in her environment, finding it eloquent in its assistance as she strives to focus and interpret her situation. She realises her inner and outer worlds together, each enriching the other, and both telling the same story, of change as the rule of all things. No such lesson comes to the poet who asks the wind if it ails still, and offers his worldly-wise patronage to it.

Only living will teach him. The dramatic tactics of the lyric set her disillusioned voice directly against the 'happy prompt Instinctive way of youth' (x), and so brings out her assent to

the rule of time. Years 'mature the mind', and he will learn to
hear the wind, as she now does:

> Nothing endures: the wind moans, saying so;
> We moan in acquiescence: there's life's pact.

(xv)

James Lee's wife, in her savage rejection of the young poet's
unrealities, shows how she has moved to face the inevitable. But
the anguish is severe, and the effort to find balm still prompts
her to speculative bursts of resistance. The creative power of
love, refusing to let 'cold spread', lifted the tone to defiance in
lyric III, and here two other attitudes are tried out, though
neither is sustained beyond a stanza—an illustration of the
increasing fluidity and explorative energy of her search for a
full reading which will meet all her impulses and capacities of
reaction. Browning's structure joins with the increased colloquial inflection in the lyric to emphasise the rhythms of self-
debate, the devious advance to clarification.

Stanza xiv proposes to see the law of change as an unmixed
good, a stimulus stretching the spirit:

> . . . Rejoice that man is hurled
> From change to change unceasingly,
> His soul's wings never furled!

But xv returns flatly to the fact, 'nothing endures'. More
tentatively, it speculates:

> Perhaps probation—do *I* know?
> God does: endure his act!

The irony in the double use of 'endure' salts the speculation.
But this stoical attitude is no more established as an answer
than the previous rejoicing. Both are offered as possible readings, neither is hailed as the sure solvent to the pain of recognising transience. The latter remains the strongest concept, for
it is felt where everything else is only formulated theoretically,
as the end of the lyric shows with its dramatic manipulation of
language to express the irrevocable slipping away of all that is
desired:

Only, for man, how bitter not to grave
  On his soul's hands' palms one fair good wise thing
Just as he grasped it! For himself, death's wave;
  While time first washes—ah, the sting!—
O'er all he'd sink to save.

(xvi)

The word order, deferring the sense, imitates the straining
grasp, and time's swamping action, while the sequence of pos-
sessives in the second line, stretching spirit out to the most
sensitive surfaces of flesh, ensures that the idea of total human
effort near to breaking-point is experienced, as the goal recedes
in the very wealth of desirable attributes which describe it—
'one fair good wise thing'.

Compared with this graphic signalling of tension, the opening
of lyric VII, 'Among the Rocks', seems a surprising, even false,
descent into a curious mood of bonhomie: 'Oh, good gigantic
smile o' the brown old earth, This autumn morning!' (i). The
earth's relaxation in sunlight like a friendly giant in a fairy tale
is a fanciful personification transposing the poetic key; this is
neither the coastal landscape of 'In the Doorway', the moaning
wind among the vines of that lyric and VI, nor the baked turf of
V. Nearer the cricket-description of the latter, it disconcerts
by its apparent frivolity. But it remains an index to the psychological adjustments of the speaker, and indeed still observes the
external scene, although it loads an elaborate fantasy on what
is, simply, an autumn day which seems like a pause in the
process of fading and chilling, inviting enjoyment of the sun
and the twittering sea-lark.

VII signifies a holiday of the spirit, and it confirms that lyric
VI marked a major effort of will and honesty, a confrontation
with the dreaded fact that 'nothing endures'. What follows is a
release, the reward of a break in misery, and such a morning
provides the mood. The playful note in the imagery points to
an abdication from strenuous and sober thought. From this
mood, however, as the second stanza shows, she is able to
gather herself to struggle another step forward in the attempt
to arrive at an understanding of love, which as she sees it
remains unreconcilable with the admitted supremacy of

change. The lyric goes on searching for a tenable position, one which, while conceding that love cannot be an experience aloof from time, none the less meets her deep belief in it as a value countering, by its creative nature, the casual implications of lives ruled by change.

Here VII takes up the idea so bluntly formulated in 'Along the Beach'. To love meant seeing the inadequacies of the beloved with more rather than less clarity, that lyric claimed; it meant embracing the realities however meagre the return, committing oneself to the total person without idealisation or illusion. But where judgment of the other loomed unpleasantly large in that lyric, here the element of suffering involved for the one who loves is stressed as an essential feature:

> If you loved only what were worth your love,
> Love were clear gain, and wholly well for you . . .
>
> (ii)

Love, that is, is not a matter of 'clear gain'. It is a trial of the spirit, a purgation of the 'low nature', part of the moral striving of life not a butterfly moment of pleasure. The mood here is more important than the rather bare formulation of this philosophy. The dogged belief in love's persistence whatever the discouragements is the outcome of a more receptive state of mind, the fruit of what has gone before, still unripened, but promising further development. Love as an ordeal rather than a joy, an arduous schooling to which disillusion and abuse are germane: only the assent to the flux of life could bring the speaker to this reappraisal of what, in loving, she undertakes. For her now, love does not succumb to temporality, but it must, she sees, bear the brunt of what temporality implies.

ᥬ II ᥬ

Lyric VII acts as a pivot, turning the sequence from unsoftened contemplation of James Lee's shortcomings to the responsibilities of his wife as one who loves him. The remaining lyrics consolidate the move and finally reach a vision, though not an experience, of a loving relationship which crowns the insights won on the journey through the nine poems. Lyric VIII is explicitly—perhaps too explicitly—one of learning a lesson. In terms of artistic activity, 'Beside the Drawing Board' symbolises the adjustments of outlook which have been taking place. The longest lyric, it is also the most laboured.

As she copies the clay cast of a particularly beautiful hand, she derides the adage, 'As like as a Hand to another Hand' (i). But she does so out of scorn for the 'poor coarse hand' (iii) of the peasant child which is the comparison. Her admiration and love is solely for the beauty which approaches perfection, and she is fired with dreams of the artist who 'placed the ring' on this hand—an ideal relationship, she declares:

> . . . here at length a master found
> His match, a proud lone soul its mate . . .
>
> (ii)

It was 'a marriage rare', with heaven rather than earth its rightful setting. Then, after these ardent flights extolling immortal beauty (blurring the fact that the hand itself is 'dead long ago'), the musing abruptly changes course. It comes down to earth:

> Little girl with the poor coarse hand
> I turned from to a cold clay cast—
> I have my lesson, understand
> The worth of flesh and blood at last.
>
> (iii)

The movement spells out the discovery of the sequence as a whole. Its progress to valuing 'flesh and blood' is difficult, blinded by bitterness at times, but here James Lee's wife articulates her new scale of values as she accepts that da Vinci would find the unlovely piece of flesh as fascinating to study as the slim elegance of the other, and indeed more rewarding.

Continuing her critical contemplation of herself, she knows she is the 'fool' da Vinci addresses, one who has deluded herself, being unable to see that life is not a matter of beauty but of rough practicalities, commanding respect as it is and not to be exalted into an aesthetic dream:

'Who art thou, with stinted soul
   And stunted body, thus to cry
"I love,—shall that be life's strait dole?
   I must live beloved or die!"
This peasant hand that spins the wool
   And bakes the bread, why lives it on,
   Poor and coarse with beauty gone,—
What use survives the beauty?' Fool!

(iii)

   She is ironic now at her own expense, not James Lee's. The
moral shift is all-important. Love is losing its conceit, its self-
regard, and forgetting itself as a special state. Learning to
reconcile its nature with the crude human facts, it no longer
cherishes itself as an insulated, timeless emotion. The moment
of leaving James Lee is imminent, for her love now has the
strength to exist outside the charmed world of the two of them.
That world in collapsing threatened to destroy her, but has not
done so because she has found love to be a state of understanding acceptance, attuned to the 'poor and coarse', and to a
life in which 'nothing endures' except such fidelity of spirit.
   The marriage has failed. The final lyric, spoken as a farewell
'On Deck', concedes the breakdown completely. Yet in it, the
proposition, 'if I were dear to someone else' returns with renewed urgency. The potential of such a relationship has almost
the last word, defying the admitted fact of its impossibility. The
resurgence depends upon her abandonment of the clay cast for
flesh and blood: the relationship she can now conceive is far
from the conventional peace of 'For the lake, its swan; For the
dell, its dove' (I). It is a naked scrutiny, each holding the other
in a gaze of love which is all-seeing, refusing to idealise. She
approached this in IV; but the great difference here is that the
clearsightedness turned at that stage towards James Lee is now
imagined as turned back on herself, by a lover who can himself
bear the realities of life. Her own love's development has
released her to stand free and, as it were, love herself in the
same rigorous way. As she imagines a James Lee who loved her
in this sense, contemplating her as she is, she reaches the height
of her assent to the world of change, ugliness, and imperfection.

She sees herself through his eyes, that is, as James Lee's wife, just as profoundly as she sees him; not hiding together in a private world, immune from coarse facts, but secure in a love which survives because it can accommodate those facts as the terms of its contract, and indeed exists because they are so.

This is the marriage which could be; and Browning particularly emphasises that each partner is the custodian of the other's identity, carrying the reality of the other person within themselves. The intimacy is pointed by the rhyme-plan of the lyric, for the first rhyme word is 'me', and the last, 'James Lee', with every verse maintaining the link by rhyming three times with this base. Every first line ends with 'me', to renew the stress and lead on to the final—and first—naming of the other, James Lee.

In describing how he might love her, she describes her love for him. The speaker seems to inhabit both bodies, to see from his eyes as they see her, to see herself receiving this gaze, and reciprocating it. It is a remarkable performance, and by it Browning lifts the sequence to an apotheosis of the idea of being dear to someone else. He shows it to be a way of discovering the self without disguise, and of bearing that discovery because it is transfigured by the love which informs it. The lyric begins, however, by approaching such insight negatively. Since her presence is now irksome to James Lee, a bondage from which her going can release him, there is none of this loving contemplation of what she is. She can be expunged from his mind —killed:

> There is nothing to remember in me,
>   Nothing I ever said with a grace,
> Nothing I did that you care to see,
>   Nothing I was that deserves a place
> In your mind, now I leave you, set you free.

(i)

The repeated 'nothing' emphasises the sensation of being annihilated, which is the reverse of love's creativity. From this, she builds her vision of the 'mutual flame' which love has kindled, or could kindle, when 'I grew the same In your eyes, as in mine you stand' (ii). Contemplating such a situation, she can accept her own lack of beauty:

> For then, then, what would it matter to me
> That I was the harsh ill-favoured one?
> We both should be like as pea and pea . . .
>
> (iii)

Yet 'growing the same' is rooted in passionate attention to the other's individual nature and appearance, everything which makes the one loved, him or her self. A learning by heart:

> How strange it were if you had all me,
> As I have all you in my heart and brain . . .
>
> (iv)

In verse v, the two aspects are merged, the exchange of identity which the lovers' mutual knowing brings about, and the intensity of the other's presence in the mind:

> Strange, if a face, when you thought of me,
> Rose like your own face present now,
> With eyes as dear in their due degree,
> Much such a mouth, and as bright a brow,
> Till you saw yourself, while you cried, "'Tis
> She!'

The intuition is complex, at once a loss and a new possession of self, a blending which is dependent on the distinct being of the other, a state of self-love which is free—as Maud's lover was not—of selfishness, an identity only recognised because it is given to the other, to be received back in the mirror of love.

The interlacing and duplicating of language in the lyric exhibits what could be if, 'As I feel, thus feels he' (vii). All culminates in her full acquiescence in her 'fading', as this might be known from his loving reflection of what she is:

> Why, fade you might to a thing like me,
> And your hair grow these coarse hanks of hair,
> Your skin, this bark of a gnarled tree,—
> You might turn myself!—should I know or care
> When I should be dead of joy, James Lee!
>
> (viii)

Between lyrics I and IX, the craving that there should be no change is itself changed, into the acceptance of the human as well as the natural wintering process and the unlovely aspects —the 'peasant hand'—of life. Love removes the anguish, not by judging or by denying, but by containing all vicissitude and coarseness.

James Lee's wife therefore reconciles her refusal to diminish love as a power in life with a capitulation to the real nature of earthly experience. But of course this is only one angle of 'On Deck'. As all the quotations show, the lyric is ironic as well as visionary and affirmative. She is well aware that James Lee's view of love is not hers; the breakdown is no less a fact because she can imagine the profundities which might be. The tension gives the lyric a strength which confirms Browning's refusal, like his speaker's, to pretend a relationship is either easy, or even likely, if much is demanded of it.

Lyric IX is a poem of love deeply valued, but it is also one of parting and finality, admitting that such love is an ordeal, a responsibility, and a severe test for the lover who is to know and be known so completely. James Lee is not going to undertake it, and as his wife rises to her certainty of what could be, so she concedes simultaneously that it will not materialise. 'Strange plea' (ii), she describes her entreaty that he feel as she does, and 'strange' is the word introducing each phase in her depiction of the reciprocal relationship. The emotion of the lyric flows not only into the vision, but equally into the awareness that the vision is refused: if 'one touch of such love' affected her husband, as it possesses herself, then, 'I should be dead of joy, James Lee!' Irony has the last word.

The sequence does not surmount the realities of the broken marriage, and it implies that a living union of the sort she believes in is improbable. Browning is both firmly pragmatic and deeply perceptive about relationships and their potential in *James Lee's Wife*, for the poem insists that human incompatibility and weakness, and the exigencies of 'seasonal' being, are facts to be accepted as the fuel of love even though they are undeniably elements which can dampen and extinguish its 'mutual flame'.

To Meredith, to be 'dear to someone else' showed itself as a fragile possibility, fortuitous and unreliable, destined to end in moral and emotional confusion. In *Maud*, the fearful hope became the ecstatic but fatal truth, and the inability of such a state to save the lover from himself was wretchedly discovered. *James Lee's Wife* explores the meaning of 'being dear' in its implications for personal identity, in its struggle to accommodate itself to time and fallibility, and, like the other poems in their different ways, the sequence puts the stress heavily on the conditional, *if* I were dear . . . In all three poems, the Victorian refusal to bypass the formidable problems and disasters of intimate relationships, once they are seen in their historical reality, is manifest, and the degree to which this perception becomes a source of varied and vigorous creative achievement is boldly declared.

# V

# 'To Marry Her and Take Her Home'

Clough: *The Bothie of Tober-na-Vuolich*;
Patmore: *The Angel in the House*

ᥩ I ᥩ

In taking Byron's poems of separation and Wordsworth's poems of loss as my points of departure for considering the Victorian treatment of intimate relationships, I stressed that to the Romantic mind, a time of crisis brought recognition of such a theme. So far, it has been apparent that commonly the Victorians followed this pattern, making their much more extensive expeditions into this area of emotional life when reflecting on bereavement or some other collapse of a relationship. This is not surprising; extremes of feeling obviously stimulate imaginative research, especially when that feeling is suffering.

What is more unexpected is the existence of poems not prompted by extremes, not centred on suffering, and innocent of violent passions. Poems which are the mirror image of *Amours de Voyage*: there, nothing happened because love never became committed; in these equally unsensational poems, nothing happens because love does commit itself and wins its goal. Of course, emotionally, as in *Amours*, a great deal happens, and this is the point. The Victorian poet is prepared to find his opportunity in the domestic, the mundane, the 'perilously ordinary and familiar', as Alice Meynell said of Patmore,[1] not because he wishes to indulge the sentimental taste of middle-class readers, but because he sees in such a sphere experience as valuable as it is commonplace.

It is not timidity but boldness, a challenge the more formidable because it lacks drama and the helpful ingredients of death, disaster and disillusion. The poet is forced to employ his

---

[1] Introduction to the Muses Library edition of *The Angel in the House* (n.d.), p. 17.

antennae with the utmost sensitivity if he is to find his way to the significance he divines within love affairs which simply succeed. What rouses his imagination is the proposition of relationship itself; not its more arresting manifestations in the wounds it can inflict, but the way one person becomes aware of one other amid the many, and both find their lives orientated as to a pole star.

Lovers experiencing this totally usual course of events are in the poets' eyes undergoing an upheaval of personality, a revision of their existence, as momentous as the lover losing his love. A whole world-picture is involved, and one thing Patmore and Clough share is a keen eye for the society to which their lovers, Felix and Philip, belong. It is not incidental, or merely coincidental, that *The Angel in the House* and *The Bothie of Tober-na-Vuolich* contain close readings of, respectively, a professional middle-class English milieu, and the translation of that culture to the Scottish Highlands where it makes contact with the indigenous society. How they live is part of the history and part of the meaning of the love affairs between Honoria and Felix, Philip and Elspie, and each couple rediscovers itself in relation to its society through the experiences of love. The values of society too are defined, tested, exposed or given new resonance by the personal revelations enjoyed by the lovers.

Just as strikingly as in the works already discussed, the poems considered in this chapter insist that the imagination is concerned with process as much as result. They are motivated by the need to depict love as it germinates and develops, to record all that affects its progress. Clough adopts a relaxed and capacious narrative form which enables him to follow Philip's course flexibly through the various loops and side-turns which none the less lead him steadily to Elspie—and each meander is shown to play its part in shaping the emotional logic of that conclusion. Patmore is more ambitious, structurally, the nature of its organisation being one of the salient features of *The Angel in the House*; here the principle of acknowledging process is observed almost punctiliously, the outcome being a long poem which refines its material into a highly distinctive union of narrative and analysis.

In both poets the impulse is critical as well as creative, or rather, a critical awareness of the situations they present is part of their creative conception. Structurally, tonally and verbally they examine the experience whose course they follow, and subject it to a dry and ironic observation as well as an inward scrutiny. The ability to combine a light touch with a deep concern, to be at once sympathetic, exploratory and amused is a gift shared by the poems of this chapter. But as in the poems of grief and disruption, there is no uniformity of mood or outlook. Clough sees his Scottish gathering with his own special clarity and wit, Patmore beholds Felix, the Dean and his daughters with a delicacy of perception which combines feeling with grace in a manner peculiarly his own, and indeed peculiar in its complete mastery to this poem.

In taking as their difficult material the quiet history of successful love, and in showing that it too is a rich and complex topic, Clough and Patmore offer their distinctive testimonies to the mature sophistication of the Victorian poetry of relationships.

ᐧ 2 ᐧ

For Philip Hewson, Oxford student, radical and poet, to marry and take home Elspie Mackaye, child of the Highlands, a great deal must happen to each of them personally, and a pathway be found through the mazes of society. *The Bothie of Tober-na-Vuolich* may be a high-spirited 'long-vacation pastoral', but its exploration of the route to such a union is sensitive to all the nuances of feeling and pressures of environment which compose its history.

Love is to be learnt, Clough says. Even sexual love is not an irresistible force sweeping all problems and fears from its track. Without denying its instinctive depths or its power on the level of what Shaw would call the life-force, Clough shows how such elements are not to be separated from other equally compelling but more individual reactions of temperament and outlook, prompting both advance and retreat. The commitment of marriage is examined in *The Bothie*, and its nature as a personal ordeal, a searching modification of being, as well as an enriching experience, is acknowledged. Clough's is no sentimental tale of Prince Charming carrying off his Cinderella, but a study of two people discovering why and how and with what consequences they can embark on a permanent intermingling of their lives.

The theme is the more emphatic because of the wide divergence of their lives before they meet and the contrasts in all ways between them. Clough makes the relationship unlikely to begin and improbable to develop, so that its growth can be plainly seen in its essentials. Neither family, shared work or interests, nor social machinery introduce Philip to Elspie, and no custom or convention in either community encourages them towards marriage. The basic situation, though not socially isolated as in *James Lee's Wife*, is one providing laboratory conditions for research into the marriage relationship, or, more precisely, into the journey to the decision to marry. The processes by which love establishes itself and lovers advance to a state of marital consent, are intricate, Clough suggests, and his poem is organised to do justice to this idea. He takes every opportunity the pastoral's holiday freedom of movement offers to further his theme of search and discovery.

The Oxford reading-party is first seen in cordial but casual contact with the native life of the region it is gracing with its presence. The irony is Clough's, and he establishes in his first Canto the limits of association between two worlds very unlike each other. In the whisky-promoted conviviality of the dinner after the sports, the Oxford party is toasted—as are all the local worthies, peasant and nobility—but as 'the Strangers'. And Clough's introduction of the group in its personal vanities and idiosyncrasies, its nicknames and intellectual in-jokes, sets the young men apart from their hosts, whose society, in its established hierarchy from Marquis to priest and minister, from gillies to Sir Hector, is there by right not by invitation. Throughout the poem, the contrast of a life which belongs, with one which has no roots in the Highlands is sustained as the context for Philip and Elspie. For instance, the landscape itself, as Clough's descriptions emphasise, is differently conceived by the two groups: to the undergraduates it is a playground, hills to walk in, 'amber torrents' (V.22)[2] to bathe in, facilities to add

[2] Quotations are taken from *The Poems of Arthur Hugh Clough*, ed. A. L. P. Norrington (1968).

to the delights of being young and on vacation; to the inhabitants of the cottages, 'peat-roofed, windowless, white' (VI.10), it is a place of work and practical service—the lakes for laundry-use, the hills for peat, the earth reluctantly yielding barley, oats and potatoes.

Philip's after-dinner speech confirms the presence of two worlds, but reveals that he is not completely identified with either. His radical politics are humbug to his friends and he is critical of the Highland society as they are not. He is aware that he differs from both groups, and to this extent, he is potentially ready for relationships which differ from the orthodox. But Clough's account of Philip's radicalism is not without irony, hinting clearly at the undergraduate idealist whose banners are painted in black and white and whose passion thrives on the uncomplicated certainties of theory. 'Hating lords and scorning ladies', he often denounces 'in fire and fury',

> Feudal tenures, mercantile lords, competition and
>       bishops,
> Liveries, armorial bearings, amongst other matters
>       the Game-laws . . .
>
> (I.125–8)

There is a heady lack of sober priorities about this assortment which points to Philip's immaturity—a 'radical hot' (125), but a radical untested by the application of ideas to life, as Arnold might put it. Thus he belongs still to the Oxford party essentially, in his commitment to an intellectual position. Theory is all, and to argue it as a thesis against the professional resistance of Adam the tutor and the rougher assaults of his friends' scepticism is his life at this stage.

The poem shows his journey from the merely academic through the experience of loving Elspie, an experience which gradually exerts a power, not so much to change him as to change his mode of expression from argument to act. Through commitment to her, he learns the deeper implications of what began as 'hating lords and scorning ladies'; and conversely, his social instincts open the way to make this love possible. Philip would not love Elspie seriously unless he were a 'radical hot', and he does not understand what it is to be a radical until he does love her.

In Canto II the party discusses the girls met and danced with the previous night. Philip is stung into a harangue on the true and false relations between men and women. His eloquent argument for equality and the sharing of labour instead of the charades of 'Offering unneeded arms, performing dull farces of escort' (58), reveals him more ardent in his ideals than versed in self-knowledge. Rhapsodising on the 'charm of . . . labour' as displayed in the toil of a bonnetless maiden 'Bending . . . in a garden uprooting potatoes' (44–5), he deserves Lindsay's sly hint that what really stirred him was her 'high-kilted' (107) appearance. The mockery of the others exposes the sexual naivety of his arguments, and more conventional reactions too than he is aware of: his 'longing delicious' (46) chivalrously to take work from the maidens (but not all of it), and his conviction that 'sweet girls' are to be admired as they do household tasks, which 'someone, after all, must do' (103–4), show a mixture of sentimentality and patronage diluting the concept of a democracy of the sexes which he thinks himself to support. His potential relationships are therefore at risk, for while he can wax lyrical on 'sweet girls' milking the cows he is only partially emancipated from the view he condemns, and he is as likely to treat them as dolls as any of the Oxford party.

The passion of Philip's argument, however, gives the Canto its impetus and, by launching the poem's explorations into 'the feelings between men and women' (39), sets it on its way to the Bothie. But he is not to go there immediately or directly. The long-vacation spirit is one of spontaneity, randomness and freedom, and Clough never violates this relaxation to impose a more earnest mood of quest on the poem. On the contrary, the poet uses the characteristics of impromptu living, the response to the hour, the company, the weather, to provide Philip with his emotional education, as he too is caught by the moment and its chance encounters. His route to the Bothie is improvised and erratic, and he only sets out on his way because 'the weather is golden', restlessness enters the party—'four weeks here we have read' (II.216–17)—and there are visits to be made 'to the westward' (III.1). Clough is a master of the delayed event: *Amours de Voyage* turns on the postponement of meetings, and *The Bothie* acknowledges this structural principle just as centrally, though more positively. That Philip be kept apart from Elspie for much of the poem is as necessary to Clough's psychological purpose as it is that Claude should remain a hesitating step behind Mary, only here the poetic object is to create the conditions for an eventual coming together, not to symbolise the impossibility of such a union. If Claude must procrastinate and lose, Philip must meet his ferry- and inn-girls, carry peats and stay reaping with Katie, and linger 'dancing with Lady Maria', before he can pass through the braes of Lochaber and win. Elspie, already met and danced with, exerts her influence in the interim, the north to his confused compass, but she cannot be answered until the disorientation has completed its disturbing but enlightening work.

### ↜ 3 ↝

From Canto III to V, Philip's journey is obliquely and intermittently traced. Clough exploits the holiday casualness by reporting on the pilgrimage at second or third hand, as other travellers hear fragments of news, by quoting letters to Adam, by sudden swoops of the muse for direct observation. The effect is a broken mosaic of impressions, a model of Philip's own experience which, while compulsive and vivid as he lives it, is incoherent to him as a whole. The key lies in the future with Elspie, and from Canto VI, Clough concentrates on the two of them together and, through their conversations, fills in and so makes sense of the events of the earlier weeks—for Philip as well as the reader. It is an ambitious narrative method but one so disarmingly disguised by the airy manner of a mere reporter of student gallivanting that its resource in subordinating story to inner experience can pass unnoticed, unlike the comparable strategies in, for example, *Maud* or *The Angel in the House*.

Straggling back from their wanderings, his companions offer to Adam a version of the still-absent Philip's activities, to the point where they left him, in a Rannoch farmer's house, 'Helping to shear, and dry clothes, and bring in peat from the peat stack' (III.103). The story is told, 'the Piper narrating, and

Arthur correcting' (151), of a sequence of female encounters, an ironic sketch of the radical whose principles decree that he make himself agreeable to every working girl he meets. The confusion of sexual instincts with championship of shared labour, is both placed and judged for what it is in Clough's indirect presentation by such witnesses, and it is important to the poet's point that Philip's escapades shall be seen in this context of his contemporaries' views. His behaviour can indeed be easily interpreted in their terms. To the Piper, his radicalism simply offers a free ticket for dalliance. Describing Philip's interest in Katie at Rannoch, this philanderer assumes that all his domestic assistance to the girl was merely his way of advancing his cause—'making fires' is 'making love' (220). Hobbes, however, equally simply reverses the situation, proposing that Philip was attracted because his principles were stirred:

> Did you not say she was seen every day in her beauty
>     and bedgown
> Doing plain household work, as washing, cooking,
>     scouring?
> How could he help but love her?
>
> (229–31)

The affair may develop because this is the lure, Hobbes observes ironically; 'Is not Katie as Rachel, and is not Philip a Jacob?' (235)—and, he adds, may not Rachel in time prove a Leah? The tutor Adam's more serious train of thought meets this interpretation rather than the Piper's: he is alarmed not because the radical has turned philanderer, but because he has not, and may be about to let his theories take him into a disastrous permanent commitment.

Clough therefore emphasises the ambiguities of Philip's behaviour at this stage by giving these various reactions, each with its element of truth, as the golden-haired Katie in her kitchen dazzles the radical into trying confusedly to relate life to principle. Elspie is to clear his head and his heart, and as Canto III ends with news of his sudden departure from Rannoch, their gradual approach to each other is markedly advanced.

The poem switches to Philip himself, his mood emerging in
his letters and soliloquies during his 'fierce, furious walking—
o'er mountain-top and moorland' (IV.33). In his brooding he
tries to retain his romance even as he has abruptly terminated
it. He wants a painless resolution for both of them, and his
dream of 'projections of spirit to spirit' and 'inward embraces'
(49) betray the fantasy and paradoxically, the sexuality, in his
relations with Katie: 'behold, for we mated our spirits'—

> Yea, if she felt me within her, when not with one finger
>     I touched her,
> Surely she knows it, and feels it, while sorrowing here
>     in the moorland.
>
> (58, 60–1)

The same mixture of anxiety, sexual disturbance and rhetorical unreality is revealed in a letter to Adam. He soberly admits
himself to have been 'Deeply, entirely possessed by the charm
of the maiden of Rannoch' (113), but his fear for Katie's possible
end as a lost woman in the 'dissolute city' (155) is a melodramatic indulgence which indicates yet does not entirely face
how uneasy he is at his motives and attitudes towards her.
Dreaming that he sees the 'dressy girls slithering-by' (156) at
their business of accosting, he thinks he understands how they
came to such a fate, being betrayed as Katie was, their 'maiden
reserve' (170) torn away and irrecoverable. 'I am the lost one'
(165), he accuses himself; but there is still naivety here as well
as a hint of a move to more realistic and responsible relations
with women.

The lack of proportion or ability to read the character or
assumptions of the girl he has just missed committing himself to
are made quite clear by Clough, in his placing of an account
of the deserted Katie between Philip's soliloquy and his letter.
The irony is generated simply by juxtaposing the high-flown
agonising with the actual situation. The pragmatic Piper,
knowing his own desires and taking their measure coolly with
no agonising, has returned to Rannoch 'for the love of gay
Janet' (82); reeling and frisking the night away with him are
others of the reading party, including Airlie of the elegant
dress—

Skipping, and tripping, though stately, though languid, with
    head on one shoulder,
Airlie, with sight of the waistcoat the golden-haired Katie
    consoling . . .
Katie, who simple and comely, and smiling and blushing as
    ever,
What though she wear on that neck a blue kerchief
    remember'd as Philip's,
Seems in her maidenly freedom to need small consolement
    of waistcoats!

(97–101)

The mating of spirit with spirit is deflated into a rivalry of
kerchief and waistcoat, and Philip's earnest courting and equally
earnest wretchedness are set incongruously against this other
world, one of dancing and conventions clearly recognised,
where to be jilted by one young gentleman on vacation is to be
free to smile at another, not to set off for the dissolute city in
maidenly shame and despair. Philip's attitudes are at once
worse, and potentially richer, in their seriousness, than this
social treaty allows for. His peers know flirtation for what it is;
he confused a holiday attraction with a passion based on high
principles, and to that extent he was a greater danger to Katie
than any of his friends could be. His exaggeration of his flight's
consequences shows a lack of balance which neither Katie nor
her other suitors would countenance, raising issues of commitment which are not relevant from their point of view. But this
is where the gauche over-emphasis of Philip becomes a criticism
of them rather than of him: by refusing to recognise a sexual
game, by following in theory at least, other rules of conduct, he
is exposing that game for the dubious pastime it is. Neither the
students nor the Janets and Katies expect more of these relationships than a summer's diversion; to Philip, permanence, concern, sharing, and growing intimacy are not only conceivable
properties in them, but the whole point of them.

    In the ironic surveys of Philip's solemnity and Katie's
resilience, therefore, Clough is defining the implications of a
rooted relationship. He crystallises the Canto's trend by making
its chief episode the influence of Elspie on Philip, albeit she is

not as yet identified by him. Her power, however, is recognised, for a glance of hers drove him precipitately from Katie. He reports the effect of her look upon him, the shock of insight it brought, in the letter to Adam. It was 'singular, very' (125); full of his 'dreamings' (127) on Katie, he was passed by a girl who fleetingly looked at him, and her look,

. . . seemed to regard me with simple superior insight,
Quietly saying to itself—Yes, there he is still in his fancy . . .
Doesn't yet see we have here just the things he is used-to
    elsewhere;
People here too are people, and not as fairy-land creatures;
He is in a trance, and possessed; I wonder how long to
    continue;
It is a shame and a pity—and no good likely to follow.—
Something like this, but indeed I cannot attempt to
    define it.
Only, three hours thence I was off and away in the moorland,
Hiding myself from myself if I could; the arrow within me.

(134-5, 141-7)

This epiphanal moment changes Philip from the idealistic traveller in a romantic dream to a man capable of living the ideals he prizes. His principles, his awareness of people and his language—so inflated while Katie was its subject—all suffer a salutary jolt, as Elspie's keen scrutiny brings home to him a real world, where girls and their work can be assessed practically and seriously, in the same vocabulary and tone as the things 'he is used-to elsewhere'. At this point in the poem Philip ceases to be a Stranger on holiday in the Highlands and becomes potentially the husband of Elspie.

But he still underestimates sexual and emotional forces, and a more emphatic demonstration is needed to show him that he does. This takes place in a move from kitchen to castle: after reaping with Katie, there is 'dancing with Lady Maria' (241), an affair which tears Philip's principles apart from his instincts in no uncertain manner. Here he cannot confuse the attractions of a woman with theories of democratic labour and mutual aid; nor can he reconcile his politics with his willing presence in the atmosphere he has castigated as 'hot-house' (II.21) and inhabited by dolls. To continue to dance with Lady Maria, he must haul down his colours and, he reports to Adam, he finds this can be done. His letter is half shamefaced, half truculent in its announcement that all is to be sacrificed for the loveliness of Lady Maria: society in its injustice is redeemed because it has produced this 'flower' (V.49). 'Be rich, O ye rich! be sublime in great houses' (70), for God has arranged things so— 'All the works of His hand hath disposed in a wonderful order' (85).

It is a caricature of contemporary tory complacency, and Philip offers it equivocally, disturbed at himself and unable to determine his own degree of conversion. Does he speak, he says, in irony or earnest? He falls back on uncharacteristic banalities to cover his embarrassment:

> You will wonder at this, no doubt! I also wonder!
> But we must live and learn; we can't know all things at twenty.
>
> (88–9)

This attack of convenient but ludicrous humility shows Philip's weakened state. A lame observation, yet it states a truth also, for by living, he is learning. Through his infatuation for Maria he discovers that a person can seem more important than ideas; that an attraction has to be admitted for what it is, and can exert its power regardless of social sympathies or political antagonisms. His affair with Katie did not teach him the independent role of sexual nature; dancing with Lady Maria does.

But the necessity he feels to wrench his social views into accord with the new love indicates the persistence of his political nature. If his principles cannot bless their union, then he must acquire new principles: he is not content simply to abandon politics. And although Philip's attempt to argue himself from radical to tory is full of unease, and doomed to pass with his infatuation, Clough shows that from this aspect of the affair too, his nature and its needs in a relationship grow clearer to himself. From a youth confusing people and theories, and sexual feeling with radical principles, he is becoming a man who can distinguish the emotional world as an area of experience valid in itself, yet not to be trivialised by being divorced from whatever else he holds important. So his mistakes all carry him forward to the Bothie.

## ᔐ 4 ᔐ

From Canto VI to IX, the poem concentrates on that part of Philip's journey which remains once the Bothie is reached. This is Elspie's journey too, and Clough's refusal to end the poem with a Cinderella finale as Philip arrives and finds her, emphasises his concern with the deeper aspects of love rather than its sentimental surface. How two people come to the point of a committed relationship is his theme and, above all, how this entails a fundamental readjustment and reappraisal in both lovers as the intimacy grows. Love, as James Lee's wife saw, provides a mirror in which both see themselves and each other with new clarity, and this can mean disaster or, as in Clough's poem, the acceptance of an enriched, though not an easy, reality. A greater understanding of the past is a further consequence; what seemed a maze shows itself a route to a destined end.

In Canto VI, the scene changes to the Bothie, a place where country life means work and the setting is bleak. Clough presents it unadorned in a suitably austere yet graphic description:

Blank hill-sides slope down to a salt sea loch at their bases,
Scored by runnels, that fringe ere they end with rowan and
    alder;
Cottages here and there outstanding bare on the mountain,
Peat-roofed, windowless, white; the road underneath by the
    water.

(7–10)

Philip as the Canto opens is a figure in this landscape, walking with Elspie by the loch. His arrival is to be related retrospectively, the emphasis falling first on his achieved presence, with a suggestion of bonds established, allegiance given, a choice made. This impression is confirmed in the tone and the imagery Philip uses in telling Adam by letter what has happened to him:

Who would have guessed I should find my haven and end of my
    travel,
Here, by accident too, in the bothie we laughed about so?
Who would have guessed that here would be she whose
    glance at Rannoch
Turned me in that mysterious way; yes, angels conspiring,
Slowly drew me, conducted me, home, to herself; the needle
Which in the shaken compass flew hither and thither, at last,
    long
Quivering, poises to north. I think so. But I am cautious;
More, at least, than I was in the old silly days when I left
    you.

(47–54)

Everything in his account points to a maturing of insight. The
'old silly days' include his passions for Katie and Maria and
now, the north surely discovered, he is sobered by the contrast.
His political compass too has reverted to its north, radical
sentiments reasserting themselves in harmony with his emotions, but less naively.

    However, Philip at this stage has much to learn of Elspie's
nature; and she has yet to find her bearings in relation to him.
Clough therefore takes two Cantos for their developing dialogue. Cantos VII and VIII 'speak with the mouth of the
lovers' (VI.102), showing them learning from past events,
present reactions and future expectations. The kernel of the
poem, the Cantos have their difficulties for modern readers,
who are too ready to seize on one aspect—the sexual—and too
prone to balk at another—the social. Neither aspect can be
fairly understood if it is isolated from the broader context, that
is, from the whole study of a growing intimacy. Philip and
Elspie are both undergoing the shock of invasion by another, a
far more complex experience than the stirring of physical
passion alone. Equally, the transition from an expectation of
each other based on their respective roles in the social order,
to the direct personal encounter of love is a formidable revision
of secure assumptions and ingrained habit. To reduce the interest
here to the presence of sexual imagery and quaint Victorian
class-reactions is to caricature Clough's theme.

180

Elspie enters the poem as Katie and Maria do not, for in this relationship, the distinct personality of the woman Philip loves is an essential feature in the situation. He must accommodate himself to Elspie as herself, not merely as a girl who is placed by sexual, or political, generalisations; she likewise must attune herself to him, yet without betraying her growing sense of self-definition. The interplay and delicate balancing of two personalities who are at once stimulated and modified by each other is finely suggested in Clough's choice of imagery, and in his whole handling of the exchanges 'by the alders, at evening, the runnel below them' (VI.103). Even Elspie's diligent knitting as they talk is a shrewd, not a banal detail, for it emphasises the practicality of her nature, her unsentimental and uncoquettish view of time, even romantic evening time with Philip, as intended for work.

This level-headed and undramatic attitude emerges pertinently in the twilight conversation of Canto VII, where they look back to their first encounters at the sports, and at the dance at Rannoch. Elspie reassures Philip on the ability of Katie to survive, and in her reading of her earlier rival's character, she shows that maturity which was so lacking in Philip's visions of ruin:

No, she lives and takes pleasure in all, as in beautiful weather,
Sorry to lose it, but just as we would be to lose fine weather.
And she is strong to return to herself and feel undeserted.
Oh, she is strong, and not silly; she thinks no further about
    you;
She has had kerchiefs before from gentle, I know, as from
    simple.
Yes, she is good and not silly; yet were you wrong, Mr
    Philip,
Wrong, for yourself perhaps more than for her.

(14–20)

This speech of Elspie, composedly knitting, is enough to establish her as a person who retains her own judgments and speaks them candidly even to the man who attracts her and whom she accepts as socially above her. There is no flattery of Philip, and though she aims to reassure him, she does not hesitate to scourge

his pride—'she thinks no further about you'—or to repeat the
moral criticism she formed, and offered him in a single glance,
at the time:

> . . . I thought it all a mistaking,
> All a mere chance, you know, and accident,—not proper
>     choosing . . .
>
> (24–5)

Appreciating now the force of that 'proper choosing', Philip
is prompted to declare his love. Elspie's immediate response is
to 'blush all over' (54), but to answer quietly—hinting at the
conjunction in her of strong feeling and restraint—with the
dream-imagery of the two sides of the bridge coming together,
'a great invisible hand coming down, and Dropping the great
key-stone in the middle' (68–9). Then, she says, she feels herself
joined to the 'other stones of the archway' and suffused 'with a
strange happy sense of completeness' (71–2). Stopping her knitting at last to ponder this, she then experiences a minor fulfilment of the dream as Philip takes her hand, so that emotion,

> Came all over her more and yet more, from his hand, from
>     her heart, and
> Most from the sweet idea and image her brain was renewing.
>
> (78–9)

But he is more overcome than she, kissing her hand and
weeping, an extravagance which sobers her and returns her to
her more dominant and admonitory role: 'Be patient, dear
Mr Philip, Do not do anything hasty. It is all so soon, so
sudden' (87–8).

This scene and its rhythms is worth tracing in detail because
the contrast of the reflective Elspie and the impulsive Philip is
brought out in it, and hence the complementary grounding of
their relationship is clearly demonstrated. So Elspie's image of
the two sides of the arch catches a perception relevant to their
whole attraction for, and dependence on each other, not merely
to the latent sexual aspect. The 'completeness' she envisages
sums up her readiness to accept the fulfilment which his
personality—not just his person—will bring to her; the image

also implies the responsibility of each to the other, the mutual dependence and supportive strength of the union. She appreciates these implications, for she shows her ability to serve him in all her observations and her concern that his behaviour shall be worthy of him. Philip's radical theories on the beauty of service take on life and validity in Elspie's attitude to him.

He is less sensitive to the reticence and slower pace of her nature than she is to his needs. She checks him partly because to her, love, however welcome, demands adjustments she cannot suddenly make. But he pleads for her to alter at once: 'Do as I bid you, my child; do not go on calling me Mr' (92). He coaxes her into 'Philip' and kisses her for saying it. This is a kind of assault upon her, a dominance which is not the equivalent of her acts of leadership in relation to him. Her response is to withdraw; but in explaining this rejection the next evening, she brings further insight to them both so that they can once more advance towards each other. By means of such rhythms, Clough is showing the subtle manoeuvring which is necessary if two people are to bring themselves into a viable and profound association: should a lover be overbearing, the outcome will be a ruinous conquest not a creative union.

Elspie's second dream-symbol sensitively explores this fear of a rape which goes beyond the physical:

You are too strong, you see, Mr Philip! just like the sea there,
Which *will* come, through the straits and all between the
    mountains,
Forcing its great strong tide into every nook and inlet,
Getting far in, up the quiet stream of sweet inland water,
Sucking it up, and stopping it, turning it, driving it
    backward,
Quite preventing its own quiet running: and then, soon after,
Back it goes off, leaving weeds on the shore, and wrack and
    uncleanness:
And the poor burn in the glen tries again its peaceful
    running,
But it is brackish and tainted, and all its banks in
    disorder . . .

(120–8)

She identifies herself with the burn, trying to sustain its own course 'through the tyrannous brine',

I was confined and squeezed in the coils of the great salt tide,
    that
Would mix-in itself with me, and change me; I felt myself
    changing;
And I struggled, and screamed, I believe, in my dream. It
    was dreadful.

(130–3)

'Quite unused to the great salt sea; quite afraid and unwilling' (136): her portrayal of an alien power which leaves her no vestige of her own 'quiet running' is not the relationship her first symbol envisaged, with its emphasis on mutual support, the completion not the swamping of personality.

The contrast is important, and to notice only the sexual suggestion from both Elspie's speeches is to blur Clough's discrimination, as well as his point that decorum and restraint play an essential role in love. This is a major theme of Patmore too, especially in *The Angel in the House,* and it is an imaginative perception influencing many Victorian poems, though often recognised in the violation or the loss rather than the observance. Elspie speaks in this context, and out of her deepest instinct; Philip's impatience must learn to accept that love decrees distance as much as intimacy.

But as she sees him cast down by her words, Elspie is able to change her attitude, and the Canto ends on a strong reversal of the symbol of sea and stream. The passion which Elspie ascribed to the ocean becomes her own eagerness to meet and mingle with the sea; the quiet stream, alive in all its being, seeks now the 'great still sea' (163) instead of fearing a usurping flood. The lines carry the confident joy of willing assent to union as the way of self-realisation, the logical destiny of all the 'myriad springs' (158) which make up the stream. Drawn but not forced by the power of the sea, the rivulets join the 'delicate rill in the valley',

Filling it, making it strong, and still descending, seeking
With a blind forefeeling descending ever, and seeking,
With a delicious forefeeling, the great still sea before it;

There deep into it, far, to carry, and lose in its bosom,
Waters that still from their sources exhaustless are fain to be
    added.

(160–5)

The vision of the new element which is sea and ever-replenish-
ing stream together leads to the first close embrace of Philip
and Elspie 'in sweet multitudinous vague emotion' (168).


ભ 5 ભ

Canto VIII continues to record the alternations of feeling
which a serious commitment to loving entails, as the search for
the reality of each in the other proceeds. It centres on the social
and intellectual differences which Elspie, and Philip too, are
conscious of, and which both must allow for and distinguish in
their false and genuine manifestations. The Canto shows how
a relationship has to shed the skins of convention and free itself
of all that is extraneous in its assumptions before it can arrive
at a true evaluation of its strength and potential as a union of
two independent persons.

Elspie's return to doubt here is based on a sense of inferiority,
as she dwells on his gifts of birth and education—'the ease of a
practised Intellect's motion' (7–8)—and her inability to rise
to these levels. Yet out of her diffidence the conviction unexpec-
tedly comes, that she herself has value; that the risk is not
simply that Philip will be humiliated by such a wife, but that
she too could be in a way betrayed by the marriage:

It would do neither for him nor for her; she also was something,
Not much indeed, it was true, yet not to be lightly extinguished.
Should *he—he*, she said, have a wife beneath him? herself be
An inferior there where only equality can be?
It would do neither for him nor for her.

(20–4)

This conviction underlines that they are in fact suited. Elspie
has reached by her own route the ideal of democracy in marriage which Philip has argued from the start of the poem. And
as she ponders about him—'daily appreciating more, and more
exactly appraising' (12)—so love clarifies not only her view of

185

him, but her sense of herself as a person of complementary qualities and affinities with him. It again works creatively, that is, to breed confidence in their relationship as one which will fulfil, not 'extinguish', the potential of both natures.

The poem's initial theories of equality in relationships have by Canto VIII ripened from adolescent intellectualism to a living experience of the complicated interplay between two people. Yet Philip still, ironically, needs to be educated by Elspie in this development. She must exercise her new confidence to counter some of his assumptions, and show him that he is less prepared to see her as herself than she is to declare and offer him that self. Their exchange on the subject of books is significant of more than its immediate topic. Elspie, asking him to leave her some books for the winter, is refused on the grounds that reading is unnecessary for women, they being wise in nature's way; he implies that men turn to women as a rest from their serious concerns: 'Lo, you will talk, forsooth, of the things we are sick to the death of' (119). So much for the sharing of lives, and Elspie sharply reminds him that he is espoused to an individual with a mind of her own, which she is used to employing:

What, she said, and if I have let you become my sweetheart,
I am to read no books! but you may go your ways then,
And I will read, she said, with my father at home as I used to.
(120–2)

His continued patronage expresses itself in the slight concession which follows this threat:

If you must have it, he said, I myself will read them to you.
Well, she said, but no, I will read to myself when I choose it . . .
(123–4)

In each half-teasing but firm contradiction she utters, Elspie comes more spiritedly to life, with her own idiom and decisive rhythms of speech, skilfully suggested by Clough to assist this self-definition.

Even the democrat's irritation at her feudal 'Mr Philip' is now schooled by her ability to defend the usage in her own way. 'Thank heaven', he says, 'that's over for ever':

186

No, but it's not, she said, it is not over nor will be.
Was it not then, she asked, the name I called you first by?
(128–30)

Theory again must yield to her teaching, this time that formality can become part of the symbolism and souvenirs of love; not a barrier to tenderness but an expression of it. But when he kisses her, he is now, voluntarily, 'Philip'. In the comedy here, Clough shows Elspie measuring exactly where she stands, sure of the relationship as she has so far known it, with Mr Philip, aware that further, unknown, degress of intimacy are to come, for which his name on its own must be the symbol. The modulation to a deeper psychological encounter which is taking place is finely shown in this detail of modes of address.

If Elspie sets up a creative opposition to Philip's shallower assumptions, she comes to meet him as an ally on fundamental principles. His radicalism is tempered in the fire of love, but Elspie endorses as well as refines his beliefs. 'Philip, she said, I will not be a lady' (136), a declaration which rouses no resistance. Neither here needs to convert or correct the other, and Philip is quick to recognise the woman he loves in this determination of hers:

God forbid you should ever be aught but yourself, my Elspie!
As for service, I love it not, I: your weakness is mine too . . .
(142–3)

In such agreement, each becomes more clearly defined and salutes the other's individuality as the sure ground of their union.

Canto IX completes the removal of Philip from the student world to the Bothie, and consolidates his growth from a serious but naive idealist to a man living his principles with emotional as well as intellectual understanding—the former having humbled, clarified and deepened the other. Echoing Elspie's imagery, he feels his convictions flowing strongly within him, taking possession of him as a tide brings the Atlantic to the creeks of Scotland:

As at return of tide the total weight of ocean,
Drawn by moon and sun from Labrador and Greenland,
Sets-in amain, in the open space betwixt Mull and Scarba,

Heaving, swelling, spreading, the might of the mighty
    Atlantic;
There into cranny and slit of the rocky, cavernous bottom
Settles down, and with dimples huge the smooth sea-surface
Eddies, coils and whirls; by dangerous Corryvreckan:
So in my soul of souls through its cells and secret recesses,
Comes back swelling and spreading, the old democratic
    fervour.

                                     (73–81)

    Philip's theories are now powering his whole personality,
tapping all the energies of his being, and he is in every sense
sure of himself. That Elspie has brought about this harmonisa-
tion is hinted in the adoption of her idiom, and in another
simile her influence is directly acknowledged as the source of
his development. In a vision of the city, he exorcises his earlier
melodramatic fantasies of prostitutes 'in the glare of the public
gas-lights' (IV.159), for this image turns on the coming of
purifying daylight to the streets, 'shaming away . . . the mis-
users of night, shaming out the gas lamps' (83–4). Its point is
that daylight seems to restore the city to 'Primal Nature and
Beauty', and such is the effect of Elspie's love on him. Despite
the ugliness in the city, the blots he finds in himself, this sense of
renewal and harmony persists:

Meantime above purer air untarnished of new-lit fires:
So that the whole great wicked artificial civilised fabric—
All its unfinished houses, lots for sale, and railway outworks—
Seems reaccepted, resumed to Primal Nature and Beauty:—
—Such—in me, and to me, and on me, the love of Elspie!
                                     (104–8)

There is no denial of realities, and the vigour of Philip's social
indignation is quite unimpaired, but in the details of the image,
which are its life, Clough conveys the stirring of the city at
morning as an innocent awakening. The ordinary activities of
life are consecrated by the dawn light, as it seems to show
humanity restored to grace and made wonderful in its most
simple tasks and routine pursuits. As the streets are 'flooded with
broadening clearness' (85),

He that goes forth to his walks, while speeding to the suburb,
Sees sights only peaceful and pure; as labourers settling
Slowly to work, in their limbs the lingering sweetness of
     slumber;
Humble market-carts, coming-in, bringing-in, not only
Flower, fruit, farm-store, but sounds and sights of the
     country
Dwelling yet on the sense of the dreamy drivers; soon after
Half-awake servant-maids unfastening drowsy shutters
Up at the windows, or down, letting-in the air by the
     doorway . . .

(89–96)

The suggestion of life emerging sleepily out of dream-worlds,
the one mingling with the other, makes the passage gentle in
contemplating a humanity as vulnerable in its fragility as it
is at the same time wholly practical and robust. An urban Eden,
the scene is one where the Fall is not denied, but in this moment
of clear light, the legacies from it are compatible with hope for
man in his most ordinary nature. Clough epitomises here, not
only the transforming power of love, the dawn light, in Philip,
but the social ideal which motivates him. In the image's
ability to see the city, for all its 'infinite jumble and mess'
(64), as the abode of these essentially innocent lives, the
poem's theme of respect for the ordinary, the workaday, is
raised to its climax. This is what 'the old democratic fervour'
means to Philip, and its articulation is made possible by his
love.

'So won Philip his bride' (138). They marry in 'gorgeous
bright October' (130), when 'shearing had ended, and barley-
stooks were garnered' (135), and their presents of 'medicine
chest and tool-box' (144) likewise emphasise the working way of
life they are to embark on. They depart for New Zealand, a
move which has been seen as a retreat by Clough and Philip
from the social courage needed to assert 'democratic fervour' in
Scotland or England. But the idea of a new world is prepared
for in the dawn vision, and the freshness of a clean start is
poetically appropriate: a transplanting of love to a suitably
unspoilt environment where the incarnate ideal may flourish as

the hopeful social and personal symbol it is. However practical Clough's emphasis on the tool-box, he is not restricted to the literal in this poem. It is not only Hobbes in his farewell letter who says, 'Which things are an allegory, Philip' (166).

And the message of this letter, that marriage is a bigamous union with 'Rachel-and-Leah' (171), and must be accepted as such, shows Clough allowing the ironic voice a last word to keep romance in its place. But if Leah in her 'earthy' (170) character is given her due, then shall 'Rachel have joy, and survive her sister' (185). This in brief is the lesson of Elspie's circumspect approach to marriage, and Philip's Highland progress, through false starts and unreal theories, to the discovery of mature loving, and the personal enlightenment it brings. To reach this individual illumination is to become a settler in a world renewed and redefined, but not softened in its fundamentals; it is to arrive with a tool-box in a New Zealand of the spirit. And 'there he built him a home' (197).

ᔕ 6 ᔕ

Of all the poems discussed in these chapters, *The Angel in the House* is the one most likely to offend modern opinion. What promoted the poem's popularity in the 1850s reduces its chances of a serious hearing now: the assumption that Patmore merely sentimentalises women, regarding them as domestic angels of sweetness and light. This view distorts the poem, in fact, but critical efforts to show that it does so have not always themselves been free from other distortions of emphasis which, while generally fair to Patmore, are not altogether beneficial to *The Angel in the House*. Frederick Page, J. C. Reid and others try to stress the angel rather than the house; that is, they show —rightly—that Patmore is concerned with sexual love in marriage as a symbol of a higher spiritual union which belongs in its fullness to eternity not earthly life. The poet's roots are deep in the mystical tradition of western Christianity and to ignore this is to misread all his work.

But it is also possible to argue that he shocks that tradition, ascetic and celibate as it is, by his literal approach to the sexual symbolism. He insists on speaking of human marriage, and doing so in terms of his own English world and its conventions, as his means of articulating a vision which at first sight seems only incongruously associated with middle-class nineteenth-century society. His Victorian readers were right, in so far as they read him as a poet of their lives: to play down the setting and contemporary atmosphere of *The Angel in the House* is as unjust to the poem as is confining it to this milieu.

To Patmore, everyday minutiae are the spirit made flesh. Love, his poem proposes, is only to be known through the customs and social details which the lovers observe; to separate it from the gift of violets or the picnic day is to deny it its proper expression. In this necessary conjunction lie the risks for *The Angel in the House*, though they are already diminished once it is seen that the poet honours the entirely ordinary for larger reasons. The banal is redeemed in his lovers' world, and the stolen glove, the new sand-shoes, the geranium-plot are all transfigured by what they imply. A lovers' commonplace, anyway, but to Patmore it symbolises the complete sanctification of experience by the feeling which holds two people together. This is a heavy load for sand-shoes and violets, certainly, and were the tone of the poem less buoyant it would sink beneath such demands. It never takes itself solemnly, however: throughout there is a light breeze of wit which, aided by the octosyllabics, acts as its wings. The tenderness, the follies and the intensities of love are all upheld by this airiness. Patmore takes his Scylla and Charybdis of the pretentious and the banal with aplomb and highly deft navigation.

As Clough showed a political principle coming fully to life in personal terms, so Patmore explores a religious world-view by realising it through the medium of two Victorian people. *The Angel in the House* is a poem haunted by the Fall of man, the sense of a dislocated order, and it sees love as an opportunity to repair that injury, since this experience is one of special harmony bred out of the response of one personality to another. If idealisation of the female partner is an aspect of this, so too is her idealising of her lover, and as Patmore pursues the personal consequences of their coming together, the word idealisation itself takes on deeper resonance and loses its common associations with falsification and unreality.

Patmore, then, finds spiritual and psychological truths within the current social convention; he also extends and revivifies a literary convention. Felix lends Honoria an edition of Petrarch during their courtship, and the Epilogue to the poem reflects how strange it would be to meet Laura, who drew from Petrarch his 'songs and . . . immortal tears' (4).[3] The presence of the courtly love tradition in Patmore's imagination is important because it points attention to the ideas of courtesy, veneration and ceremony which are so central to what the poem is saying about relationships. Equally important, however, is the Victorian poet's divergence from the Renaissance as he connects the old 'remote, romantic' ideal with the more prosaic convention of matrimony and family life. 'Think you, if Laura had been Petrarch's wife, He would have written sonnets all his life?' asks Byron in *Don Juan* (III.8), inviting the negative. But Patmore's answer is yes: rather than opposing the two kinds of love, he fuses them.

If he has an ancestor here, it is Spenser. *The Angel in the House* proves to be a Spenserian poem in its values and its imaginative goal of a married Britomart; chastity is not a converse to sexual love, but a vital element within it. The restraints conferred by love are one with its freedoms, and honouring a woman need not be divorced from, and must not be lost to, intimacy with her. The paradox braces the whole poem, as fourteenth-century Laura becomes Honoria, eldest daughter of the Dean, and her suitor Felix becomes her husband taking her to Green's Hotel at the seaside for their honeymoon.

## ⌒ 7 ⌒

The structure of *The Angel in the House* illustrates very well the experimental pressure exerted upon Victorian poets by their poetry of relationships. Patmore's appreciation that he is offering a narrative which is not a narrative but a psychological exploration has already been quoted:

[3] Quotations are taken from *The Poems of Coventry Patmore*, ed. F. Page (1949). References are given to Cantos and sections within them, small roman numerals indicating Preludes; arabic, narrative sections.

The Song should have no incidents,
They are so dull, and pall, twice read:
Its scope should be the heart's events . . .

How to give form and substance to these events is the
problem he shares with his contemporaries and, like them,
he is concerned with capturing not just a single state of
mind but an emotional journey of changing landscapes and
perspectives.

His solution is a scheme of twenty-four short Cantos whose
titles highlight either some particular moment of importance
to Felix and Honoria in their courtship and early married days
—'The Violets', 'Sarum Plain', 'Accepted'—or some significant
mood of their relationship—'Aetna and the Moon', 'Sahara',
'Love in Idleness', 'The Revulsion'. The twenty-four are split
into two Books, 'The Betrothal' and 'The Espousals'. Thus
attention is fixed both on spots of time, which illuminate the
inner world of the lovers, and the dialogue between them as it
develops.

To ensure the inward emphasis, Patmore divides each Canto
into two sections, a set of general Preludes followed by an
episode about Felix and Honoria. The nature of love, the power
of relationships, the paradoxes of courtship are all set forth and
established as leading themes in the Preludes. Each usually
contains three or four titled sections, ranging from extended
meditation to brief emblems or gnomic quatrains. They direct
how the Canto's episode is to be read, and once it is read, the
Preludes in their turn take on further implication. The relation
between the two can be seen as a union of spirit and body, for
the advance to the specific story can simply be termed an act
of incarnation. Patmore declares his theology of human life and
love in the structure as well as the matter and tone of his poem:
Preludes and episodes blend together in a harmony which is the
inspiration of the whole. Nothing palls, twice read.

ᔍ 8 ᔍ

Like an overture, Canto I, 'The Cathedral Close', touches
lightly on what is to come:

> Moving but as the feelings move,
>     I run, or loiter with delight,
> Or pause to mark where gentle Love
>     Persuades the soul from height to height.

(iii)

Solemnity is set aside—'my words are gay As David's dance'—
but 'New truths' will be discovered, 'like new stars'. This is the
first example of a recurrent cosmic imagery, and so here the
scale as well as the tone of the poem is hinted; parochialism is
rejected even though the cause of the particular and the local
is to be promoted.

The narrative section begins this promotion appropriately
with Felix returning to the Dean's house after six years absence:
he like the poet is to revalue the familiar. It is a house whose
inmates,

> Kept their own laws, which seem'd to be
> The fair sum of six thousand years'
>     Traditions of civility.

It has a 'temple-like repose', an air,

> Of life's kind purposes pursued,
>     With order'd freedom sweet and fair.

(5)

The poem is to learn the height and depth of such 'civility' and
'order'd freedom' in their full Christian implications for 'a
world not right', and it is not accidental that Felix's first men-
tion of Honoria is a memory of his lack of civility, when she,
'kiss'd at Christmas, call'd me rude, And, sobbing low, refused
to sing' (4). Their future relationship will suffer similar blunders
before the ideal of civility can take firmer shape and meaning.

Adjusting himself to the strange young ladies he left as girls,
Felix recalls his old arguments on religion with Mary, who,
'heavenly overmuch', had scorned the world and thought that
'bliss Was only for a better clime'. This too is a significant
recollection, for the poem is to set itself absolutely against such
puritanism and argue passionately for a heaven rooted in

earth. Thus the introductory Canto launches Patmore's main preoccupations and establishes the emotional rhythms of 'David's dance'.

'Mary and Mildred' which follows is a Canto of subtle patterning, with Patmore's wit mediating between ideal and actual, balancing the opening tribute to 'The best half of creation's best' (i) with the episode's follies of the young man falling regularly in love as a general gesture to the sex, but ignorant of his own heart as he does so. The Preludes themselves adroitly steer the Canto through several moods, so that the high note on which it begins is not allowed to go on too long or become too intense. Its final lines carry the first Prelude, 'The Paragon', from praise for women and lovers to the reason why they merit such esteem:

> Our lifted lives at last shall touch
>   That happy goal to which they move;
> Until we find, as darkness rolls
>   Away, and evil mists dissolve,
> The nuptial contrasts are the poles
>   On which the heavenly spheres revolve.
>
> (i)

But in the second Prelude, 'Love at Large', the idea of sexual response as a doorway to an understanding of life is transposed into a lighter sketch of youthful susceptibilities. Patmore's control and his skill in tonal modulations are well shown here, for 'Love at Large' relaxes the mood without trivialising it or losing touch with what has gone before. There are Ancient Mariner echoes in the imagery, working seriously to extend suggestion despite the obvious incongruity of linking a severe ordeal of privation with the undramatic situation which is this Prelude's subject— 'Whene'er I come where ladies are'. Patmore rides the irony, inviting it as part of the mood, but he is also saying unironically that life without the potential of love is a 'ship frost-bound and far Withheld in ice'. Prelude ii must be quoted in full, to show how its dancing rhythms and their momentum contrast with a dragging, heavier beat to contribute to its psychological point; likewise the sustained and vivid handling of the image:

Whene'er I come where ladies are,
　　How sad soever I was before,
Though like a ship frost-bound and far
　　Withheld in ice from the ocean's roar,
Third-winter'd in that dreadful dock,
　　With stiffen'd cordage, sails decay'd,
And crew that care for calm and shock
　　Alike, too dull to be dismay'd,
Yet, if I come where ladies are,
　　How sad soever I was before,
Then is my sadness banish'd far,
　　And I am like that ship no more;
Or like that ship if the ice-field splits,
　　Burst by the sudden polar Spring,
And all thank God with their warming wits,
　　And kiss each other and dance and sing,
And hoist fresh sails, that make the breeze
　　Blow them along the liquid sea,
Out of the North, where life did freeze,
　　Into the haven where they would be.

(ii)

So the Preludes, typically, contrast, yet corroborate each other;
together they exhibit Patmore's easy movement between his
most difficult Christian concepts and the cheerful, simple
impulses of life. And by this interplay in the Preludes, the
episode of 'Mary and Mildred', at once serious and flirtatious,
is prepared for. In it, Felix rejoices in being 'where ladies are'
and confuses his momentary inclinations with genuine commitment. Of the three girls, it is Mildred who attracts him most, he
decides. And yet he cannot help but observe that

　　Honoria, less admired the while,
　　　Was lovelier, though from love remote.

(4)

　　Taking its cue from that ending, Canto III, 'Honoria', leaves
flirtation behind and in its episode traces the process of falling
seriously in love, while establishing the paradoxes and reiterating the import, moral and psychological, of this state in its

Preludes. In Prelude ii, for instance, Patmore formulates one of his chief insights, opposing the popular view that force of passion is an unruly flood, overwhelming the will and beyond control. He declares this to be a misconception of love's nature, its proper character being harder to appreciate because it lacks the self-assertion and turbulence, though not the strength, which passion is supposed to entail:

> Ice-cold seems heaven's noble glow
> To spirits whose vital heat is hell.

Patmore's meaning here can be amplified by a passage from his prose notes, *Magna Moralia*, where, defining virtues as 'ordered passions', he stresses the 'great decorum' which characterises love at its highest:

> In vulgar minds the idea of passion is inseparable from that of disorder; in them the advances of love, or anger, or any other strong energy towards its end, is like the rush of a savage horde, with war-whoops, tom-toms, and confused tumult; and the great decorum of a passion, which keeps and is immensely increased in force by, the discipline of God's order, looks to them like weakness and coldness.[4]

*The Angel in the House* depicts the advance of love's strong energy towards its end, and by all it says and is the poem exemplifies the working of the great decorum as part of that love's essence. The paradox broached in Prelude ii is active throughout.

In the Canto's episode, Felix is brought to recognise that his feeling for Honoria is love by the catalyst of discovering a possible rival in her cousin Frederick. So the strong energy begins to exert its power. He is in love and knows that he has met his 'destined maid' (i).

∽ 9 ∽

What this means is explored in the following Cantos, all of them showing how the daily minutiae and the fundamentals of loving relate to each other, either happily as in Canto IV, 'The

[4] *The Rod, the Root and the Flower*, ed. D. Patmore (1950), p. 146.

Morning Call', which moves felicitously from thoughts of Eden and the 'Rose of the World' to a stroll in a trim Victorian garden, or more tensely as in V. Being in love is not a state of untroubled blessedness. Patmore is as much concerned with the instability and rapid alterations of mood which mark this condition as he is with the depths below the ever-changing surface. For one person to unite with another is a precarious as well as a profound undertaking, and the lover is a being morbidly aware of all that can go wrong. Canto V, 'The Violets', shows an irritable Felix in the shadow of these fears, affected as they are for better or worse by whatever the moment brings.

But first the Preludes attend to the fundamentals as such, considering fallen human nature. 'The Comparison' does so by emphasising sexual difference. In man, the legacy of selfishness, conceit and arrogance is manifest; in woman, the gentler virtues survive to temper and diminish the ugliness of fallen life. And in her, the prime restorative value of love finds its fullest expression:

> And therefore in herself she stands
>     Adorn'd with undeficient grace,
> Her happy virtues taking hands,
>     Each smiling in another's face.
> So, dancing round the Tree of Life,
>     They make an Eden in her breast,
> While his, disjointed and at strife,
>     Proud-thoughted, do not bring him rest.
>
> (i)

Love's capacity to harmonise the whole psyche is Patmore's theme, and his contrasts of male and female, here and elsewhere, bring out, on the one side, the need for this, and on the other, the rich rewards of achieving the dance of the virtues. In what he says of women, that is, Patmore expresses the potential of all human nature—'creation's best'—its self-divisions healed: and his nuptial goal symbolises the absorption of the two sexes into the one creature of grace.

That goal can seem remote. Felix, love's martyr, lapses into self-pity, seeing how many things can lead to the frustration of his desires. Patmore exploits the comedy in the melodramatic mood, but he is also pointing out how fragile love is as it faces the hazards of day-to-day living. It may be a spiritual force of great power, promising to cancel the legacy of fallen nature, but it is also subject to the whims of the moment as well as the particular enigmas of the personalities it would join together. What must express itself in and through time, place and person is inevitably threatened by these incalculables. Felix broods:

> How, many times, it comes to pass
>     That trifling shades of temperament,
> Affecting only one, alas,
>     Not love, but love's success prevent;
> How manners often falsely paint
>     The man; how passionate respect,
> Hid by itself, may bear the taint
>     Of coldness and a dull neglect . . .
>
> (1)

'Heaven its very self conspires' against love, it seems. Only a blind faith can make it worth pursuing such a hopeless quest. The appreciation of the high odds against fulfilment are reminiscent of Clough's *Amours de Voyage*, where those 'trifling shades of temperament' loomed so fatally large.

The perception of how important the whole fabric of life's detail is in determining the outcome of a love affair, is endorsed by the Canto's final reversal of mood, for this too is achieved by a detail, and a trivial event is enough to turn all cursing of fate to rejoicing at its favours. Honoria's note arrives, inviting Felix to dinner. Violets, 'two white, one blue', are enclosed:

> She and her sisters found them where
>     I wager'd once no violets grew;
> So they had won the gloves. And there
>     The violets lay, two white, one blue.
>
> (2)

Eden is recovered in a moment. The comedy of the young lover blends with the implications announced in the Preludes, that love commands the secrets of harmonious living—the dance round Eden's tree.

As Felix in Canto VI takes his first practical step towards his goal and gains the Dean's consent to woo Honoria, the poem begins to experience more actively the paradoxes of love, inseparable as they are from its deepest nature. Meeting Honoria after his interview with her father, Felix becomes intensely aware of the tension between his desire and her untouched chastity. The lightly personified summer breeze which, blowing against her dress, 'loved her shape, and kiss'd her feet', reveals his own eagerness for such intimacy, yet the very strength of this physical impulse prompts him to value as part of what he loves, her 'young trust' and 'chaste and noble air'. The latter gives to 'love's feast',

> . . . its choicest gust,
> A vague, faint augury of despair.

(4)

At the height of hope and ardour, Felix salutes that sense of distance and inviolate being which is for Patmore not the doom but the necessary component of the 'elect relationship' (ii), a 'despair' which ensures that love's energy does not destroy.

Ensuing Cantos develop this concept as a key feature in the lovers' growing communion; and Canto VII immediately illustrates it further, as its title, 'Aetna and the Moon' suggests. The more volcanically roused Felix is, the more does the counter-image of calm light and untouchable beauty become an intrinsic part of what he loves. His desire to possess, his fear of failure, the overwhelming force of his passion are all calmed by the quiet presence which stimulates them: his love thrives on the paradox. Experiencing attraction and repulsion, the lover responds to both, as passionately aware of his need to be united to her as he is deeply conscious of the need to behold and preserve her as she is, apart from himself.

Canto VIII, the visit to Sarum Plain, is an episode which stands as the first climax in the courtship, and in earning this status it draws on the preparation of the preceding Cantos as well as the usual source of its own Preludes. At this vantage point, it is possible to begin to appreciate the dovetailing of all sections in the poem; references forward and back become rewardingly apparent in the way the summer outing is presented. The first two Preludes emphasise once more the ineffable quality of love, its illumination of every life it enters with a hint of heaven's splendour. Then Prelude iii firmly connects the high moments of intuition with the commonplaces of life. 'The Spirit's Epochs' is one of Patmore's most characteristic successes, the oblique approach to the positive statement, and the lift of rhythm and tone towards the conclusion both collaborating neatly with his point:

> Not in the crises of events,
> > Of compass'd hopes, or fears fulfill'd,
> Or acts of gravest consequence,
> > Are life's delight and depth reveal'd.
> The day of days was not the day;
> > That went before, or was postponed;
> The night Death took our lamp away
> > Was not the night on which we groan'd.
> I drew my bride, beneath the moon,
> > Across my threshold; happy hour!
> But, ah, the walk that afternoon
> > We saw the water-flags in flower!

Prelude iv returns to theological language. 'Female and male God made the man', and sexual union is seen as a reunion, for 'in our love we dimly scan The love which is between Himself'. But this is cause for gaiety not awe; wisdom 'laughs and plays' —like David—rather than kneels before such an insight, and Patmore here encapsulates the distinctive quality of his poem. It is a religious work whose tone is carefree not because the vision is shallow, but because its profundity springs from joy, sexual joy, the bond between earth and heaven. Prelude v, 'The Praise of Love', crisply sums up in a quatrain:

> Spirit of Knowledge, grant me this:
> > A simple heart and subtle wit
> To praise the thing whose praise it is
> > That all which can be praised is it.

The 'subtle wit' is then called on to capture the nuances of the day on Salisbury Plain. Various 'moods of love' are to be traced, and so are the unspoken but major developments between the lovers. For Felix, what will end as one of the water-flag days

begins in fact with dark meditations in a 'close and sultry lane'
(4) as he reacts to the proximity of Honoria with a passion which
is half despair. Patmore does not overlook the sometimes
devious, even perverse, emotional routes to epiphanies; the
elusiveness of a lover's logic is a theme, and an influence on
structure, throughout—'The moods of love are like the wind,
And none knows whence or why they rise' (2).

As they all emerge to the actual breeze of the Plain, the mood
lightens too and the pleasures of the moment take precedence.
That the lifting of spirits is also a physical response is hinted with
appropriate delicacy, as in Canto VI, by the agency of the wind,
which, caressing her hair and vexing 'the ribbon at her waist',
also blows her dress in folds round him. The interplay here of
weather and mood is raised to a fusion of the two as Felix
describes the peace which gradually possesses him:

> Till, one vague rack along my sky,
>   The thought that she might ne'er be mine
> Lay half forgotten by the eye
>   So feasted with the sun's warm shine.

Stonehenge above them,

> ... On a little mound
>   Sat the three ladies; at their feet
> I sat; and smelt the heathy smell,
>   Pluck'd harebells, turn'd the telescope
> To the country round.

>                                        (5)

The holiday relaxation of the occasion is its strength as a setting
for the love which is to grow from it. Patmore stresses the
contrast between the human figures and the 'scowling' Druid
rocks, their pagan mood of 'chill gloom' disapproving and failing to understand 'the lightness of immortal love'. Thus the idea
of gaiety of spirit as the true human wisdom is brought out once
more, to lead in to the emotional climax of the Canto which is
one of just that lightness, discovering itself for the first time in
the demeanour of the other person. The reciprocation here
marks the advance of love from a private condition to a

conscious, though mute, relationship with all the expansion of feeling which this involves. A new dimension is opened up to Felix and Honoria in the tender elation of the hour:

> And, as we talk'd, my spirit quaff'd
>     The sparkling winds; the candid skies
> At our untruthful strangeness laugh'd;
>     I kiss'd with mine her smiling eyes;
> And sweet familiarness and awe
>     Prevail'd that hour on either part,
> And in the eternal light I saw
>     That she was mine . . .
>                               . . . and there grew
> More form and more fair stateliness
> Than heretofore between us two.

Here the love of Felix and Honoria is established as mutual, and a pledging of self, a new hope for wholeness of being, arises out of a happy outing on a fine day. Patmore in Canto VIII combines delight and depth with no falsity of touch, and with deceptive ease. His limpid but 'sparkling' verse is itself an incarnation of the spirit in the hour, as in language both relaxed and dignified, in tone both stately and familiar, he shows a growing intimacy breeding a greater courtesy.

### ↜ 10 ↝

After the water-flag day, Canto IX comes as anticlimax and reaction. Entitled 'Sahara', it depicts Honoria's departure for London, with the prospect therefore of a desert to be crossed by Felix during her month's absence. The Canto plays off the emotional against the factual reality to illustrate how love creates its own scale of value and transfers the individual's centre of awareness from himself to the other. Honoria's presence is everything—'She near, all for the time was well' (1); 'What should I do, where should I go, Now she was gone . . . ' (4).

He wanders past the Deanery, 'one sad window open yet' (5), and his Sahara is conveyed, as ever, through the minutiae on which he dwells:

> I wonder'd, would her bird be fed,
> Her rose-plots water'd, she not by . . .
>
> (6)

And minutiae are his comfort too as he visits all her haunts: 'Her dress had brush'd this wicket'. The balance is finely kept between a quietly ironic view of the behaviour of the lovelorn and the serious record of a desolation of spirit wholly justified because 'The glory from the world was gone' (4). The Canto ends more peacefully with an enlarging symbol in which the minutiae are absorbed and their implication epitomised:

> . . . the blackbird, in the wood,
> Talk'd by himself, and eastward grew
> In heaven the symbol of my mood,
> Where one bright star engross'd the blue.
>
> (6)

This symbol provides the keynote for Canto X, where the title, 'Going to Church', introduces a more reflective movement. Felix places his idea of Honoria and his love for her into a specifically religious context, and the Preludes contemplate the Christian notions of grace and purity in their human incarnation. The Preludes, that is, see the spirit embodied, while the episode sees Honoria as the woman nearest the harmonies of angelic nature. To put it linguistically, Canto X takes the two, usually separate, aspects of the word 'grace', the secular and the religious, and demonstrates their essential unity. This is Patmore's vision in a word: as he sums up, 'all grace is the grace of God' (i). The Canto is an astute piece of poetic manoeuvring which gives all the connotations of the term their full rights, yet brings them together to reveal a single ultimate quality of being.

Such is the 'Joyful Wisdom' in the Prelude having that title. The persons who truly embody heavenly values, those who draw us as 'oases in our waste of sin', are souls where 'everything is well and fair', controlled and marked by a considerate courtesy in all their dealings. Theirs is not a cruel asceticism, but a disciplined living none the less:

> They live by law, not like the fool,
>> But like the bard, who freely sings
> In strictest bonds of rhyme and rule,
>> And finds in them, not bonds, but wings.
>
> (1)

Patmore shows in all his language, and especially in this favourite paradox, the merging of one whose person is graceful with one whose life is full of grace. The qualities of poise, ease, balance and harmony, blending law with freedom, spring from the same root as the elements of a spiritual beauty—continence, unselfishness, love. This rare, well-ordered, responsive soul is transfigured humanity: 'They shine like Moses in the face'.

The lover's eye reads the signs. Stirred and influenced by the personal graces, he perceives their spiritual corollaries, and finds there is no unbridgeable gulf between the values of earth and heaven. The episode shows Felix experiencing this enlargement of his religious, as of his lover's sensibility. His Sunday morning meditation presents Honoria to him as one of the rare creatures the Prelude describes. In her the implications of grace serenely meet and become one harmony of nature:

> Her beauty was a godly grace;
> The mystery of loveliness
>> Which made an altar of her face,
> Was not of the flesh, though that was fair,
>> But a most pure and living light
> Without a name, by which the rare
>> And virtuous spirit flamed to sight.
>
> (4)

Contrary to Puritan fears, God expresses himself through the created:

> . . . Him loved I most,
> But her I loved most sensibly.

There is no dichotomy, and this insight allows Felix to 'take' his 'passion into Church' in every way. The Canto soars finally into a state of complete calm, in which the passions of the flesh are at one with the idea of purity, the Fall overcome as love

rests assured that its energies and desires are compatible with
its spiritual intuitions:

> And all through the high Liturgy
>   My spirit rejoiced without allay,
> Being, for once, borne clearly above
>   All banks and bars of ignorance,
> By this bright spring-tide of pure love
>   And floated in a free expanse,
> Whence it could see from side to side,
>   The obscurity from every part
> Winnow'd away and purified
>   By the vibrations of my heart.
>
> (6)

But the vibrations of the heart can lead to blunders and the
loss of such inner security. Felix has not yet learnt the full import of a love relationship, which indeed can only be discovered
as the two impinge more urgently on each other. Canto XI,
'The Dance', furthers his education and the relationship. First,
however, it returns the poem to the fallen world which Felix
momentarily transcended. The two Preludes both emphasise
the frailties of human nature, and the greater need for 'respect'
in love if harm to the individual from the demands of intimacy
is to be avoided:

> Angels may be familiar; those
>   Who err each other must respect.
>
> (ii)

Felix agrees, and goes further. Building on his Salisbury Plain
experience, he sees that distance is indispensable to intimacy, not
merely a safeguard—it is 'The space which makes attraction felt':

> He who would seek to make her his
>   Will comprehend that souls of grace
> Own sweet repulsion, and that 'tis
>   The quality of their embrace
> To be like the majestic reach
>   Of coupled suns, that, from afar,
> Mingle their mutual spheres, while each
>   Circles the twin obsequious star;

And in the warmth of hand to hand,
    Of heart to heart, he'll vow to note
And reverently understand
    How the two spirits shine remote;
And ne'er to numb fine honour's nerve,
    Nor let sweet awe in passion melt;
Nor fail by courtesies to observe
    The space which makes attraction felt . . .

(1)

The cosmic imagery, at once succinct and spacious, honours
the perception and extends it with its own dignity, precision
and power. And what can be suggested by the laws of the cosmos
can also be communicated through the metaphors afforded by
the ballroom. Music and dancing provide Felix with more
images of harmony as he watches 'where she danced Native to
melody and light'(2). He sees music as the language of love,
and Honoria, one whose spirit is 'lantern'd by her body'(1), as
the living interpreter of that language: 'I ne'er knew what
music meant Until I danced to it with her'(3).

Nevertheless, despite his quickened appreciation, Felix
lapses into the erring lover who presumes angelic familiarity.
His passion imposes upon Honoria, making its desires his sole
governor. To object that he only presses her hand is beside the
point, for the message of assault and unbridled demand is
poetically clear:

My passion, for reproof, that hour
    Tasted mortality's alloy,
And bore me down an eddying gulf;
    I wish'd the world might run to wreck,
So I but once might fling myself
    Obliviously about her neck.

(3)

The descent towards violence here is dramatically apparent in
the contrast of language and imagery with the earlier cosmic
and human dancing. The surrender to feeling which 'bore me
down an eddying gulf' is the antithesis of disciplined musical
emotion, and the world running to wreck suggests a menacing

207

breakdown of that planetary order and saving distance, a collapse into chaos which is a judgment on the abandonment of 'fling myself obliviously'. Rightly, Felix sees himself as a 'deranger of love's sphere'. However, his abuse has turned vision into the pain of experience, and his nature as a lover is to that extent developed.

So is hers. The final paradox shows that Honoria is being drawn into a stronger response and commitment because of the gaffe she does not condone: 'Her farewell did her heart express As much, but not with anger, moved'(4). It is only because she is attuned to Felix that she registers the force of passion in him which threatened her, and her shock is one of assent as well as defensive resistance. That profound readjustment of the private or virginal being to the idea of union, which Clough showed Elspie undergoing, is here initiated in Patmore's Honoria. Her conflicting feelings make her face, 'the jousting field Of joy and beautiful alarm'.

From such a climax Patmore is able to move swiftly to the declaration which crowns Book One of the poem. He has brought both lovers to the point where the implicit must become explicit, the relationship must acknowledge itself and become an audible dialogue, with further discoveries dependent on this advance. Canto XII surveys the state of betrothal and sees it as a happy yet delicately balanced condition for both partners, the outcome of an intricate procedure of pursuit and capture on both sides.

The Canto's title, 'The Abdication', and the use of the image 'The Chase' in the first Prelude emphasise the tensions and risks in the devious but persistent move towards intimacy which all the previous Cantos, but particularly XI, have noted. 'The Chase' looks back to the end of XI and expands the ambivalence in the female attitude summarised there. Courtship is a subtle tactical exercise, a war which becomes a tacit conspiracy as she 'takes warmth from his desire'. But there remains for her an element of assault: 'She's chased to death, undone, surprised, and violently caught'. And for her successful suitor too, there is a 'strange alarm'(1) in the victory, and loss in the knowledge that she is willing to renounce her independence, 'By love unsceptred and brought low'.

So Felix finds as Honoria consents to marry him. 'The summit won, I paused and sigh'd'(5). He has to adjust himself to the Victorian rather than the Renaissance situation, as it were. The 'mistress' of his 'reverent thought' is now inviting him to regard her as one with whom he is to share a life, not asking that he lay his at her feet. The irony that he has himself brought this about, that it is indeed a 'meeting of desires'(4), does not lessen the pain of recognising that he has irrevocably changed her by loving her and pleading that she admit his love:

> Her soul, which late I loved to invest
> With pity for my poor desert,
> Buried its face within my breast,
> Like a pet fawn by hunters hurt.
>
> (5)

Her sovereign self-sufficiency is gone. But he too is changed and brought into a new dependency, for he is conditioned by what she asks of him, her need for cherishing. The hunter, having gained his prey, is now her refuge. The chase is over and each, in short, is the prize of the other, each is undergoing a surrender and a change of attitude. The new note of tenderness in the imagery of the chase's end points to this development, with a promise of deeper intimacy arising out of it.

In Canto XII, the love leading to partnership emerges as more humbling and more responsibly demanding then the homage of courtly love. The prospect of union is formidable as well as blissful. Lovers who commit themselves to each other do so out of need; they are both vulnerable humans and must learn to see and treat each other so, replacing the veneration of actual distance with its spiritual equivalent. The courtesies of love must heal the wounds of love; the giving of self and the receiving of the other must be an exchange in which both 'shine remote' if there is to be no hurtful tyranny.

Thus Felix and Honoria, after their private ordeals of preparation, stand at the beginning of their shared experience, and the way from 'The Betrothal' to 'The Espousals' is to Patmore a further journey of exploration, in which the lovers' relationship becomes ever more lucid in its happiness as it discovers the depths of the waters it so buoyantly navigates.

ဢ II ဢ

Twelve Cantos take Felix from choosing to declaring his love.
It is therefore no surprise that twelve more are needed to carry
him from declaration to marriage, nor that the Prologue to
Book Two should underline the historical approach. It features
the poet, his wife and their children in a light sketch of normal
family uproar and hilarity, occasioned by the finding of a
hedgehog. That is, the two stages in the courtship of Felix and
Honoria are divided by a scene from the life of the older Felix—
the poet ten years married. As Book One was a gift for Honoria
on the eighth anniversary, so this Book is also deliberately
integrated into the continuing experience of love, at once confirming the values the poem advocates and refusing to romanti-
cise them. Before the progress of young Felix and Honoria is
resumed, the Prologue establishes cheerfully and unequivocally
that these are the terms in which their relationship will express
itself, and that domestic trivia are the language of love when it
is most, not least, itself in earthly life.

Canto I, however, redresses the balance, in its Preludes
reiterating the larger view which gives the homely details their
value, and in its episode, 'Accepted', taking up again the
psychological complexities in more observations on the ambiguity of response to the happiness of betrothal, as does Canto
II, 'The Course of True Love'. Here Prelude i, 'The Changed
Allegiance', explores the reorientation which is necessary for
the woman in the process of discovering and accommodating
hitherto unknown emotions. That it is a movement from a
restricted to an enlarged consciousness, which none the less
cannot be casually undertaken, is apparent from the opening
image, where her situation is compared to a bird hesitating to
leave an unfastened cage. He 'fears the freedom of his wings'
and ventures forth only by degrees until he finally 'confides
himself to air'. Just so, she, offered love, 'First doubts if truly
she is free',

> Then pauses, restlessly retired,
> Alarm'd at too much liberty . . .

But the alarm is countered by an impulse of willing consent;

the force and suppressed power of these confused feelings—aspects of love's strong energy—are implied in Patmore's notable choice of images and of verbs in this long Prelude. Her response, for instance,

> Comes with alternate gush and check
> And joltings of the heart, as wine
> Pour'd from a flask of narrow neck.

The doubt is essentially whether she may trust herself to believe her declaration, 'I am in love, am his'. She fears self-betrayal; but once conceding the truth of her commitment, she 'Lets run the cables of reserve, And floats into a sea of bliss'—a nautical image which captures the sensation of joyous release, balancing another sea-simile which suggests the first sensations of strange and threatening feeling. A new element is suddenly discovered through her whole being:

> A touch, her hand press'd lightly, she
> Stands dizzied, shock'd, and flush'd, like one
> Set sudden neck-deep in the sea.

But she is ready to learn to swim. Thus Honoria's side of the ballroom incident in Book One, XI, is glossed, and the woman's approach to betrothal vividly amplified.

In 'his flattering look' she finds herself. Loving involves an encounter with one's own being as well as with the other person; identities are mingled, yet become each more distinct, and self is revalued through the other's love for it. This complex blending and transfiguring of self-experience is summed up in Prelude iii:

> The beauty in her Lover's eyes
> Was admiration of her own.

Patmore's gift of condensed expression serves him well in conveying these elusive psychological perceptions. For instance in Prelude i, he is able to give the necessary tautness and strength to another aspect of the woman consenting to love. She appreciates the hunter role of her lover, but must hope that his predatory threat will discipline itself to gentleness. She likewise

must lower her customary defences of independence and aloof-
ness, to yield to him. The two, that is, voluntarily disarm themselves in the interests of love. Patmore's lines resort to the tension
of paradox to bring out how positive a gesture this is on her
part—a submission which is neither meek nor coy:

> Her will's indomitably bent
> On mere submissiveness to him.

The ideas of service and mastery take on new implications in
these Preludes, as the guiding question remains, 'what were love
should reverence cease?'(i).

Canto III continues to examine 'Love Ceremonious'(i),
through the spectacle of Honoria dancing, as in Canto XI of
Book One. But the increased sensuous ardour in Felix's observation of her at 'The County Ball' leads to no lapse of conduct,
emphasising on the contrary the mutually supportive association of growing passion and reverence. He celebrates her beauty
in words which resolve all friction between flesh and spirit,
without over-refining the one or coarsening the other:

> Her ball-dress seem'd a breathing mist,
>   From the fair form exhaled and shed,
> Raised in the dance with arm and wrist
>   All warmth and light, unbraceleted.
> Her motion, feeling 'twas beloved,
>   The pensive soul of tune express'd,
> And, oh, what perfume, as she moved,
>   Came from the flowers in her breast!

The impressions of sense are rendered almost intangible, dissolving through the agency of 'breathing mist', perfume, and
the aura of light which surrounds her form. But their tangible
physical reality is equally felt in the 'unbraceleted wrist', which
subtly throws the stress onto the warm and living arm. Spirit
here is indeed 'lantern'd' in the body. And as her motion in the
dance communicates her love to Felix and he responds with a
mounting tide of feeling, the intimate dialogue intensifies
in the very experience of 'love ceremonious'.

But in the episode of Canto IV, 'Love in Idleness', Patmore
shows that the state of betrothal is still one of incompleteness,

breeding inactivity and unsettled confusion of purpose in the lover. Great schemes of self-betterment are generated but the energies which encourage their inception prevent their coming to birth. The engaged lover is leading a kind of larval existence, not yet the fulfilled being he will become when married, but no longer the independent and lesser creature he was before; love and its transforming operations command his whole nature:

> The soul, its wingless state dissolved,
>   Awaits its nuptial life complete,
> All indolently self-convolved,
>   Cocoon'd in silken fancies sweet.

(6)

The inertia and the state of engrossed surrender which characterises courtship is well caught in this image, and Patmore implies both the positive and negative aspects of the interim condition. It is a creative phase; to be absorbed in love is part of its blessing, and a necessary concentration if the metamorphosis of personality is to be achieved. But equally, it is a period of immaturity, of love as the romantic dream, a phase which must pass. The poem's marital momentum is preserved and the implications of the 'nuptial life complete' are pointed: the goal is not life become love, but love become life, informing and expressing itself through all activities, not preventing them.

#### ᨳ 12 ᨳ

It follows logically enough that Canto V's mood is one of restless emptiness awaiting fulfilment. The scene is Felix's house, its rooms ready to receive his wife, but as yet mere stage-sets before the play begins. The growing urgency of feeling and its object, not simply to love Honoria, but 'to marry her and take her home', are exemplified in a Canto which balances frustration with hope. And similarly, Canto VI, 'The Love Letters', highlights the fretful dissatisfactions of the unmarried lovers' state.

The written dialogue between them is anxious and uneasy, aggressively expressing itself by provocations and contraries.

They question each other, constantly testing, seeking reassurance, begging for signs, and finding their joy in being miserable. All reveals the richness and poverty of the unripened relationship. Prelude i, 'Love's Perversity', is nicely double-edged to set the ironic tone which befits the oddness of such behaviour:

> How strange a thing a lover seems
> To animals that do not love! . . .
> . . . how his great devotion mocks
> Our poor propriety, and scares
> The undevout with paradox!

The lover is ridiculous in his folly; but his state is enviable, for he is more boldly human than the rational and circumspect who look askance at the new horizons folly discloses. An alien creature, the lover arouses distrust, the panic of being assailed by a reversal of all prudent values. But the symptoms of this venture into more adventurous living are, none the less, those of extravagance, and there is a torment in its negotiations which is not to be envied. That this is true for both parties, the episode makes clear as the brisk exchange of notes ends with passion gathering strength, charging Honoria too with its tensions:

> Adieu! I am not well. Last night
> My dreams were wild: I often woke,
> The summer-lightning was so bright;
> And when it flash'd I thought you spoke.
>
> (3)

Love's perversity knows its remedy, and the fever of VI is immediately, in Prelude i of VII, contrasted with the matrimonial state in its combination of security and order: 'Can ought compared with wedlock be For use?' The note is unromantic, if Cantos IV and VI typify romantic love in its absorption in itself and its need for dramatic assertion and crises. 'Use' is a sturdier idea altogether, and points firmly to the everyday domesticity seen throughout as love's proper destiny. The Prelude, 'Joy and Use', promotes the quiet value of permanence by contrasting it with transient affairs, whose 'sorry raptures rest destroys', and the final lines bring together the cosmic and the domestic in a typical Patmore affirmation that the most commonplace is the most valuable. The Don Juans must 'like comets . . . roam', whereas,

> On settled poles turn solid joys
> And sunlike pleasures shine at home.

The composure of this looks back to the 'summer lightning' of VI, and so criticises the betrothed condition as well as passion which denies any permanent bond.

The episode, called 'The Revulsion', combines the growing concentration on marriage with the continued record of the psychological tides of engagement as they ebb and flow. Lying 'Abandon'd to delicious thought', Felix responds to the 'spousal time of May'(1). But then mortality casts its shadow and his musing brings 'A dream that shook my house of clay' (2). He imagines a time when the only bleak comfort might be that misery for the partner's death has fallen to his lot, not to hers. So he turns to confront the idea: 'Rehearsed the losing of a wife, And faced its terrors each and all'. Patmore notes the dash of lover's cunning at work in this sombre move—it is an investment against the eventuality being realised, for 'blows foreseen are slow to fall'.

At first Felix whips up his imagination with the more obvious trappings of death, but then something of the utter emptiness and disorientation is divined:

> At morn remembering by degrees
>     That she I dream'd about was dead;
> Love's still recurrent jubilees,
>     The days that she was born, won, wed;
> The duties of my life the same,
>     Their meaning for the feelings gone . . .

His imaginings prove so effective that he is persuaded he may be featuring an 'actual harm'(3), rather than insuring himself against it. The lover's uncontrollable and illogical instability is again demonstrated. He rushes to Sarum Close in a state of 'chill alarm', to find he has after all only wept for an hypothesis.

But the interlude has advanced Felix: he is conscious of a sadness at the heart of love, for the possibility of bereavement has entered in, and henceforth is to be taken into account. The

Canto moves from a boyish ecstasy, careless of anything but its lyrical moment, to a man's more complex love, where time's role is acknowledged and its import recognised. This is a step towards marital responsibility, the love which carries the burden of mortality. So Felix looks on his living Honoria with a relief which contains rather than cancels his premonition. What he sees is

> The light and happy loveliness
> Which lay so heavy on my heart.

### ∽ 13 ∽

Canto VIII explores further the strange diplomacies and strategies which are necessary for love to create its truth. The alchemy which is worked in both lovers, the complexities of their exchanges and responses, transforming such terms as mastery and submission, hunter and hunted: these elements of the theme of two people growing together are again rehearsed and developed, while Canto IX in its second Prelude uses the metaphor of its title, 'The Foreign Land' to reiterate the otherness of the beloved person and the need for this to be entirely respected.

After these reminders of the momentous landmarks and the characteristic terrain of the lovers' journey, the poem moves with quickening expectation to its matrimonial goal. Canto X, twelve hours before the wedding, stresses the central values of the married state, its special joys and responsibilities, and the episode, 'The Epitaph', adds to these reflections the lovers' complex mood as they anticipate the event.

Prelude i observes that the ceremony and worship apparent during courtship tends to fade away in the familiarities of domestic life—'The halo leaves the sacred head'. Yet the girl who, 'mistress of her maiden charms', took on the role of wife is even more worthy of respect than she was when independent:

> He never enough can honour her
> Who past all speech has honour'd him.

The submission of consent is a free delivery of self into the hands of another, a compliment of trust. If this responsibility is accepted, then the joys and mutual service of the relationship are beyond expression; Prelude ii exclaims at the sheer 'felicity' of the proposition, 'To marry her and take her home'.

So the 'last farewell' of Felix and Honoria before they meet in church is weighted by the Preludes with the awareness that the state of singleness they are about to leave is one of less responsibility as it is one of less reward. The brink of marriage is an awesome as well as a happy moment. Honoria feels it, seeking reassurance by the apparently silly question, ' "Oh, Felix, do you love me?" ' Why does she ask?—' "I cannot tell" '(1). The tension is well conveyed in this simple exchange, emphasising that love can only trust itself to love, and fears its own vulnerability.

Felix too is oppressed with the last prejudices of the Petrarchan lover. The role of bridegroom seems like presumption, a blasphemy against love's deity or a human violation of cosmic harmonies:

> What law, if man could mount so high,
> To further insolence set bars,
> And kept the chaste moon in the sky,
> And bade him not tread out the stars!
>
> (2)

Intimacy must prove destructive, robbing love of its decorum, depriving its strong energy of the control distance imposes. The Preludes' theme recurs in his conviction that ceremony is essential yet is not easily compatible with passionate union. Thinking of his wedding, theoretically the consummation of his desires, Felix is overcome by the loss and debasement it could mean for both of them, so that all

> Which should have been delight and health,
> Made heart and spirit sick and sere.
>
> (3)

But love asserts itself and sees its nature more clearly. The responsibilities of reverence are fully admitted, but as integral to the husband's role, not at war with it. The Preludes' ideals

217

are brought into focus as Felix interprets and anticipates his
marriage vow:

> And swore her welfare to prefer
> To all things, and for aye as now
> To live, not for myself, but her.

The shift of centre is the secret and, appreciating this, Felix's
mood changes to one of 'peace' and 'gaiety ineffable'. Recognising marriage as the reconciliation of realised desire and self-
lessness, he can affirm the poem's dominant harmony: 'Bright
with the spirit shone the sense'.

The joyous confidence bred by the insights of X—themselves
prepared for in the whole dialogue of courtship—is manifest in
the tone of the first Prelude of Canto XI, introducing 'The
Wedding'. Here, 'Platonic Love', the love which is reverence
only, a distant adoration confined to the spirit, is rejected
completely. Always for Patmore, spirit shines in sense and
is lanterned by the body, and such a certainty releases the lover,
not to the selfish boldness of license, but to an assured freedom of
the flesh, emancipated from puritanical restraints as from
lustful appetite. This is the love which, 'Angelic, dares to seize
her hand', welcoming the human situation in the completeness
of its nature and thus discovering the potential of that nature.
To live and love in this way is to

> Live greatly; so shalt thou acquire
> Unknown capacities of joy.

Equally insistent on the sexual union as the highest human good,
Prelude ii shows that it is at once a completion and a trans-
mutation of identity, an experience which intensifies self-
awareness but does so through the stronger experience of being
another: she is the 'strange, sweet half of me'; 'I more than love
thee, thee I am'. Giving self is finding it.

But these shafts of light into the meaning of marriage are too
bright for the occasion itself. Faithful as always to psychological
truth, Patmore shows Felix going through the motions of the
wedding service, 'In apathy of heart and will'(1). As the earlier
Prelude remarked, the day of days is not the day, and this one
is anticlimax and a check on all the feeling it is supposed to

sanction. Simply, the marriage day, in its embarrassments and social rituals, is 'To those before it and beyond, An iceberg in an Indian sea' (2). The discomfort of the intensely private becoming public is caught in the whole sketch of the wedding. Even when they are alone again, Felix is not able to believe the day's meaning and feel that free delight and confidence which 'dares to seize her hand'. He is suffering from what the Dean drily called, 'the weak alarms Of novel nearness' (3). Patmore fixes this malady to an exact degree to close a neat protrayal of the ironies of the longed-for day which in the event bears no comparison with the water-flag afternoons.

True to the emphasis throughout, the final Canto, 'Husband and Wife', begins with a Prelude which reasserts the tenacity of the virginal being, exerting its magnetic attraction, never to be invaded:

> Why, having won her, do I woo?
> Because her spirit's vestal grace
> Provokes me always to pursue,
> But, spirit-like, eludes embrace . . .

So the space between is preserved, stimulating love because it quells any grosser notions of possession. The union is the more complete because the root answer to the question above is, simply, 'because, in short, She's not and never can be mine'. The poem rests once again on paradox.

The second Prelude balances the first as it declares the unceasing growth of love and joy in the experience of living with someone so closely:

> But truly my delight was more
> In her to whom I'm bound for aye
> Yesterday than the day before,
> And more today than yesterday.

This tribute to continuity and the accruing returns of marriage puts the honeymoon episode which follows into the right perspective. With the Epilogue, the effect is to diminish the sense of the poem coming to a climactic ending. Rather, Felix and Honoria are now beginning their relationship in its fullness, and Patmore ensures that this is properly appreciated.

As always, domestic detail impresses on Felix the momentous change in his life. Paying for Honoria's sand-shoes, he is acting the social role of her husband, and so he realises that such indeed he is:

> How light the touches are that kiss
> The music from the chords of life!
>
> (1)

It is the water-flag argument again. Stirred to his soul by the fact that this 'Stranger' is now his 'three days' Wife', Felix can only approach his feelings obliquely and adjust to his situation through the small incidents of their days together. Patmore suggests this, economically, in the shopping and the sea-shore walk where the new shoes leave their prints, and she collects stones for him. All is charged with implication simply by being so quiet and unspectacular: they are living together and dis-covering what this means. Their first days together at Green's Hotel are important because of this.

The Canto crowns the whole poem with a final thanksgiving for the blessings of marriage, emphasising its complete ease, its growing confidence, and its mutual peace. The 'weak alarms' have faded away as Felix and Honoria talk together of 'this and that' in exchanges which are 'familiar, unaffected, free'. Then, 'after tea',

> As doubtful if a lot so sweet
>     As ours was ours in very sooth,
> Like children, to promote conceit,
>     We feign'd that it was not the truth;
> And she assumed the maiden coy,
>     And I adored remorseless charms,
> And then we clapp'd our hands for joy,
>     And ran into each other's arms.

What they relive are the twenty-four Cantos of *The Angel in the House*. In the poem Patmore has traced the process by which the happy climax of confident union and delight in unreserved commitment is achieved, and he has set out the lifelong implications. Through the courtship, the goal has become more clearly seen and more deeply understood. So Felix and Honoria traverse the way again, to win the full savour of their love's fruition, the 'familiar, unaffected, free' embrace of husband and wife.

A merely romantic poet would end the poem there, with the tableau of the accomplished relationship. But the Epilogue follows so that there is no mistaking Patmore's evolutionary conception: no peak is the highest. Felix says that he has only shown the first stage of love, which is easier to describe than the later time, when its 'flames intensest glow' (1). The 'ten-years' Wife' is preferable to the girl, he declares, for her 'customary love is not Her passion, or her play, but life'. Love is now life; and girlish charms are as 'apples green' to 'apples gold'. However much he has extolled her, she is 'still unpraised Honoria' (3), and all he can hope for is to continue to be properly conscious of the great good which is his.

Demonstrating the robustly unromantic reality of love's incarnation, the Epilogue is invaded by the family in 'full-cry' (1), and the poem draws most unobtrusively to its close on an encounter with a friend who, greeting their son, enquires, ' "Is he yours, this handsome boy?" ' (4). It is anticlimax not conclusion. But Patmore can afford to come to rest on the commonplace, having turned the searching gaze of a profound religious and psychological vision on his lovers, as he conducts them through the complexities of the heart's events to their union of 'settled joys'. His achievement in *The Angel in the House* is to bring the Victorian poetry of relationships triumphantly home to the domestic world without allowing it to decline to the level of an unsophisticated idyll of the hearth.

# CONCLUSION

# The Heart's Events

'The Victorians responded to the sequence of time, to its motion and unfolding perspectives'. This observation appears in the preface to a recent collection of essays on Victorian poetry,[1] and the unifying theme of the essays, the editors say, is 'the Victorian sense of the past'—the past here meaning an awareness of historical periods, and the movement of history on this scale. My concern in these chapters has been to show that the sense of time, history, and the relation of past to present is equally fundamental to the poets of the age in the sphere of personal experience, and particularly in their attempts to explore the phenomenon of intimacy. In so far as this aspect is alluded to in *Victorian Poetry*, my conviction that it is a preoccupation running right through the century, from the beginnings of *In Memoriam* in the 1830s onwards, is supported by J. Hillis Miller's essay on Hardy's poetry, which points to the importance of personal relationships in general, and of the experience of falling out of love in particular, in the poems as well as the novels. Hardy, Hillis Miller says, tries to characterise 'human time', and to convey the experience of temporality in its 'natural yet discontinuous change', the strange relation not just of one being to another, but of the present to the past self.[2]

It is obvious even from this summary that Hardy's version of these themes is as individual as that of each poet in whom I have shown them active. There is no stereotype response to time, to the encounter with another person, to the changing self, and least of all to the imaginative challenge of constructing

---

[1] *Victorian Poetry*, ed. M. Bradbury and D. Palmer (*Stratford upon Avon Studies* 15, 1972), p. 8. I read this interesting collection after beginning my own study.

[2] 'History as Repetition in Thomas Hardy's Poetry', *Victorian Poetry*, pp. 242, 238–9.

a poetry which can capture the events of the heart as a developing psychological process, and one involving the interaction of two people. The common elements stimulate the poets to highly individual creativity, and this is as true structurally as it is tonally and linguistically. The nature of the vision impels an expansion from the single lyric unit, and the result, as I suggested in my introduction, is a period of vigorous and fresh research into the concept of the long poem, taking it in a creative direction as vital as, yet distinct from, that of the contemporary novel.

'People much prefer *Vanity Fair* and *Bleak House*', said Clough in 1853, comparing the relative prestige of poetry and the novel.[3] He called for poetry to take its cue from the novel, to be 'substantive and lifelike, immediate and firsthand', to deal with 'general wants, ordinary feelings'. The novelist, unlike the poet, he claimed, tries to build 'a real house to be lived in', acknowledging that his readers are people, not 'gods' or 'marble statues' to be offered an 'Ionic portico'. I hope that this study will be seen as an attempt to demonstrate that Clough's views were too pessimistic. His own poems were in existence by 1853, as were *In Memoriam* and the 'Marguerite' lyrics; within three years, *The Angel in the House* and *Maud* appeared, to be joined in the 1860s by *James Lee's Wife* and *Modern Love*, and by Patmore's odes a decade later.

Here are many real houses to be lived in, I suggest, though not, certainly, of the same architecture as the novelists' buildings. The poets do not compete with the story-telling art, yet in turning away from incident, they remain just as firmly in touch with the social and psychological realities of the day. In their choice and their treatment of the heart's events, they are not at all remote from the urgent preoccupations of those with 'ordinary feelings'. On the contrary, the Victorian poetry of relationships speaks movingly to such feelings, and is manifestly not written for or by marble statues. Both substantive and lifelike, it rewards its readers with a highly sensitive scrutiny of the varied events which shock, delight and school the human heart when it involves itself with another.

[3] In a review of 'Recent English Poetry', *North American Review*, July 1853; quoted in *Victorian Scrutinies*, ed. I. Armstrong (1972), pp. 154–6.

# Index

Editors are not included unless quoted.

# DATE DUE